KENNEDY

Lord Longford takes a fresh look at Kennedy : his personality, his political achievement and his reputation. He examines the growth of his powerful Irish Catholic family and the roots of his immense drive and ambition. He describes the Kennedy family's pursuit of power, the construction of the Kennedy myth and the fight for the presidency. He chronicles the thousand days of the Kennedy administration : the Bay of Pigs and the Cuban crisis, the involvement in civil rights, the escalation of the Vietnam conflict, the assassination that still remains largely unexplained and the subject of continual controversy.

Kennedy is a new biography of one of the greatest political figures of our time.

KENNEDY

Lord Longford

A STAR BOOK

published by
the Paperback Division of
W. H. ALLEN & CO. LTD.

A Star Book
Published in 1978
by the Paperback Division of
W. H. Allen & Co. Ltd
A Howard and Wyndham Company
44 Hill Street, London W1X 8LB

First published in Great Britain by
Weidenfeld & Nicolson, 1976

Printed in Breat Britain by
Hazell Watson & Viney Ltd
Aylesbury, Bucks

ISBN 0 352 30147 3

To Elizabeth

Contents

Acknowledgments

Anyone who writes about President Kennedy must acknowledge a large debt to Arthur Schlesinger and Theodore Sorensen, more particularly for the former's *Thousand Days* and the latter's *Kennedy*. Both of them knew Kennedy well (Sorensen longer and more closely). Both of them served him faithfully and loved him dearly. In addition Arthur Schlesinger is one of the outstanding American historians, of fine literary talents; Theodore Sorensen has since become a distinguished public man in his own right. Their books are of high and enduring quality.

But the authors would be the last to claim that their biographies could be 'unbiassed', whatever that could mean. They were written under the first impact of the assassination and published in 1965. Plenty of scope was left for further contributions and of these there have indeed been plenty, favourable and unfavourable, high class and less respect-worthy.

In my short bibliography, I have listed close on fifty of the books that I found most useful, though some were much more useful than others. The revisionist writers – debunkers would be too harsh a word – have not been neglected, but inevitably most was to be learnt from those who knew him best and not infrequently loved him most. In addition to Schlesinger and Sorensen, *Times to Remember* by Mrs Rose Kennedy and *Johnny We Hardly Knew Ye* by Kenneth P. O'Donnell and David F. Powers with Joe McCarthy, provide an indispensable flavour. So does Richard Whalen's *Founding Father*, which is by no means soft on Joseph Kennedy.

The time, however, seemed to me to have come to attempt a dispassionate biography, with some advantage to be derived if it were written by an 'outsider', in my case by a British minister of Irish background, whose family home is still in Ireland. David Nunnerley's specialist study *President Kennedy and Britain* is quite excellent. But apart from that and the sparkling impressions of Henry Fairlie (*The Kennedy Promise*), there has been hardly any British writing about Kennedy, in spite of the unique honours accorded him in Britain when he died. The last two volumes of Harold Macmillan's autobiography throw exceptional light not only on Macmillan's relationship with Kennedy, but on Kennedy himself. One day it is to be hoped Lord Harlech will write his own autobiography, or deal in some other way with his years in Washington. As things stand, it seemed high time for a British writer to attempt a new biography of Kennedy.

In writing this book I have received much kindness from Mr Harold Macmillan and Lord Harlech, also from Lord Caccia who was British Ambassador in Washington during the early months of the Kennedy Presidency. My son-in-law, Mr Hugh Fraser, whose friendship with the whole Kennedy family goes back forty years and has continued to flourish, generously read the manuscript, as did Professor Arthur Schlesinger. None of those mentioned bears any shadow of responsibility for any statements of fact or opinion.

Two significant American books came into my hands while I was correcting the proofs. On a first reading neither leads me to modify what I have written in any important way, but I would certainly have made fuller use of them if they had reached me earlier. The first, called *The Promise and the Performance* by Dr Lewis Paper, is a thoughtful academic analysis of Kennedy's achievements as President in comparison with the expectations created. Not surprisingly the final conclusion is guarded. 'It is, of course,' writes Dr Paper, 'impossible to determine whether Kennedy would have succeeded in fulfilling the promise he offered in 1961 if he had survived two terms in the White House. But there is much interesting argumentation en route.'

One particular criticism must be quoted: 'Kennedy devoted little time to establishing long range strategies which would guide his administration's policies and programmes, strategies which could give more substance to the far-sighted rhetoric of many of his speeches. For Kennedy the questions usually had to be specific, concrete and immediate'. A criticism of this kind which could be applied to plenty of Presidents and Prime Ministers will occur to many as they read the following text. But once we concede, as we should, that Kennedy was a late developer and developing fast when he died, we cannot rule out the possibility in this sphere also of a great improvement.

The second book, *The Search for J.F.K.* by Joan and Clay Blair, is, on the face of it, much more controversial. The authors have been at great pains to break through what they regard as 'the cover-up' surrounding some aspects of Kennedy's life, and to introduce reality instead of myth and legend. 'We believe', they say, 'that these [omissions and distortions] constitute overwhelming evidence that shrewd manipulation of the media can make a man President of the United States.' Personally I believe such a proposition to be quite untenable. But even if it were true, it could not be demonstrated by the book under discussion, which stops short thirteen years before Kennedy was elected President.

No one interested in Kennedy, however, could fail to read large parts of *The Search for J.F.K.* with fascination. The Blairs devote nearly six hundred pages to twelve years of Kennedy's life (1935–1947), when he was passing from 18 to 30. I myself cover the same period in less than twenty pages (Chapters 2 and 3). It goes without saying that there are all sorts of things worth noticing in the longer book which are not to be found in mine. But the detailed studies of the Blairs do not force me to reconsider my standpoint. They say, for example, that the 'impression was given that Jack was a robust young man' and they take enormous trouble to prove, I would think conclusively, that in fact he suffered from Addison's disease. Whether his illness should be described in that way does not seem to me of much importance now. What does matter is that all his life he contended with pain and sickness. In this respect the Blairs concede that he was truly heroic, but that conclusion will be reached by anyone who reads his mother's book or, for that matter, mine.

Secondly they say that 'the impression was fostered that Jack was a dedicated and brilliant scholar'. That impression if it ever existed had long disappeared by the time I began to write about Kennedy. In my own mind I judge him to have been a man of very high intelligence, but as I said just now a late developer. Something like a third of the Blairs' long book is devoted to Kennedy's war performance. They insist that he was, to use their own words, 'a manufactured war hero'. Even the Blairs, however, admit that he 'performed bravely'. They cannot take away from him the fact that he was decorated for valour and that when those who served under him were interrogated, they expressed un-qualified devotion.

Finally they have much to say, and they say it without prurience, about Jack Kennedy's endless friendships with women, in the period in question. In my own concluding chapter I summarize my point of view in regard to that aspect of his life. Out of the many opinions quoted by the Blairs, one has a special ring of truth. It comes from George Smathers, a very close friend of Jack Kennedy's and the only politician among the ushers at his wedding. 'Jack', writes George Smathers, 'liked girls. He liked girls very much. He came by it naturally. His daddy liked girls. He was a great chaser. Jack liked girls and girls liked him. He had just a great way with women. He was such a warm, lovable guy himself. He was a sweet fella, a really sweet fella.'

Also at the eleventh hour, I was visited by Mr Peter Dawnay, who has spent several years on research into the assassination.

He is convinced that the murder of the President was plotted by a group whose names he supplied to me, mostly composed of Texan oil men and Southern politicians, coordinated by operatives connected with the CIA and military intelligence. Their aim in his view was not simply to kill Kennedy, but incidentally to put the blame on Castro and the Communists generally, in order to gain popular support for a full-scale invasion of Cuba.

Mr Dawnay rejects the whole idea that Lee Oswald shot the President, though he accepts the possibility that Oswald was made use of in one way or another. He considers that there were four or five assassins and that seven or more shots were fired, some of them from the front.

I am not as yet convinced by his theory in advance of studying his evidence. We must await a book on the subject from Mr Dawnay. The mystery is not yet solved.

Once again I am immensely grateful to my Personal Assistant, Gwendolen Keeble. She has helped me at every turn, most particularly in regard to the chapter about Jacqueline Kennedy; to Barbara Winch and also Elizabeth Abbott for their admirable typing of the manuscript.

My family have assisted me in their distinctive ways. My wife's virtues as a biographer are known on both sides of the Atlantic. I can only hope that some of her merit has rubbed off on my work.

I

A long way from County Wexford

Background

John Kennedy has many claims to historical recognition. In one respect he is unique. In London there are the statues of three American Presidents – George Washington, Abraham Lincoln and Franklin D. Roosevelt. In the case of President Kennedy, the British people have gone further and raised a memorial to him on the hallowed grounds of Runnymede; they have established a scholarship scheme which will for ever bear his name.

At his death an immense wave of admiration and poignant sorrow poured across the world. Yet his Presidency had lasted for less than three years. He himself was only forty-six. Making every allowance for the appalling circumstances of his assassination, his was by any possible standard a stupendous achievement.

His world reputation had been rising continuously and was higher at his death than ever previously. When he visited Ireland during his last summer, the whole island, as was said to his mother and later quoted by her, 'appeared to be in a tumult of admiration and celebration'. Vast crowds welcomed him in Europe, over a million people in West Berlin alone. No post-war political figure, even de Gaulle, has approached John Kennedy in his power to inspire alike the mighty and the humble, the sophisticated and the simple, above all the young.

Even the most ordinary mortals cannot be explained as mere products of heredity and environment. In the case of a superlative figure like Kennedy, his personality would naturally owe far more

I

than usual to elements all his own. Yet the formative influences brought to bear on him were immensely powerful. This accident of his birth and upbringing was more potent than that attending any major statesman in this century, with the possible exception of Winston Churchill. But in Churchill's case there was no question of the father's promoting the son's career. He died when the young Winston was twenty, having consistently neglected and disparaged him. Contrariwise, after the death of Joe Kennedy, the elder son, John Kennedy's father never rested until he saw his son installed as President. This same father had not only been Ambassador to Britain in 1938–9, but also one of the wealthiest and most powerful men in his country, and was discussed at one time as a possible President.

The Kennedy family are described by Mrs Rose Kennedy (*Times to Remember*, 1974), the President's mother, as an American family of Irish descent. Her paternal grandparents (who became the Fitzgeralds) both emigrated from County Wexford in the 1840s, but did not meet until they reached Boston, where they married. Her husband's grandfather also emigrated from County Wexford to Boston and also married an Irish immigrant girl there. The year 1914 saw the marriage of the President's parents, Rose Fitzgerald and Joseph Patrick Kennedy. By this time both fathers had lifted themselves into the middle class, were quite rich and were distinctly influential in the Irish politics of Boston.

But of the two, 'Honey Fitz', Rose Kennedy's father, was more prominent in politics; Patrick Joseph Kennedy, father of 'Joe' Kennedy, as a business man. Honey Fitz had sat in the United States House of Representatives and been elected Mayor of Boston. For many years he was one of the great Irish political 'characters'. Patrick Joseph Kennedy was three times elected to the Massachusetts House of Representatives and also to the State Senate. He had made himself a key figure in the control of local Democratic politics. But his major concern was with his banking and 'tavern' interests. The last association stuck to his son. Despite his education at the élitist Boston Latin School whose alumni included five signers of the Declaration of Independence, and at Harvard, long after 'Joe' Kennedy had become immensely rich and powerful, he was still referred to slightingly by the 'Brahmins' of Boston as the son of 'Pat the tavern keeper'. Be that as it may, by the time the future President was a young man, the Kennedy family had achieved a position of wealth and social status loftier than that of any family of Irish-American origins.

John Kennedy was born on 29 May 1917. He had eight brothers and sisters: Joe (b. 1915), Rosemary (b. 1918), Kathleen (b. 1920), Eunice (b. 1921), Patricia (b. 1924), Robert (b. 1925), Jean (b. 1928), and Edward (b. 1932).

Robert was Attorney-General in his brother's administration and was aiming at the Presidency when assassinated in 1968. 'Jack' Kennedy himself, as all the world knows, was assassinated in 1963. Jack Kennedy's birthplace was a modest house at 83 Beal Street, Brooklyn, in the suburbs of Boston. With the arrival of the fourth child, Kathleen, the family moved to a larger house in Naples Road. But in 1926, when Jack was nine, the father transferred the whole family to Riverdale, New York and three years later to Bronxville. The move to New York was actuated by Joe Kennedy's belief that an Irish-Catholic family would have much more limited scope if they remained in Boston. No doubt business reasons here combined with those of social advancement.

Rose Kennedy, the future President's mother, is said to have asked: 'When are the nice people in Boston going to accept us?' Joe Kennedy, the father, put his side of the argument just as succinctly: 'Boston is a good city to come from, but not a good city to go to. If you want to make money, go where the money is.'

A year before, Joe Kennedy had bought a house at Hyannis Port on Cape Cod, in what was to become the famous 'family compound'. A large part of their summers was spent there. Hyannis Port more than anywhere else was the family home. Even after many years' residence, the native-born Cape Codders were allergic to their presence.

From 1933, the Kennedys enjoyed a third home described by Richard Whalen in *The Founding Father* (New York, 1964) as 'comfortable winter quarters on North Ocean Boulevard in Palm Beach'. The house was set on two acres facing the ocean.

Links with Boston were maintained, if only through Mrs Kennedy's devotion to her father Honey Fitzgerald. But with an education at Choate, a crack non-Catholic school, and Harvard, John Kennedy did not grow up among Irish influences outside his family. Mrs Rose Kennedy gives a list of his favourite books in boyhood, most of them tales of chivalry or romance: Robert Louis Stevenson, Conan Doyle, King Arthur's knights. There is no trace of an Irish interest there. The greatest of all his favourites a little later was John Buchan's autobiography, a delightful book by a greatly gifted man. But John Buchan was about as little Irish as anybody could be.

One cannot however question Rose Kennedy's statement many years later that 'Jack delighted in his Irish heritage'. By the time he made his presidential tour of 1963, that was plain to the meanest eye. I myself met him once only, and then very briefly, at a reception given for him by Mr de Valera in the Irish President's residence in the Phoenix Park, Dublin. I watched in fascination as he moved throughout the afternoon among the enchanted crowds with Mr de Valera beside him like a benignant uncle. By this time he may well have felt – he certainly looked – as Irish as any man or woman there. It is left for his devoted but always shrewd biographer, Theodore Sorensen, to point out that his earliest interest in the land of his forebears was largely literary and political. His companions on a youthful visit there were mostly English or Anglo-Irish.

While his father was Ambassador in London, Jack developed lasting friendships among the English and Scottish aristocracy, including David Ormsby Gore (later Lord Harlech), Hugh Fraser, the Cavendishes and the Cecils, the last two interlocked by marriage. His sister Kathleen, in spite of the religious sacrifice involved, married the much-loved young man who, if he had not been killed leading his men, would have become Duke of Devonshire. Mrs Kennedy does not forbear to point out, in spite of much personal goodwill, that in Irish circles no two families were deemed to have obstructed the march of Irish nationalism more powerfully than these same Cavendishes and Cecils. No two statesmen could have done more than Hartington (Cavendish) and Salisbury (Cecil) to defeat Home Rule in the eighties and nineties.

These upper-class British friendships endured and played no small part in producing a warm relationship during his Presidency between John Kennedy and Harold Macmillan, who had married the aunt of Kathleen Kennedy's husband. But Kenneth O'Donnell, whom we shall come to in a moment, repeats something of significance that Kennedy said to him on the 1963 visit to Ireland. He said he had been staying with his sister Kathleen at Lismore Castle, County Waterford, which belonged to the Duke and Duchess of Devonshire, the parents of her deceased husband. One day he drove to Dunganstown, New Ross, County Wexford, to find the house which his great-grandfather had left in 1848 to emigrate to Boston. He took with him an English lady who was staying at Lismore. They found some Kennedys, who proved to be second cousins of his father, in their white-washed thatched cottage, drinking a cup of tea in the kitchen. When they were driving back to Lismore the English lady commented: 'That was like Tobacco Road.' Now the President recalled the scene and added: 'I felt like kicking her out of the car. For me the visit to that cottage was filled with magic sentiment.' That night at dinner he looked round at the other guests, Anthony Eden and Randolph Churchill among them. He thought about the cottage where his cousins lived and said to himself: 'What a contrast.' By 1963 the experience obviously meant much to him. But sixteen years had passed without his attempting to repeat it.

He had returned to Boston with his entry into politics in 1946 and his election from Massachusetts to the House of Representatives. Arthur Schlesinger (*A Thousand Days*, 1965) suggests that this return to Boston must have involved a 'culture shock'. 'While born a Boston Irishman, he had never been a member of the Boston Irish community and his life had carried him far away from his roots. Now he was back among his own people, yet not quite of them . . . he fraternized for the first time with the men and women from whom the Kennedys and Fitzgeralds had sprung.'

Three in particular of the Boston Irish became his intimate and greatly valued advisers: Kenneth O'Donnell, the old football captain, fiercely loyal and protective; David Powers, lovable and entertaining at all times; and Lawrence O'Brien, the master politician. They and others of their fraternity were nicknamed 'the Irish Mafia'. Schlesinger assures us that 'the Irish Mafia did not possess Kennedy any more than anyone else did. They were his instruments in politics as Ted Sorensen was his instrument on issues.' David Powers, however, in *Johnny, We Hardly Knew Ye* (Boston, 1972) by himself and Kenneth O'Donnell, brings out a point overlooked by most others. 'Much as he personally disagreed with their viewpoint, Jack enjoyed the positive Irish pols [i.e. political professionals], and they liked him from the beginning. He was a completely new type of Irish politician himself, but he was *very Irish* [my italics], and he loved everything about politics, including the old pols and their stories and political jokes.'

The mutual interaction between Kennedy and a constituency where the Irish influence was so strong had been at work for seventeen years by the time he visited the 'old country' in 1963. By that time his dormant love of Ireland had been thoroughly awakened. His wife Jacqueline wrote a touching poem about him soon after they were married, which brings out his mixed inheritance:

He would call New England his place and his creed
But part he was of an alien breed
Of a breed that had laughed on Irish hills
And heard the voices in Irish rills . . .

The lilt of that green land danced in his blood
Tara, Killarney, a magical flood
That surged in the depth of his too proud heart
And spiked the punch of New England so tart.

I cannot resist adding four more lines from the same poem:

He would find love
He would never find peace
For he must go seeking
The Golden Fleece. . . .

For some years before 1963 he had been making notes for a book about the migrations and the many national, ethnic, political and religious groups that had taken part in the composition of the United States. The title he had in mind was *A Nation of Immigrants*. He had published a pamphlet under this title in 1958. He was, in short, an American through and through, but an American who remembered the island of his father's origins with ever-increasing pride. How far he himself felt discriminated against in the United States as an Irish-American is a point we shall touch on later.

The influence of his family continued long after he grew up but operated most obviously in his boyhood. His mother mentions that she has often been asked 'what has made the Kennedy children strive so hard for individual excellence?' And she begins her answer by quoting something that her husband used to say to the children: 'We don't want any losers around here.' They were encouraged to be winners, leaders, victors in whatever they set their hands to and to develop the habit. Their daughter Eunice has recalled: 'Mother and Dad put us through rigorous training in athletics. Dad wanted his children to win the sailing and swimming races (I remember racing fourteen times a week when I was twelve years old).' Mrs Kennedy tries to defend this approach by claiming that 'the main point of the whole exercise was not winning *per se*. It was rather that we wanted them to do their absolute best.' But that is somewhat unconvincing in view of the passage quoted above, or this further advice, for example, from Joe Kennedy: 'Don't come in second or third – that doesn't count. But win!' Few families in any country have been urged forward so strongly from their earliest days.

Whatever the ultimate purpose in the minds of their parents, there is no doubt that the children grew up in the conviction that they had to win if they were to satisfy their parents whom they admired and loved.

Competition between the children was encouraged. The endless fights between Jack Kennedy and his older and stronger brother, Joe, were treated as natural. But as Mrs Kennedy points out: 'In later years people remarked about the unity of the family, the close bonds of loyalty and faith among them and their spontaneous understanding of each other.' And in this she rightly takes pride. How far however the 'clannishness' which she repudiates in fact existed is more disputable. Jack Kennedy came to say this: 'We soon learned that competition in the family was a kind of dry run for the world outside.' The real competition was between the Kennedys and the rest.

But these two tremendous characteristics of the Kennedys, the intense mutual devotion flowing over into mutual admiration, and the undying determination to win any contest they embarked on, can be studied from various angles. They owed not a little to the fact that in a sense the Kennedys were a solitary phenomenon. They had ascended out of the Irish-American society without being fully accepted among the leaders of the dominant Anglo-Saxon Protestant culture. That would not be relevant in England where American class distinctions would be of no interest provided that those involved had plenty of vitality and charm, not to mention plenty of money. But in America the failure to be accepted on level terms in the best circles haunted the Kennedys till Jack's election to the Presidency – perhaps even after that. The urge to close ranks, find still more virtue in themselves and snap their fingers at the silly snobs outside supplied a strong additional dynamic.

Professors Schwab and Shneidman lay very heavy stress on this factor in their recent life of John Kennedy (*John F. Kennedy*, Boston, 1974). This is a valuable book, stimulating and controversial. In regard to the President's father their case seems irresistible. Joe Kennedy, they point out, 'was a millionaire many times over, but the money while giving him and his family material well-being did not give him or them a social standing. No matter how wealthy he was, he was still the son of an Irish tavern keeper . . . the élite would never elect him to the Harvard Board of Overseers. With all his wealth he could not be elected to the Cohasset Country Club.' The general effect was undoubtedly to strengthen his ambitions on behalf of his family.

It may well be, however, that Professors Schwab and Shneidman overstate the strength of this influence on the future President. They quote effectively, it is true, a saying of Senator George Smathers, a close friend during the time when both were bachelors, who stated, 'I think that he felt that as an Irishman somewhere along the line he had been discriminated against.' A room-mate of Jack Kennedy's at Harvard has recalled that he and two of his friends had to insist that Jack Kennedy should be invited where they were invited during the 'Club punching season'. Jack Kennedy was unwelcome, largely because he was a Catholic and partly because he was the grandson of the 'not soon forgotten' Honey Fitz. But this type of theory, which attributes to Jack Kennedy a chip on the shoulder as part of his motivation, does not seem borne out by the opinions of those who knew him best.

On one occasion Bobby Kennedy drew the British Ambassador Harold Caccia (now Lord Caccia) aside after a dinner at the British Embassy. He asked him provocatively: 'Why are we, the Kennedys, in America; why are we here at all? It is because you, the British, drove us out of Ireland!' Commenting on this incident to me Lord Caccia remarks: 'Jack Kennedy would never have said such a thing to me and, what's more, I don't think he was apt to dwell on such thoughts.' Schwab and Shneidman argue that it was Jack Kennedy's experience of being rejected by the Anglo-Saxon élite that enabled him to sympathize so perfectly with the downtrodden everywhere. They go so far as to call Kennedy the 'social outcast'. This would seem to be exaggerating the point. But the hereditary wrongs of the Irish in Ireland and the social discrimination against them in the higher circles of Boston must be allowed some psychological influence.

The immediate impulsion as already indicated came from the father, Joe Kennedy himself. The main facts of his career can be given briefly. They are powerfully amplified in *The Founding Father*. An early anecdote is symbolic of much that followed. Joe Kennedy was brought on as a substitute near the end of the Harvard *v.* Yale baseball match of 1911, by a surprising decision of the Harvard captain. The game ended with the ball in Kennedy's hands. The captain asked him to hand it over. But Joe Kennedy stuck to it: 'I made the put out, didn't I?' he retorted. He lived up to that standard of obstinacy in his own interests and those of his family.

A much later story is irresistible here. Joe Kennedy was getting very irritated on the golf links by a slow player in front of him. Finally, he shouted: 'Bill, if you want us to go through, just let us know.' Bill was seen to nod. 'Before the depression,' said Joe Kennedy to his companion, Paul Fay (John Kennedy's great friend from naval days), 'that guy used to be worth thirty-five or forty million dollars. Now he would be lucky if he could scrape together two or three million, and he is still acting like he had it.' 'The poor fellow,' said Fay, tongue in cheek, 'how does he manage?'

Joe Kennedy, born in 1888, was by 1923 in business in New York on his own account, behind a door marked JOSEPH P. KENNEDY — BANKER. Already well-versed in stock market manipulation, he advanced rapidly, but at first unobtrusively, as a clever 'lone-wolf' operator. Then in 1926 came his first great opportunity when he entered the film industry with staggering success. 'Look at that bunch of pants-pressers in Hollywood making themselves millionaires,' he had remarked somewhat earlier. 'I could take the whole business away from them.' Over the next three years, in Whalen's expression, 'he almost made good his boast'.

His absorption in films involved prolonged trips to California, where he rented a house in Beverley Hills. He went for long periods without seeing his wife and children, though his devotion never flagged and he was never out of touch on the telephone. By October 1928 he was almost out of the film business, several million dollars richer. When the great Stock Exchange crash came

9

in 1929, large numbers of rich men and poor men were ruined, but not Kennedy. Financially speaking, he was at a safe distance with large holdings in cash. 'Only a fool,' said Joe Kennedy in a typical comment, 'holds out for the top dollar.'

Joe Kennedy was one of the relatively few rich men to come out strongly for Roosevelt from 1932 onwards. 'I think,' he said later, 'I was the first man with more than twelve dollars in the Bank who openly supported him.' For a long time he felt cheated of his reward. He was widely regarded as outstandingly unscrupulous even in the harsh world of business competition. No charge of downright dishonesty was ever proved against him, but there could be little question about his ruthlessness. And in business circles his support for Roosevelt earned him the title of 'Traitor'.

So he had to put up with his frustration as best he might. He undertook important tasks for the President but no high position in Government came his way. His friendship with Roosevelt's son Jimmy brought however good dividends. When Joe Kennedy visited Britain with Jimmy Roosevelt in 1933, Prohibition was 'on the way out' and the opportunities for large-scale importations into America were wide open. The British distillers were much impressed by Kennedy and the company he was keeping. He was appointed the U.S. agent for Haig and Haig, John Dewar & Sons and Gordon's Dry Gin Company. Thirteen very profitable years later he severed his connection with liquor to improve Jack's prospects in politics.

In December 1937 the news broke that he was becoming American Ambassador in London. (He was to be dubbed by one writer later on as 'our Ambassador to the Court of Haig & Haig'). At the same time he acquired the impression that if all went well, he might become Secretary of the Treasury. He had worked hard for Roosevelt; he had plenty of cash, could afford the very expensive post and was regarded as a good all-round negotiator. It was a glorious moment for Joe Kennedy. He served in London till the end of 1940, with certain breaks at home. His mission opened brilliantly. His accomplished wife and nine gay, high-spirited and handsome children contributed strongly to the glamour.

Soon the Kennedys were spending a weekend at Windsor Castle. There were numerous servants in evidence, in full livery, and one who, in Mrs Kennedy's words, 'as well as livery wore a perruque, was especially appointed to attend us and lead the way whenever we left our suite'. After a few minutes of contemplating the scene, as he dressed for dinner with the King and Queen, Joe Kennedy turned to his wife and said: 'Well, Rose . . . this is a helluva long way from East Boston, isn't it?'

Several times he spoke to his wife of settling later in England. But long before the end, he was utterly disgruntled and yearning to escape.

In his usual fashion, he 'got close to the man at the top'; he developed a genuine friendship with the Prime Minister, Neville Chamberlain. In spite of obvious differences in their backgrounds their outlooks were in many respects similar. As businessmen they both hated war for its appalling wastefulness, its threat of social revolution and the advantages it would bring the Communists. On the human side Chamberlain's innate pacifism was matched by Kennedy's horror at the threat to his own four sons. He stood by Chamberlain's policy of appeasement though in the end Chamberlain himself was forced to abandon it for Britain. Kennedy, an Irish-American, was ambivalent, to say the least, towards Britain's rôle in the world. He became more determined than ever that America should not be sucked into the conflict. These views were not likely to make him popular in war-time Britain; still less his unconcealed conviction that Britain was certain to be beaten.

His family returned to America at the outbreak of the war. They did not experience therefore, as he did, a final year of mutual disenchantment in London.

When Joe Kennedy went back to America, he laboured desperately to keep his country out of the war. But events thrust him and his opinions aside. When the United States 'came in', he was anxious to serve Roosevelt but his offers were not taken up. As some compensation he made vast sums of money in a new business career in real estate.

No stroke of fortune, good or bad, ever affected Joe Kennedy half so powerfully as the death in action of his eldest son Joe, his pride and joy, in July 1944. From that he never recovered, though he was not the man to fold his hands in adversity.

No family in a single generation was ever crowned with so much glory or hit so hard. Three out of the four sons were to die violent deaths, the fourth to be involved in a tragic episode. Kathleen was to meet death in an aeroplane crash; Rosemary was mentally retarded. She was presented at Court in London, but afterwards became more seriously afflicted. The family showed her at all times limitless devotion and have promoted far-reaching research into mental retardation.

According to Joe Kennedy's friend Cardinal Cushing, Archbishop of Boston, people mistakenly thought of him as a man completely interested in accumulating money. But Joe Kennedy told the Cardinal that 'his idea in life was the success of his children', which the Cardinal accepted as the truth. At what *point* in his life that became the dominant factor it would be hard to specify. In the thirties, when his eldest son Joe was studying under Harold Laski, there was talk of Joe Jr being trained to be a future President. But until the gloomy end of Joe Kennedy's Ambassadorship and perhaps for a while thereafter, Joe Senior must be credited with political aspirations of his own. Gradually he redirected them to the careers of his children. Mr Whalen give his biography of Joe Kennedy the sub-title: 'A study in power, wealth and family ambition'. By the time Jack Kennedy was making his way in Congress, the last of the three had taken over.

When immense success had been achieved, when Jack was President, Bobby Attorney-General and Ted a senator, Mrs Kennedy insists that the central strategic rôle of their father should never be overlooked, and the historians of the various campaigns bear her out. The Ambassador came to be looked upon in Britain as the most unhelpful representative that the United States had ever sent us. Far more nasty things than nice ones are said about him in the various books, though Theodore Sorensen (*Kennedy*, London, 1965) appears to have found him likeable, and there is no denying his acid wit. He had collected many enemies in America, as he was the first to recognize, and he took infinite pains that his reputation should not interfere with the growth of Jack's. He found a plausible excuse for being out of the country during the presidential election.

But Mrs Kennedy describes in moving terms the last meeting between Jack and his father. Ambassador Kennedy was on the porch in his wheelchair. The President went to him, put his arm round the old man's shoulder and kissed him on the forehead. He moved away, then came back and kissed him a second time. When the President was inside the helicopter for the take-off, he looked out at the figure in the wheelchair and his eyes filled with tears. 'He's the one who made all this possible,' he said to David

Powers, 'and look at him now.' At that time, Joe Kennedy had been incapacitated for two years following a severe stroke. He lasted another six years. Mrs Kennedy was kneeling by his bedside, holding his hand, when he died. 'Next to Almighty God,' she writes, 'I had loved him, do love him with all my heart, all my soul, all my mind. But I felt now that it was God's blessing which took him.' Joe Kennedy, with all his defects, some of them blatant, had the power of arousing deep love where he valued it most.

By and large, Rose Kennedy has been appreciated as emphatically as her husband has been disparaged. The title of Nancy Gager Clinch's book *The Kennedy Neurosis* (New York, 1973) speaks for itself. But even Nancy Clinch recognizes in her own words that 'to include Rose Kennedy in a Kennedy neurosis is certain to offend many people. She alone of the Kennedys has aroused almost universal respect and admiration, even among otherwise hard critics of the family.' The tremendous courage, dignity and resilience under a series of shattering blows are fully recognized. Nancy Clinch refers to Rose Kennedy as 'a strong, stoical woman'. She acknowledges the deep religious faith which has upheld her through all adversity. *The Kennedy Neurosis* was written before the publication of Rose Kennedy's autobiography. No one who has read this carefully compiled and absorbing volume will fail to credit her with these qualities, along with others. Near the end comes a passage, often quoted, in which she tells us that if God took away all his blessings and left her faith alone, she believes she could still be happy – leaving all to his inscrutable providence; 'When I start my day with a prayer of consecration to Him, with complete trust and confidence, I am perfectly relaxed and happy, regardless of what accident of fate befalls me, because I know it is part of His divine plan and He will take care of me and my dear ones.'

'The Ambassador' (Joe) did not lead the kind of life when he was in full vigour that one associates with piety. His attitude to women was predatory. His friendship with Gloria Swanson was not charitably interpreted. But his Catholicism was unquestioned throughout even though he insisted on the sons going to non-Catholic schools and Harvard. Rose Kennedy remarks that this was one of the few occasions when they had an important difference of opinion. When the news of the President's ﹍ssassination reached him, he took the news, to quote Cardinal Cushing again, 'with extraordinary resignation and confidence in God'. Rose's belief was no doubt altogether deeper. Jack Kennedy was a Catholic President and a practising Catholic in good standing. His mother tells us of an occasion when she entered his room in the White House and found him on his knees. The influence of his early religious upbringing is incalculable, but cannot have been small.

It has been said by critics that Rose Kennedy, consciously or unconsciously, developed an assumption that God was on the side of the Kennedys. In so far as the family developed a belief that the Kennedys were a 'super-family', she must presumably share some of the responsibility. Those who suspect the motives of all politicians will find grounds for criticism in her extraordinary skill in the electoral arts originally acquired from her father. 'In 1946', says David Powers, 'she had a greater understanding of precinct politics than anyone in our organization.' But he adds this comment, which should be pondered over by all who seek to analyse the extraordinary charisma of her son Jack: 'She not only loved meeting people, but she cared about the people she met.' That was the key. Her key and his.

2
A second son:
the making of a hero

Youth

When America came into the war in December 1941, Jack Kennedy was already in the navy. He had been accepted two months before, and by now he was twenty-four years old. What sort of mark had he made by this time?

The question does not admit of an unqualified answer. One could say that he had taken comparatively little advantage of his rare opportunities. Contrariwise it could be claimed that he had already revealed unusual promise. No one questioned his charm.

Rose Kennedy provides a vivid picture of the family life and upbringing of her young children. On an earlier occasion, when asked what kind of child was President Kennedy, she replied: 'By and large he was not any different from any other little boy in the neighbourhood. He liked to play and he had a terrible way of misplacing things like items of clothing. Sometimes he disobeyed and then he was spanked.' But even so early, his winning ways were undeniable: 'Sometimes I would punish him by sending him up to bed with only bread and water. Then he would slip downstairs and charm the cook into feeding him.' When he was about ten we get a glimpse of his style in a 'poem' dedicated to his father:

A Plea for a Raise
by Jack Kennedy
(dedicated to my father Mr J. P. Kennedy)

Chapter I
My recent allowance
is 40c. This I used for aeroplanes
and other playthings of childhood but now I am a scout
and I put away my childish
things. Before I would spend
20c of my c.40 allowance
and in five minutes I
would have empty pockets
and nothing to gain and
20c to lose. When I became
a scout I have to buy
canteens, haversacks, blankets
searchliagts [sic] ponchos things
that will last for years
and I can always use it
while I cant use a
chocolate marshmellow
sunday with vanilla ice
cream and so I put in
my plea for a raise of
thirty cents for me to buy
out things and pay my
own way more around.

Finis

John Fitzgerald Francis Kennedy

'I don't know', writes Mrs Kennedy, 'why he included "Francis" in his signature. Perhaps it was to invoke the blessing and help of that gentle saint.' His father granted the 'raise' – John Kennedy's charm and shrewdness already served him well!

Jack went first for a year to a Catholic school, Canterbury in Connecticut, where he did not prosper. Then to Choate, a real 'establishment' school where his brother Joe was immensely successful. There is no doubt that he heartily disliked Choate. During his Presidency, his old school unveiled his portrait as Choate's most distinguished son. He could not withhold the comment, 'This is the most ironic celebration of which I have ever heard.' In spite of sickness and injury he threw himself with the utmost vigour into various sports, including football, in which he made the Choate 'varsity' team. The coach recorded of him later, 'The most burning thing I can remember about Jack was that he was a fighter. You take Joe, he was a real athlete, but Jack made up for what he lacked in ability with his fight.'

But apparently he reserved his 'fight' for football. His mother records that she and her husband were anxious about his physical health in those years and accustomed to the idea that every now and then he would be laid up by some disease or accident. 'What concerned us as much or more was his lack of diligence in his studies or, let us say, lack of fight in trying to do well in those subjects which didn't happen to interest him.' His academic record was in short unsatisfactory.

He made some effort to improve. 'I really feel', he wrote to his father, 'that I have been bluffing myself about how much real work I have been doing.' And to his mother: 'Maybe Dad thinks I am alibiing, but I am not. I have also been worrying about my studies.'

But additionally he set out at one point to make himself a bit of an all-round nuisance. At Choate to be what was called a 'mucker' was to be everything that was not wanted there. Kennedy and a friend deliberately organized a 'Muckers' Club' to show what they thought of the prevailing atmosphere. Much trouble duly followed. Yet even at that stage, with nothing much to point to, there was a feeling abroad that Jack would turn out all right. Although his cumulative grades placed him slightly below the middle of the class, he was voted *most likely to succeed*. The Headmaster writing to his parents acknowledged that he could not feel seriously uneasy or worried about him. 'The longer I live and work with him, and the more I talk to him, the more confidence I have in him.' And he had already revealed the capacity for winning and retaining friends that came so easily to him at all times of his life.

Throughout his childhood his health was never satisfactory. While a high proportion of his physical sufferings in later life sprang no doubt from his war injuries and the long exposure involved in his heroic exploits, it is a fact that before that he suffered from all sorts of ailments and at Harvard seriously damaged his back at football. 'We used to laugh', wrote Bob Kennedy, 'about the great risk a mosquito took in biting Jack Kennedy – with some of his blood the mosquito was almost sure to die.' He passed a surprising amount of his childhood sick in bed. At least one compensation resulted. He was the only one in the family who was fond of reading. Loneliness and sickness made him read all the more, especially history, biography, the Arthurian romances, and later Churchill's *Marlborough*, when he was in his 'teens.

The loneliness in Schlesinger's view came from 'a frailness and sensitivity which set him somewhat apart from the extroverted and gregarious family'. Bearing in mind his ill-health in boyhood and the constant pain which followed his war-time injuries, it is easy to understand his later preoccupation with courage and, it may be added, with death. When he returned from his wedding trip he read his young wife what he said was his favourite poem ('I Have a Rendezvous with Death' by Alan Seeger):

> It may be he shall take my hand
> And lead me into his dark land
> And close my eyes and quench my breath . . .
>
> But I've a rendezvous with Death
> At midnight in some flaming town,
> When Spring trips north again this year,
> And I to my pledged word am true,
> I shall not fail that rendezvous.

By that time he was thirty-six years old and had been brought close to death in all sorts of ways in war and family bereavement. Yet he harmonized what might seem a somewhat morbid preoccupation with a love of living which endeared him alike to his intimate circle and later to far-flung millions.

One other feature of his boyhood must be touched on – the impact of his elder brother Joe. The devotion of the Kennedys to each other was so unqualified that it is difficult to take all that they have said about each other at its face value. After the death of his elder brother, Jack published a collection of essays about him by people who had known him well, and said, no doubt with total sincerity: 'Joe did many things well, but I have always felt that he achieved his greatest success as the eldest brother.' Yet Mrs Kennedy herself recalls that during the earlier years of their boyhood there were fights, 'some of which I have been told were *real* battles. Joe was older, bigger, stronger and better co-ordinated; but Jack, frail though he was, could fight like fury when he had to.' What psychological effect these battles had she does not seem concerned with.

Richard Whalen in *The Founding Father* provides a different angle. 'Joe', he says, 'was patient and gentle with the small ones, a good athlete who became their hero as he taught them to throw a ball, ride a bicycle and sail a boat.' But with 'the slight, willowy Jack, the only rival for his throne, he was a severe taskmaster and a taunting bully. They fought frequently. The fights usually ended with Jack pinned and humiliated.'

On 23 April 1935 Jack, now nearly eighteen, applied for admission to Harvard. The headmaster of Choate in spite of his personal goodwill was unenthusiastic, though he looked out for an excuse. 'Part of Jack's lack of intellectual drive is doubtless due to a severe illness.' In reply to a question about any unusual ability the headmaster answered 'No'.

The next year and a half was a frustrating period. Joe Kennedy decided that Jack, like Joe before him, should go to London and study with Harold Laski at the London School of Economics. Joe detested Laski's views but wanted his sons to know 'the other side of the story' to combat it more effectively. Jack, however, became ill in London with either hepatitis or jaundice, did not study with Laski and returned to America. Now he wanted to go to Princeton instead of Harvard. Yet in the following summer, 1936, we find him re-applying for admission to Harvard in a letter which sets out to explain what happened in the meantime.

I then decided to go to Princeton, due to its proximity to New York, where the doctors who were treating my illness were located . . . Again, due to sickness in the early part of December, I left Princeton to go south, after spending more than two months in the Peter Bent Brigham Hospital in Boston, under the care of Dr William P. Murphy. After my return from the south, I went out to Arizona.

According to another account, his real reason for going to Princeton was to be with his Choate room-mate LeMoyne Billings. There seems no doubt, however, about the ill health which interrupted his studies.

From 1936 to 1940 Jack was a student at Harvard. Impressions of him afterwards were mixed, but a distinguished American ambassador, a year younger than Kennedy, recalls him as 'mousey'.

His career, to use his mother's apt expression, was considerably 'fragmented between his first and second years'. In the summer of 1937, he made a prolonged tour of Europe, commenting sensibly but unexcitingly on the situation in Rome, and in Madrid where the Civil War was raging. He returned to Europe in the summer of 1938 and spent most of the time with his family in England, where his father was now Ambassador. In 1939 he obtained leave from Harvard to spend time in Europe. Acting in an unofficial way as his father's 'eyes and ears' during the last months of peace, he spent six weeks in Paris, a month in Warsaw and also visited Moscow, Leningrad, Jerusalem and Madrid. He was in Berlin at the time of the Hitler–Stalin pact; he was in the gallery of the House of Commons to hear Chamberlain announce the British decision to go to war on 2 September 1939.

On 4 September the British liner *Athenia* was torpedoed by a German U-boat with 300 Americans aboard, twelve of whom lost their lives. Jack was sent by his father to comfort the survivors and help them aboard the US relief ship *Orizaba*. This was his first real test in the adult world and he came through well. Then he returned to Harvard.

Taking his period there as a whole, and making obvious allowances, there was a noticeable though by no means dazzling improvement in his academic work. Already in 1936–7, his first year, his father commented on the marked change for the better. His tutor was moderately optimistic: 'Though his mind is still undisciplined and will probably never be original, he has ability, I think, and gives promise of development.' One wonders what that tutor made of his assessment in after years. In the second year his grades improved slightly. His tutor in government, Dr Bruce Hopper, was still rather patronizing: 'He is surprisingly able when he gets down to work. His preparation may be spotty but his general ability should bolster him up. A commendable fellow.'

It was not until his last year at Harvard that he gave any signs of possessing higher talents than those of a bright undergraduate. At last he took advantage of his special opportunities to produce a piece of work that did him lasting credit. *Why England Slept* was written as a thesis for his Harvard degree. It helped him to graduate with what in England would be called 'Honours', though there is no suggestion that he got what we would call a 'First'. It was his own analysis of why England failed until it was almost too late to face up to the Nazi peril.

After he took his degree in 1940, the thesis was published as a book of over 200 pages under the title *Why England Slept*. He makes handsome acknowledgments to Professor Bruce Hopper and Dr Paysan Wild of Harvard, and Mr John (the late Sir John) Wheeler-Bennett for their help. Incidentally, it was republished by Sidgwick & Jackson, Ltd., of which I am Chairman at the time of writing.

Sir John Wheeler-Bennett's recollections are of particular interest in relation to this stage of Jack Kennedy's life. He gives an arresting little picture of an informal dinner party during what he calls 'Mr Joseph Kennedy's disastrous period as United States Ambassador in London':

'I'll tell you about these boys,' said the Ambassador to me in his rasping nasal voice, pointing to Joe, Jack and Bobby on the other side of the table, 'there's young Joe – he is going to be President of the United States; and there's Jack – he's going to be a University President; and there's Bobby (tapping his nose in a cunning manner) – he's the lawyer.'

Jack Wheeler-Bennett had forgotten about this conversation until he was back in America and addressing a class at the invitation of his friend, Bruce Hopper, when 'a most pleasing, open-countenanced, blue-eyed young man came up to me afterwards'. He introduced himself to me as Jack Kennedy and recalled the meeting in London. Could he come and talk to Wheeler-Bennett? They met by arrangement at the Hopper's house the following afternoon.

What followed was of mutual pleasure and benefit. Hopper asked Wheeler-Bennett whether he would supervise Jack Kennedy's thesis for his Master's degree; at first Wheeler-Bennett was cautious. The following afternoon he and Jack Kennedy walked for two hours along the banks of the River Charles, 'at the conclusion of which I had decided that here was a highly exceptional young man, who surely merited all the help that I could give him'. Wheeler-Bennett seems to have been one of the very first people to look beyond Jack Kennedy's charm and recognize his intellectual capacity.

Wheeler-Bennett discusses *Why England Slept* with inside knowledge. He mentions that Jack Kennedy had not only done some research on his own initiative, but had drawn widely on the views of his father who 'was an arch-appeaser and an extreme admirer of Neville Chamberlain'. 'Not unnaturally, the boy had arrived at a definitely prejudiced point of view and it fell to my lot, without trying too hard, to prejudice him in the opposite direction, at least to expound the other side.'

Joe Kennedy, with his usual shrewdness, guessed that some such process might be at work. He would telephone at frequent intervals to ask, 'What's that Limey been telling you?'

Over twenty years later, President Kennedy asked Sir John Wheeler-Bennett, then staying with the Ormsby Gores, to call on him. 'We've both come quite a long way since the first edition of this book was published,' he said as he signed a copy of the second. This, in Wheeler-Bennett's words, 'was undeniably endearing'.

Reading the book today by a youth who had hitherto made no academic or literary mark, one is astonished at its overall self-confidence and maturity. As we have already seen, he had travelled by now quite extensively in Europe and acted there and elsewhere as his father's eyes and ears. Even so, one is struck by his intimate grasp of the inner realities of British politics. One is not suggesting that it was not his own handiwork. But with the help of unusual advantages he had penetrated recesses of knowledge and discussion not available to the ordinary student.

He paid some price for his special advantages. Schlesinger points out that ostensibly writing to prepare America for its own crisis at a moment when British survival was uncertain, he remains agnostic about the choices open to America. He certainly does not insist that America should intervene before too late, though by this time he may have held such a view. Whether or not he was under the direct influence of his father, one must detect an understandable desire to say nothing to embarrass the latter in his non-interventionist exertions.

After much well-informed and powerful analysis the conclusion is disappointingly vague. The reluctance to blame individuals is not unqualified. 'England was admittedly unfortunate to have a man like Baldwin, with his lack of vision, in office at a particular period when vision above all else was needed.' Even Chamberlain, a close friend of his father's, is referred to as 'a man who wished so intensely for peace and had such sincere and strong hopes in the possibility of achieving it, that he failed completely to estimate the dire need of his country to prepare for war.'

But far more insistence is laid on the weaknesses inherent in capitalism and democracy, though he expresses the more or less confident hope that they prevail in the long run. 'The people', he said, 'for a long time would not have tolerated any great arms programmes'. . . . and much more to the same effect.

At this stage of his life and thinking, John Kennedy appeared to find no scope in politics for the heroic individual. Six years later in *Profiles in Courage* (New York, 1956) he was to preach a very different gospel.

Mrs Kennedy tells us that at a certain point she had to explain to the children that they belonged to an immensely rich family and must appreciate the special responsibilities of those with great possessions. It is tempting and indeed irresistible to look on her husband as possessing a much cruder form of ambition than hers. But we must not forget that in his eyes his great wealth was, or became, a stepping-stone to supreme public office and supreme public service for his sons. When the war came, he did not hound his sons into the danger zone, but brought up as they had been, with an outlook in which dreams of service and dreams of glory were blended, they took the only course one could conceive of their choosing, and he applauded their choice.

Rose Kennedy provides a mother's reaction. 'One may wonder what I thought about all this. I hated it. War has always seemed to me the ultimate insanity. There was nothing I could do but put on a cheerful face. To hope and to pray.'

The war years 1939–45 fell for Kennedy into five phases. During the first (1939–40) he was completing his studies at Harvard and writing *Why England Slept*. In the second phase, after dabbling in business administration and drifting around South America, we find him early in 1941 attempting to join the army. Having been rejected for that service and for the navy because of his injured back, he was finally accepted by the latter after five months of therapeutic exercises. By the time of his acceptance, Pearl Harbour and the American entry into the war (December 1941) were only two months away. During the third phase (October 1941 to August 1943), he was at first engaged in intelligence work. His friendship with the glamorous Inga Arvad, suspected of Nazi affiliations, seems to have led to his transfer from Washington to Charleston under something of a cloud. There followed serious trouble with his back, training as a line officer, volunteering for PT boats, more training and some instruction. By February 1943, after pulling every string, he was at last allowed to proceed to active service in the South Pacific, but did not arrive 'at the front lines' until July.

The fourth phase was very short and very glorious (2–8 August 1943). On the night of 2 August 1943 his torpedo boat PT/109 was cut in half by the Japanese destroyer *Amagiri* as it patrolled in the dark waters of Blackett Strait, west of New Georgia in the Solomon Islands. By 8 August he and the ten survivors out of his crew of twelve were safe.

The fifth phase (August 1943 until the end of the war in August 1945) is one of hospitalization and attempted recovery from injuries. A year after the destruction of PT/109 his elder brother Joe was killed in an action for which he was posthumously awarded the Navy Cross ('for extraordinary heroism and courage'). Not long before, his sister Kathleen's husband, the Marquis of Hartington, had been killed in France.

By this time Jack Kennedy himself was out of the war. Physically he never recovered from his injuries, malaria taking a long and additional toll. But in a political and still more in a deeper, psychological sense, the experience brought him lasting advantage. At last he had achieved something without benefit of wealth and family, absolutely and entirely on his own.

John Kennedy's heroic adventure on PT/109 has been described in more than one book and in many magazine articles; a film exploited the episode, not unnaturally, for political purposes. But it was undoubtedly 'the real thing'.

It was about 2.30 am 2 August when the Japanese destroyer emerged out of the blackness. Some reports from the survivors are more vivid than any indirect speech. Radioman Maguire recalled:

The destroyer hit us like the *Queen Mary*. . . . Kennedy went slamming down, smack on his back. And I went down with him. The destroyer didn't even slow down. Its bow carried along our starboard side, shearing away the middle two-thirds of PT/109. Our boat snapped in two and we never saw the after half again. . . . I was trying to stand, and I was praying harder than ever I'd done before in my entire life. Kennedy kept trying to get up. He said 'Are you all right, Mac?'. Kennedy gave the order to abandon ship, as the flames from the gas tanks of the PT/109 seemed about to engulf them. But this did not in fact occur. Kennedy and some of the others were able to climb back on the remaining half of the boat. There were still survivors in the water.

At this point comes a recollection from the gunner's mate, Charles Harris. 'Somewhere I could hear McMahon yelling for help. He had come up smack in the flames of our own high octane gasoline. I yelled for Kennedy: "Skipper, Skipper, McMahon is burned bad! Can you give him a hand?" In a couple of minutes he reached us. He half lifted McMahon out of the water, so that others could get him aboard; then started back for us.' It took three hours to get all the survivors back aboard.

Next day a memorial service was held at Rendova for Kennedy and his crew. Joe Kennedy Sr received a wire from the Navy Department informing him that his son Jack was missing. He put it in his pocket and said nothing to Rose and his children. He clung to the hope that there was still a chance.

The next stage in the astonishing story was the tremendous swim which, after hours in the water, brought Kennedy and his surviving crew to rest on a small island in enemy-held territory. For all of them it was an immense effort. But for Kennedy it was almost super-human. Handicapped throughout by a damaged back, he dragged the injured McMahon along with him over the whole three miles. The latter is the best of all witnesses.

'We're going to that small one,' Kennedy said, pointing to a tiny island about three miles away. 'I'll take McMahon.' He was very matter-of-fact about it, like he was talking about the weather.

He took the two long straps of my kapok . . . tied them together and eased me into the water. Then he put the damn straps in his mouth, holding them with his clenched teeth, and started swimming. I was on my back, my head towards him, trying to push my feet to help him. I wasn't much good to him. I couldn't believe the skinny kid would get very far with me. . . .

But he got the whole way with him. McMahon heard him say, 'Pappy, we're going in.' He thought he had never heard such happy words in his life. 'Then Kennedy half towed and half carried me ashore. I tried to help myself and walk in, but coral cut both of us bad and when we got on the sand, Kennedy and I collapsed.'

In the hectic four days which followed, there were more heroes than one, but our concern is with Kennedy. The details are still subject to dispute; the main lines of the story are clear enough. Kennedy and his men could not stay where they were without food and drink (apart from coconuts – of doubtful value to them). There seemed no hope of rescue. Kennedy spent many hours next day in the water, frantically trying to intercept any PT boats that might be passing. He came back utterly exhausted and slightly feverish, with nothing accomplished. Under Kennedy's leadership, with McMahon in tow, they swam to another island, Olasana. They were little better off.

Kennedy and 'Barney' Ross, another officer, then swam to a third island, known by various names, referred to as Naru-Groos by Joan and Clay Blair (*The Search for J.F.K.*), the latest investigators. There they found a small canoe, food and fresh water. Kennedy returned to Olasana. 'Here,' to quote the Blairs, 'he was astonished to find a fire going and two natives snuggled in for the night, helping the survivors and feeding them C-rations – astonished and relieved beyond measure.' It was obvious that the natives could be employed as messengers. Back on Naru-Groos, they showed Kennedy where a two-man native canoe was hidden. He scratched a message on a green coconut husk:

> Eleven alive Native knows posit and reefs
> Nauru Island (*sic*) Kennedy

It was taken by the natives to Rendova and was destined to become famous. But rescue came about in a different fashion.

The Australian coast-watcher, Lieutenant Evans, had been energetically combing the area through native scouts in search of survivors. The two natives referred to above passed on word about Kennedy's position which reached Evans. Meanwhile Kennedy and Ross continued their desperate struggle to obtain help. Now after further appalling vicissitudes they awoke on the shore of Naru-Groos to find four big natives standing over them.

In Ross's words, 'I shook Kennedy and he sat bolt upright. They looked mean. Then one stepped forward and in a beautiful British accent said, "I have a letter for you, Sir".' It ran as follows:

On His Majesty's Service: Friday 11 pm
To Senior Officer Nauru Island.

Have just learnt of your presence on Nauru Island and also that two natives have taken news to Rendova, I strongly advise you return immediately to here in this canoe and by the time you arrive here I will be in radio communication with authorities at Rendova and we can finalise plans to collect balance of your party.

R. A. EVANS
Lieut. RANVR

Will warn aviation of your crossing Ferguson Passage.

Evans, with some help from Kennedy, made the necessary plans for rescuing the whole party. Evans, on first meeting Kennedy, offered him a cup of tea and remarked of him: 'He was certainly a nice guy whose first thought was for his crew.' When eventually PT/157 came alongside and Kennedy climbed aboard his first question was understandable but not, we are told, popular: 'Where the hell you been?'

Kennedy in later years, when asked how he became a war hero, was known to reply whimsically 'They sunk my boat.' The Blairs argue strongly, as have done plenty of others, that his seamanship was at fault in the first place. But those who served under him were loud in their admiration. Even the Blairs admit that the long swim with McMahon on his back 'was an extremely gutsy performance'. In the final citation, when Kennedy received the Navy and Marine Corps medal, reference is made to his 'extremely heroic conduct'. 'His outstanding courage, endurance and leadership we are told contributed to the saving of several lives and were in keeping with the highest traditions of the United States naval service.'

3

The pursuit of power

The young politician

It took Kennedy fourteen years from his entry into politics in 1946 to reach the Presidency in 1960. At forty-three he was the youngest President ever elected. Some British analogies may be offered. Hugh Gaitskell, with whom Kennedy came to find a growing rapport, was ten years older than Kennedy but a political contemporary. He entered the House of Commons in 1945, was Chancellor of the Exchequer in 1950 and leader of the Labour Opposition in 1955. If he and Kennedy had not both been smitten down in 1963, they would have been leading their respective countries at the same time. Harold Wilson, born a year before Kennedy, became leader of the Labour Party on Hugh Gaitskell's death, and in 1964, the youngest British Prime Minister of modern times.

Gaitskell and Wilson, however, made their way to the heights primarily by parliamentary performance. They had to be successful outside, but it was in Parliament they outstripped their rivals. The same cannot be said of Kennedy. Sorensen, 'the pale, bespectacled intellectual' of Harlech's first recollection – his background Nebraska, Unitarian, pacifist, the very antithesis of Kennedy – became his first personal assistant and leading speech writer in 1954. He recalls that Kennedy's election to the Senate from Massachusetts, after three elections to the House of Representatives (1946, 1948, 1950) 'had not inspired any predictions of greatness in the national press, or in Democratic Party circles'.

His astonishing feat of overcoming the long-established

Senator Lodge in 1952, against the national trend, was lost sight of or played down. Much stress was laid on his physical glamour and on his audacious new methods of electioneering, including maximum use of his family and above all on the amount of money expended to secure his election.

According to one story, Joe Kennedy had claimed in 1946 that with the amount of money he was spending he could elect his chauffeur to Congress. Joe's cousin, Joe Kane, had played a prominent part in introducing Jack Kennedy to Boston politics. 'Politics,' he said, 'is like war . . . it takes three things to win – the first is money and the second is money and the third is money.' The political merits of the new senator aroused less attention at that time.

The use of money and the cult of the family cannot be easily paralleled in England, but the establishment of a national, ahead of a parliamentary reputation, coupled with personal glamour, makes one think of the Anthony Eden of the 1930s, who was incidentally Foreign Secretary by the age of thirty-eight. Eden, if not a spectacular war hero like Kennedy, had had a splendid record on the western front. In each case the war experience had contributed not a little to the idealistic determination that 'it must never happen again'.

Kennedy had considered various careers before entering politics; for example, the law, journalism, academic history or political science, and the foreign service. But with the death in action of his brother Joe, politics was the obvious life's work. 'Everything seemed to point to it in 1946,' he said. His father's father had been a member of the state legislature. His mother's father Honey Fitz, the former Mayor of Boston, had been a potent politician for many years. His father the Ambassador had ruled out business discussions in the home but promoted unending political arguments. In spite of (or because of) his own immense but questionable success in business, he brought up his family to think of public service as a superior way of life. We can slightly discount some of the statements attributed in connection with Jack's entry into politics to the Ambassador and to Jack himself. 'I got Jack into politics; I was the one. I told him Joe was dead and it was therefore his responsibility to run for Congress. He didn't want to. He felt he didn't have the ability and he still feels that way. But I told him he had to,' said Joe. 'It was like being drafted. My father wanted his eldest son in politics. "Wanted" wasn't the right word. He demanded it. You know my father,' said Jack. 'We're going to sell Jack like soap-flakes,' Joe said.

Schwab and Shneidman have convinced themselves on very little evidence that Jack Kennedy had, since a boy, cherished a passion consciously or unconsciously for a political career. He was well aware that this was impossible for him while his elder brother lived; hence on this theory he concealed these aspirations and his political views from family friends 'and perhaps even from himself'. This subordination of his career to that of Joe Jr produced, according to Schwab and Shneidman, a reluctance to succeed at school or college in any direction at all. We need not accept this particular hypothesis. It is simpler to rely on certain quotations which they themselves offer and which in themselves neither prove or disprove their thesis. 'If Joe were alive today,' said John Kennedy of his brother, 'I wouldn't be in this. I'm only trying to fill his shoes. . . . My brother Joe was the logical one in the family to be in politics, and if he had lived, I'd have kept on being a writer. . . . I never would have run for office if Joe had lived. . . . Just as I went into politics when Joe died, if anything happened to me tomorrow my brother Bobby would run for my seat.' There is no doubt at all that if Joe had lived the energies of the entire family would have been concentrated on pushing him to the highest places, in fact the Presidency. Beyond question Jack would have had to choose another profession. That and nothing else is certain.

In a mood of deep seriousness Jack Kennedy confronted the post-war world. In February 1945 Harry Hopkins, Roosevelt's closest adviser, published an article in which he said, 'Let America be the strongest nation in the world and no-one will attack her.' He called for a massive build-up of American arms. A message of this kind might have been expected to appeal to the author of *Why England Slept*. It was the more notable, therefore, that Kennedy was at pains to write a deliberate eight-page reply. It was never published but it contained at least a germ of his subsequent international thinking.

He did not renounce his earlier emphasis on the need for military strength but he supplemented it with careful proposals for international disarmament. 'What I propose', he wrote, 'is that there be worked out between the United Nations – and chiefly the

British, Russians and ourselves – an agreement for limiting our post-war rearmament plans.' But if plans of this kind failed to fructify he was as insistent as ever that the United States must be the strongest military power.

In the spring of that year, 1945, he began to work for the Hearst Press and as a special writer went on their behalf to San Francisco to watch and describe the founding of the United Nations. Some of his hopefulness was already beginning to fade. He wrote sadly afterwards: 'When I think of how much this war has cost us, of the deaths of Cy and Peter and Orv and Gil and Demi and Joe and Billy and all of those thousands and millions who have died with them – when I think of all those gallant acts that I have seen or anyone has seen who has been to the war – it would be a very easy thing to feel disappointed and somewhat betrayed.' He referred to battlefields where sacrifice had been the order of the day, but could see little evidence of national sacrifice at San Francisco. Yet he found himself wondering whether it could reasonably be expected. He made a note at the time with regard to the United Nations: 'mustn't expect too much. A truly just solution will leave every nation somewhat disappointed. There is no cure-all.' In a still more depressed mood he replied to the questionnaire addressed to members of his Harvard Class of 1940: 'I am pessimistic about the future of the country.'

He described himself to his wife as 'an idealist without illusions'. His closest associates emphasized repeatedly his joy of life. No one as sophisticated as he was, in the best sense, could be free from darker moments, but they seldom prevailed for long.

Still a journalist he covered the British General Election of 1945, finally forecasting a narrow win for the Tories. His old friend Hugh Fraser was the Conservative candidate for the Stafford and Stone constituency, which he has ever since represented. He writes as follows:

Jack had a memory which after many years could be sparked into almost total recall! In 1945 he had done a roving report on the British election for *The New York Times*. He stayed a couple of nights with me in Staffordshire and attended an adoption meeting.

A neighbouring Tory candidate had been quoted as boldly saying that striking miners should be shot, so at our packed meeting on the edge of Stoke-on-Trent, five hundred miners just allowed me a hearing, but howled down the Conservative Home Secretary. The proceedings were more hilarious than riotous. In my turn I attended some of Jack's public meetings in Boston when he was fighting Cabot Lodge for the Senate. Certainly compared to our meeting at the Meir, they were immemorably tame and boring. In all the visits or meetings in Washington, London, Palm Beach or New York, neither of us even referred to Jack's vicarious electoral experiences.

The last occasion when Hugh saw him was when they were flying together in the presidential plane in the summer of 1963 to the U.S. Air Force passing out parade at its Academy in Colorado.

Arguments we were having about the Concorde aeroplane and Walt Rostow's idea of a multi-national manned NATO fleet seemed to spark his memory. After eighteen years he reeled off in his flat New England voice his description of my adoption meeting: the shouting, the discomfited Home Secretary, but above all my chairman, whom he made the pivot of his argument, imitating accent, mannerisms and voice of that long-forgotten declaration as to how lucky the audience were to have me, Hugh Fraser, as their candidate. 'You see,' he ended, 'what you British can't understand, no one in this country ever thinks they're lucky to have anyone as a candidate, even less as a President. That's the difference between our systems.' It was total and managed recall, funny, and a homily from a proper democrat.

Next year, 1946, there was a clear opportunity for Jack to be elected to the House of Representatives for Boston's eleventh district. His mind was by now made up – his career would be in politics. And he knew his imperative duty. 'Kennedys didn't come in second.'

He would win, win, win! Jack, in his mother's words, by this time 'knew about politics, but very little about the actual mechanics of organizing and operating a campaign'. The story of his first entry into the field is vividly related by David Powers in Mrs Kennedy's book, where it should be read in full.

David Powers had agreed to work for a certain John Cotter:

... then I got this call from Bill Sutton and a few nights later, it was 21 January 1946, somebody knocked at the front door.... I saw this tall, thin, handsome guy. He introduced himself, said he was Jack Kennedy and could he talk with me for a few minutes. I invited him in. We started talking and he said he was running for Congress. I said: 'Gee, John Cotter's running for that seat. I am going to be with him. We grew up together and we stick together.'

But Jack Kennedy was not to be put off so easily. He set to work to pick Dave Powers' guidance. In Powers' language: 'He was sort of shy', but he was 'aggressively shy'. He said: 'Well, what would you do if you were like me a candidate running here for Congress?' He was soon asking Powers about everybody and everything. He was interested in boot-blacks, how many shoes they shined. 'He was incredible, this guy.' As he was going out of the door, he said to Powers: 'Dave, will you do me a favour? I'm speaking to a group of Gold Star mothers at the American Legion Hall next Tuesday. I don't know anyone in Charlestown. Will you come over with me?'

'Well,' said Powers, 'you'd do that for anybody, but can you imagine that, imagine feeling sorry for a millionaire's son? And I said "All right, I will".' We shall find Khrushchev later informing us that he felt sorry for Kennedy after their Vienna meeting. Sympathy may or may not have affected the Russian's ruthless policy. It certainly affected Powers, who became as close as anybody to Kennedy. Artifice or natural instinct, how shall one describe it? Under whatever name the magic worked.

Powers' account of the meeting with the Gold Star Mothers is a classic. 'So we go over there and he is talking to these Gold Star Mothers. We had an awful lot of boys die in the war and there were several hundred in the hall.' Now this is worth noting, for Kennedy was no stripling; he was twenty-nine years old, and already an acknowledged war hero, who had met politicians of all kinds and travelled widely. 'It seems to me he's making the world's worst speech. He's talking about the need for peace and the sacrifices of war, but he's certainly no orator. And I am getting nervous as hell. I'm the only other man there, they're all women. At the end he looked out at all those wonderful ladies, and in a kind of awkward but direct way he said, sort of blurting it out from deep inside, "I think I know how you feel because my mother is a Gold Star mother too." The effect was overwhelming. Every woman there seemed to be saying "he reminds me of my own." The son they had lost.' When he finished his little talk, the Charlestown ladies smothered him with gratitude and devotion. 'In all my years in politics,' says Powers, 'I have never seen such reaction.' As they walked away, Kennedy said to him, 'How do you think I did?' Powers spoke as he felt: 'You were great.' Kennedy went on, 'Then you'll be with me?' He put out his hand and, says Powers, 'in the excitement of the ordeal (his word), I shook his hand and said "I will".' Later, when Powers was not unnaturally criticized for his defection from Cotter, Kennedy would cheer him up by saying, with what Powers calls 'one of his classical jokes', 'Just think, Dave, some day you can say you were with me from the beginning.'

The organization, the floods of voluntary helpers from inside and outside the family, the incredible zeal and energy put into the campaign, with Joe Kennedy keeping a close watch on matters in the background, all this has been described a hundred times. But when he won the heart of David Powers, he was well on the way to winning the heart of America.

Kennedy was now a member of the House of Representatives. In retrospect it is rather strange to discover the mediocrity of his performance in his six years in the House. We can see this as part of a pattern. No eminent man in our day has proved more capable of rapid evolution. Put otherwise, he was a late developer. He once compared his political growth with his scholastic performances. 'The fact of the matter is', he said, 'that I fiddled around at Choate and really didn't become interested until the end of my sophomore [second] year at Harvard.' Sorensen adds the suggestion that he fiddled around as a congressman and really didn't become interested until his 'sophomore' year in the Senate.

Then comes a passage in Sorensen's recollections of exceptional interest: 'It seemed to me in 1953 that an inner struggle was being waged for the spirit of John Kennedy: a struggle between the political dilettante and the statesman, between the lure of luxury and lawmaking.'

Most observers had considered his performance in the House of Representatives to be largely undistinguished. Ill-health and one form of travel or another had produced a record of absenteeism which had been 'heightened by indifference' (Sorensen). The Blairs bring out the neglected point that he made a fine start in Congress and, after just seven months in public office, had become a phenomenon. Then severe illness set him back a long way. They are certainly right in stressing his independence of the Democratic Party leadership. In home affairs, he usually voted with the liberals in favour of the underprivileged, although on 18 February 1952 he declared, without giving reasons: 'I am opposed to any nationalized health plan.' Subsequently he maintained that position except that he was later ready to offer a form of nationalized medicine to the old and sick.

Regarding strikes he used strong words before and after election. He said for example on 16 April 1947, 'I believe that this country should certainly be in a position to combat a strike that affects the health and safety of the people. Therefore I feel that the President must have the power to step in and stop those strikes.' Nevertheless he came out against the Taft–Hartley Labour Management Relations Act which the trade unions regarded as most unfair to labour.

Contrariwise, on foreign policy he usually voted with the conservatives, repeatedly stressing the Soviet danger. Overall there seems no reason to differ from Sorensen's assessment. We are forced to the conclusion that in 1953 Jack Kennedy had not yet found his true identity or ultimate purpose in life.

A small digression is necessary. No biography, indeed no book, was more admired or more widely recommended by Kennedy in his maturity than Lord David Cecil's biography of William Lamb (Lord Melbourne), British Prime Minister throughout the last half of the 1830s. Most brilliant of all in that book are the first chapters describing Whig society in the eighteenth century, and the later chapter which paints the portrait of William Lamb, aged forty-seven, at a time when he had not yet 'achieved anything of significance in the world'. There are two connected but distinguishable points here for the biographer of Kennedy.

On the one hand British Whig society held for Kennedy an undeniable glamour. As already mentioned, he no sooner arrived in London than he, his brother Joe and his sister Kathleen plunged as to the manner born into the nearest approach to it that London could offer in the 1930s. The fact that Kathleen married the potential head of the greatest Whig family extant (by that time they were officially Conservatives) is surely no coincidence, though it was a love match if ever there was one. And of course Melbourne could be looked on as a Whig of Whigs, although a survivor who illustrated to an uncomprehending generation the charm of the past.

'The Whigs', David Cecil tells us, 'were the most agreeable society England has ever known. . . . The character of their agreeability was of a piece with the rest of them. It had all their vitality and all their sense of style. It was incomparably racy, spontaneous

35

and accomplished . . . it had its grace, a virile, classical grace.' All this could be said of Melbourne, and Kennedy could identify himself with it. But at one point the analogy becomes more complicated. Melbourne was cool, rational, urbane and witty, and so was John Kennedy. But Melbourne's chronic passivity towards government, whether he was in it or out of it, was utterly opposed to Kennedy's overwhelming activism. It is hardly possible to imagine two men who behaved more differently in supreme office. A similarity would seem to be discoverable rather in the fact that each had when young a divided nature. 'Melbourne's disposition', says David Cecil, 'was fundamentally divided against itself. He found his heart stretching out to an idealism which his reason told him was visionary illusion.' Kennedy's conflict, we have just been told by Sorensen, was a struggle between the political dilettante and the statesman, while his wife detected it in the clash between New England and Ireland. He may be held to have resolved his attitude in heroic action; his life was too short for that to be settled finally.

But there was nothing complex, let alone half-hearted, in his approach to the winning of elections. The technique of high powered organization with every possible refinement of public relations was steadily developed from the campaign of 1946 to the Presidential election of 1960. A peak was reached and then surpassed in the campaign for the Senate in 1952. The sitting senator, Cabot Lodge, came of one of the greatest Protestant families, the very people who had looked down on such as the Kennedys from time immemorial. He seemed a cast-iron fixture. Joseph Kennedy rightly advised his son that Lodge was the very man to go for; if he beat him he would have beaten the best.

Every kind of relative and friend was mobilized for the contest. Never had so many tea-parties been provided for women voters. The glamour of the Kennedys led by Rose, the matriarch, was a major attraction. Jack Kennedy himself soon realized that, to quote Schwab and Shneidman, 'the best thing going for him was himself'.

A huge map of Massachusetts hung in his apartment. He let it be known that he planned to speak in every corner of the state. Every place he spoke in would have a pin stuck into its name on the map. He told David Powers, 'When we've got this map completely covered with pins that's when I'll announce that I am going to run statewide.' He was thoroughly well-known before he delivered his open challenge and long before Lodge got to work. He accumulated an index file of young people who could be of future use. Kenneth O'Donnell and Lawrence O'Brien were added to his campaign staff and went forward from strength to strength. He deliberately worked in complete independence of the Democratic organization. He owed nothing to them when the result was announced.

And what a triumph it was in a year of Eisenhower and Republican Party victory! Standing for President, Eisenhower carried Massachusetts by 208,800 votes for the Republicans. The Republican nominee for Governor won by 14,456 votes. Yet Kennedy, relying on his personal machine and his personal charisma, won by 70,737 votes. The achievement was his and his only, if ever that can be said in politics.

Looking ahead for a moment one should notice that he was still not altogether satisfied. In 1955 O'Donnell and O'Brien obtained control on his behalf of the State Democratic organization. By the time of the Convention of 1956 Kennedy was not only Senator for Massachusetts but its Democratic boss.

To return to 1953. He married Jacqueline Bouvier, a girl of surpassing beauty, a Catholic like himself, but of a completely different culture from any of the Kennedys. In a prize-winning essay in 1951 she wrote that the three men she would most like to have known were Baudelaire, Wilde and Diaghilev. She had been totally uninterested in politics up to that time and never felt truly at home in them. Some of Kennedy's closest supporters remained uneasy with her, but Kennedy loved her as she was. Hitherto his friendships with young women, usually beautiful, had been legion. There seems, however, to have been a general awareness that he was not yet ready for marriage. Now, at last, he embarked wholeheartedly on a life's commitment. Still, if the central question of his career was to be whether he was to turn out 'political dilettante or statesman', it was not obvious which way her influence would operate.

The years 1953 to 1955 proved to be crucial to him. Sorensen can hardly be expected to assess his own impact on his master, friend and hero. But Lord Harlech supplies this closely-observed estimate: 'It was immediately clear to me that this was a rare and very special association. Kennedy had come to trust and to confide

37

in Sorensen absolutely . . . for eleven years, Sorensen served at his side with exceptional skill and with utter devotion.' Sorensen must therefore be given no small credit for the triumph of the statesman-like side of Kennedy.

But also of incalculable importance were the appalling physical experiences that he went through between September 1954 and May 1955.

When America came into the war, he was rejected, as I have related, by the army because of a back injured at football. It was re-injured when his PT boat was rammed. He underwent a disc operation in 1944 which had no lasting benefit. He frequently needed crutches during the 1952 campaign. In 1954 he decided that an extremely dangerous spinal fusion operation would be better than life as a cripple. But malaria had followed the war-time exposure and shock. From then on, he had suffered from an inadequate adrenal system, which led to many rumours (now, it would seem, confirmed) that he was suffering from Addison's disease. The effect of surgery on this adrenal shortage produced severe post-operative complications. Twice he was placed on the critical list and his family summoned. Twice the last rites of his Church were administered. Again, as in the Pacific and on another occasion since the war, he fought his way back to life. A Dr Janet Travell gave him new hope for life free from crutches and he remained eternally grateful to her.

But he did not return to Washington till May 1955. From then on he always kept a rocking chair in his office, wore a cloth brace and corrective shoes and slept with a bed board under his mattress. Yet at the same time he was a creditable exponent of his own famous doctrine of vigour. No one could outlast him in the most strenuous campaign. He was six feet tall, of athletic build and muscular, good at games and swam backstroke for Harvard. When he was in the Navy he was still being referred to as 'skinny', but in his maturity his weight varied round a point a little over twelve stone. His medication at times made his face a little puffy but never affected his graceful figure.

His brother Bob said after his death that he was in pain during half the years of his life. That was certainly true of more than half his years with Jackie. Yet his zest and gaiety remained for all who knew him an abiding memory.

But the sufferings of 1954 and 1955 were not by any means

wasted. During those months, with no little help from Sorensen, he wrote his book *Profiles in Courage*. His Harvard thesis *Why England Slept* had been published in book form and sold heavily. But *Profiles in Courage* is of an altogether higher calibre. The achievement brought him at least three lasting benefits – the sheer creative effort completed the intellectual and mental development that had never come to its proper flowering at Harvard. The conclusions he reached regarding political courage and integrity came to form a vital part of his own approach to statesmanship. And the huge success of the book, its translation into many languages, culminating in the award of the Pulitzer Prize, lifted him at a bound out of the ordinary run of 'freshman senators'. It removed any suggestion that he was little more than a projection of his father's family ambition and gave him a permanent standing among those best qualified to judge.

The bulk of the book consists of eight episodes, each describing the political heroism of an American senator as interpreted by Kennedy. The first was John Quincy Adams, the son of a President and later himself to be President, but at this time a young Federalist member of the Senate. When the American frigate *Chesapeake* was fired upon by the British man-o'-war *Leopard* the incensed Adams was convinced that the time for forceful action had come. In 1807 he strongly supported the Republican leader Jefferson in an embargo against the British to the fury of his own Federalist Party and his own State of Massachusetts. The next two selected men of courage were Daniel Webster and Thomas Hart Benton. Both men supported the famous Henry Clay Compromise which postponed for eleven years the final confrontation over slavery. Webster was held in the North to have sold out to the forces which favoured slavery. Benton was denounced in the South for exactly the opposite reason. It is hard to say which of them incurred the greater obloquy.

Four years later a final effort was made to produce yet one more compromise which would save the Union. Senator Sam Houston, the fourth man of courage, knew well that it would pass but he regarded it as a betrayal of the 1850 Compromise; he recorded against it what he called later 'the most unpopular vote I ever gave, but the wisest and most patriotic'. Texas, his own state, cried aloud for his scalp as one who had betrayed 'his state in the Senate'.

The next example of political courage is the most dramatic of all. Whether or not President Andrew Johnson was going to be successfully impeached depended on a single Senator. Only the vote of Senator Ross was necessary to convict the President. His own state Kansas was the most radical state in the Union, i.e. the strongest for impeaching. The pressure brought to bear on him was enormous. Describing the moment afterwards he would write, 'I almost literally looked down into my open grave.' Yet he gave the firm reply 'Not Guilty'. He was never re-elected to the Senate. When he returned to Kansas he and his family suffered social ostracism, near poverty and physical attack.

The sixth and seventh political heroes, Lucius Lamarr and George Norris, were separated by a good many years but resembled one another in defying public opinion at crucial moments over a lengthy period. Lamarr resisted immense pressure from his own state on behalf of the policy of Free Silver. George Norris supported Al Smith as a presidential candidate in 1928. Not only did Al Smith belong to the opposite party but he was a Catholic and a 'Wet' (anti-prohibitionist) while Norris was a Protestant and a 'Dry'. 'The storm which followed', recalled Norris later, 'was more violent than any I had ever encountered. It was well that I had some training in the matter of abuse.'

Senator Robert Taft came eighth and last on the list. In October 1946, at a time when he was a likely nominee for the Presidency in 1948, he had this to say about the Nuremberg Trials: 'About this whole judgment there is the spirit of vengeance and vengeance is seldom justice. The hanging of the eleven men convicted will be a blot on the American record which we shall long regret.' Made during a heated election campaign, the speech caused enormous indignation in his own (Republican) Party as well as outside it. It destroyed his chance of ever becoming President.

Kennedy sets out to analyse political courage with partial success in his opening and concluding chapters. Hemingway's definition 'Grace under pressure' is introduced not very helpfully. The eight senators selected (plus some supplementary examples) give us a better idea of the virtue under discussion than any theorizing. Yet the theorizing throws useful light on Kennedy.

At the very beginning of the book he calls courage 'that most admirable of human virtues'. And at the very end he almost equates it with conscience: 'A man does what he must – in spite of personal consequences, in spite of obstacles and dangers and pressures –

and that is the basis of all human morality.' But his general attitude does not carry him so far.

He has been accused of being obsessed with courage, due, it has been said, to a self-distrust – a doubt of his ability to live up to his father's infinite expectations. Whether or not this be in any way true there was enough suffering in his life to make it natural for him to brood on courage intensely; his ill-health as a boy, his war-time plunge into extreme peril, his proximity to death in the months before writing his book and the long, slow, painful recovery. We need not be surprised that he admired this virtue above all others.

But in the political context we ask again, what does he mean by it? He tells us a number of things that it was not. It had no necess-ary connection with wisdom or sound judgment either in terms of an *ad hoc* issue or a political philosphy. 'I make no claim that all of those who staked their careers to speak their mind were right . . . these men were not all on one side. They were not all conserva-tives or liberals.' Nor did they necessarily stand for absolute principle against compromise. Each in his different way, Webster, Benton and Houston, discovered their sacred cause in the Com-promise of 1850.

Nor did Kennedy claim for his heroes any special dose of general virtue. Some of them may have been pure and generous and kind and noble throughout their careers, in the best traditions of the American hero; but most of them were not. Norris, the unyielding bitter-ender; Adams, so irritating to so many; Webster, the businessmen's beneficiary; Benton, the bombastic bully – of such stuff were our political heroes made.

The more one examines courage as defined by Kennedy the more it narrows itself down. The chosen senators acted on their personal conviction in the face of violent hostility and abuse. That is the common factor. Moreover the denunciation came from those who might well have had it in their power to destroy each man's whole career and life's prospect of usefulness. Sometimes they triumphed in the end and sometimes they didn't. But they were ready to take their stand against the likelihood of total disaster. The courage in Kennedy's mind seemed to involve a kind of indepen-dent initiative, a readiness to face isolation which gave it an extra dimension beyond sheer determination or 'guts'.

Kennedy is quick to point out that 'courage' in his meaning of the word could never become the working rule of day-to-day politics. Politics is a collective process in which there must be much coming together of minds and fusion of personal attitudes. But he leaves us with the final impression that courage, if not equivalent to conscience, is the clearest expression of it in politics and it is the men of courage above all others who keep alive the national soul.

Did he, one wonders, ever think of *Profiles in Courage* as any kind of reply to the philosophy which underlies *Why England Slept*? In the earlier book individual statesmen are not altogether spared, but their responsibilities, their power for good or evil, are treated as relatively minor. It was the system, in that case the Capitalist Democratic System, which was to blame. In *Profiles in Courage* individual personal responsibility as exemplified by the eight senators comes fully into its own. Again, is it permissible to think of Kennedy preparing himself during this period of enforced withdrawal for the great contest ahead in one respect in particular? Whatever psychoanalysts may surmise he must have had little doubt by now, after his demonstrated war heroism, about his capacity to endure. Was he so sure about his capacity to act independently, 'to dare' like Daniel to stand alone? The next few years were to be devoted to acquiring popularity over a vast area among many millions of his fellow citizens. Did he consciously or unconsciously seek to establish within himself his own identity before commending it to countless others?

There is a striking but rather strange passage near the end of the book. He quotes approvingly a saying of President John Adams: 'It is not true in fact that any people ever existed who loved the public better than themselves.' Kennedy affirms this of his eight senators. 'It was precisely because they did love themselves', in what he regards as the highest sense, that the statesmen acted as they did. Each man's respect for himself was more important to him than his popularity with others. Would Kennedy have used quite those words nine years later? By that time many millions of men and women inside and outside America loved him and believed that he returned the feeling. Whether he loved them more than he loved himself, who by that time would presume to say?

The picture of Kennedy as a senator does not come through very clearly despite its comprehensive and expert treatment by Sorensen. 'Kennedy' he says bluntly, 'was not one of the Senate's great leaders. Few laws of national importance bear his name.'

Various excuses can be offered for the meagreness of his contribution, including the fact that in his later years there his energies were primarily concentrated on the presidential goal. But Sorensen tells us that on one occasion Kennedy asked him which ministerial portfolios he would enjoy holding. Sorensen mentioned Labour, Health, Education. Kennedy told him that none of these would interest him much. He would want Foreign Affairs or Defence. One is driven to feel that his interests during these years were still somewhat limited.

By this time, however, his basic duties were well attended to. His wealth gave him exceptional opportunities of employing assistance: 'a tremendous amount of staff work', we are told, 'preceded every Kennedy talk. He was known in the Library of Congress as the heaviest borrower of the reference works.' Perhaps the speech of his which aroused greatest interest was an address in 1957 when he outlined the interests of America and the West in a negotiated solution for eventual self-determination in Algeria. Whatever else he was, he was not a 'party hack'. He showed an independence of spirit which won him increasing respect while leaving him less popular with party professionals.

There remained considerable uncertainty about where he stood on the broadest issues. Arthur Schlesinger tells us of the approaches made to himself, as one who was close to Stevenson, about the candidature for the Vice-Presidency in 1956. It is striking that so soon after the uncertainties of 1953 Kennedy should be already setting his sights on a position so near the summit – or perhaps Sorensen was setting them for him. According to Schlesinger, Kennedy, 'without finally committing himself, had decided to let Sorensen test the wind'. In the event, Kennedy was defeated for the Democratic nomination for the Vice-Presidency by Kefauver. But from then on, there was no doubt that he would be going all out for the Presidency in 1960.

In 1958, he came up for re-election to the Senate and won by 875,000 votes, the greatest margin up to that point in Massachusett's history. So the going looked rather good. But many liberal Democrats still regarded him with suspicion. Schlesinger analyses this attitude at some length. In part it went back to the days of Senator Joseph McCarthy in the early 1950s. Kennedy's actual position there, however, was no better and no worse than that of most Democrats. He never gave the slightest support to

43

McCarthyism and, if he had not been laid low by grave illness, he would have joined in the Senate's vote of censure.

It could not be forgotten, however, that Kennedy's father had always treated McCarthy as a friend and that Bobby Kennedy had worked for him for a short while. Mrs Roosevelt, sometimes described as 'the conscience of the liberal community', was distinctly scathing: 'I feel that I would hesitate to place the difficult decisions that the next President would have to make with someone who understands what courage is and admires it, but has not quite the independence to have it.' Old New-Dealers, it may be added, retained an intense suspicion of Kennedy's father. They disliked with equal intensity the manner of his making his vast fortune and his isolationism during the war. Schlesinger adds that Kennedy's candidature 'touched uglier strains in the liberal syndrome, especially the susceptibility to anti-Catholicism'.

Schlesinger, a professor at Harvard, was well-equipped to form a better opinion than most of Kennedy as a Massachusetts senator. He considered that the liberal distrust of Kennedy was altogether unreasonable; he himself was clearly more and more attracted by him. It had remained broadly true that Kennedy in the Senate, as in the House of Representatives, had taken a liberal line on domestic and a conservative one on foreign issues. For example in August 1957 he supported the Civil Rights Bill and in March 1960, a closure motion to end the southern filibuster on the Civil Rights Bill. He supported bills to improve the lot of senior citizens, bills to improve the unclear United States Immigration policy, increases in unemployment benefits and the revision of the (reactionary) Taft-Hartley Labour Act. On the domestic side his one big change was that he came round in 1960 to supporting price levels for milk and butter fat. He realized after the Convention of 1956 that he had underestimated the strength of the farm lobby.

On foreign matters he had become a little more sophisticated and a little less bellicose (Schwab and Shneidman). He had emerged as a strong critic of imperialism, whether French in Algeria or Soviet in Eastern Europe. In 1954 he had insisted that Indo-China be given immediate independence but left the subject alone thereafter. It was to rise again to haunt him and still more his successors!

Schlesinger realized that Kennedy looked on his Catholicism as a handicap. Nothing could be 'done about it' in the sense that he had no intention whatsoever of whittling it down for political purposes. But he was anxious and willing, as events were to show, to dispel irrational fears about its implications in the event of his becoming President. After the overwhelming defeat of Al Smith in 1928, it was widely assumed that no Catholic could become President. Kennedy set out from the beginning to challenge that assumption and to challenge it as early as possible, so that by the time he ran for President, people would have got used to, at any rate, the possibility of a Catholic in the White House. His greatest need, so he told Schlesinger, was to distinguish his appeal from that of his rivals and to suggest that he could bring something unique to the service of the country. Schlesinger, basing himself on an essay by his father twenty years earlier, had written a memorandum to argue that after a period of passivity and acquiescence in national life, a new time of affirmation, progressivism and forward movement was on the way. The thesis greatly appealed to Kennedy and from then on the idea of 'getting America on the move' was in one version or another a large element in his message.

If Kennedy's strongest purpose at this time was to make his way to the summit, he was moving rapidly towards the conception of an alliance between the world of power and the world of ideas. He had not been a great senator, but a man of potential greatness was emerging from the Senate.

4

The hell of a candidate

The making of a President

On Wednesday morning, 28 October 1959 at Hyannis Port, Massachusetts, sixteen people attended a crucial meeting in the house of Robert Kennedy. For three years now, ever since Eisenhower's defeat of Adlai Stevenson in 1956, the Kennedy drive towards the Presidency had been under weigh. With the elections still a year ahead, the meeting on 28 October was to see 'the final assault plans laid'. Sorensen was to become national policy chief and Bobby Kennedy operational and practical campaign manager. Kenneth O'Donnell, Robert Kennedy's former football captain at Harvard, and Lawrence O'Brien, the political expert from Springfield, Massachusetts, were the other two key members. We are told that these two thought in almost identical terms and when they expressed an idea, it was impossible to say whether it had come first from one or the other. They had been working now in harness for John Kennedy for eight years. O'Donnell generally handled the candidate's person, transmitting the directives to O'Brien who 'commanded the base of organization'. Schwab and Shneidman state dogmatically and convincingly that this group of men would together 'revolutionize the American political process'. The advertising techniques of Madison Avenue, the technology of the computer, the scientific techniques of public opinion polling, the hiring of public relations firms, the staggering impact of television, the techniques of data-processing – all were utilized by Kennedy in new and dramatic fashion. They would be copied and developed by subsequent campaigns, and the new style introduced by Kennedy would establish itself for good or ill. The idea of the 'image' would become dominant. The candidate could be adapted to the requirements of the public or, if that proved impossible, the public to the requirements of the candidate. The implications would be profound, though even now it is too early to assess them with confidence.

One decision of strategic principle was dominant. The nomination had to be won by the route of the state primary. In Theodore White's words (*The Making of the President 1960*, 1962): 'Not until he showed primitive strength with the voters in strange states could he turn and deal with the bosses and the brokers of the North East who regarded him fondly as a fellow Catholic but, as a Catholic, hopelessly doomed to defeat.' In the event it was in the field of the primaries that Kennedy put himself so far ahead of the other Democratic possibilities that by the time the Convention was reached (first week of July 1960) there was no catching him. There was a belated challenge from Stevenson, who could never bring himself to compete unreservedly for the nomination. But in retrospect it is clear that by the time Kennedy had won the two carefully selected primaries of Wisconsin and West Virginia, the nomination was his.

At the beginning of 1960 five men had in theory some chance of becoming Democratic candidates – Kennedy himself, Hubert Humphrey, Stuart Symington, Lyndon Johnson and Stevenson. Wisconsin was not an unfair test. Coming from the next stage, Humphrey would have considerable appeal, but 31% of Wisconsin were Catholics; thus the national disadvantage of being a Catholic was cancelled. Both candidates threw all their energy into Wisconsin. We are told that each spent about the same amount of money. But Kennedy's friendships and social background provided him with a large advantage. His sisters and brothers operated all across the state. As Humphrey phrased it: 'I was like a corner grocer running against a chain store.' On the face of it Kennedy won a handsome victory, but he himself felt keen disappointment. His margin of 56% of the popular vote was not decisive. The mysterious 'bosses' who controlled the delegates of the East would not be convinced that he would be an ultimate winner. He had lost all four predominantly Protestant districts. His popular margin had come entirely from four heavily Catholic areas. There was no evidence here that a Catholic could win a contest fought across the whole nation. 'What does the result mean?' he was asked by one of his sisters. 'It means', he said quietly yet bitterly, 'that we have to do it all over again. We have to go through every one and win every one of them – West Virginia and Maryland and Indiana and Oregon, all the way to the Convention.'

But in fact it was only necessary to win West Virginia. If he had not been challenged there by Humphrey and been given a walk-over, the 'bosses' of the party might well have remained unconvinced. The fight in West Virginia therefore turned out a blessing. Yet West Virginia was on paper a much tougher proposition than Wisconsin. The population, among other characteristics, were white and Protestant. Negroes in West Virginia came to about 4% of the population, Catholics in West Virginia to 5% as compared with the 31% for Wisconsin. It was the West Virginians' religion that engaged the chief attention of all concerned with politics.

Once again the Kennedy organization swung into action under Larry O'Brien. Kennedy's personality proved more and more charismatic, yet the religious issue remained. There was some division in the candidate's entourage about how it should be tackled. Kennedy made an unequivocal decision. He would meet the religious issue head-on. He did so with extraordinary adroitness, turning it into a winning card. In what White describes as the 'finest TV broadcast he ever heard', Kennedy replied at length to a question planted by Franklin J. Roosevelt, who still carried with him a large share of his father's glory. 'So', said he, 'when any man stands on the steps of the Capitol and takes the oath of office of President, he is swearing to support the separation of Church and State; he puts one hand on the bible and raises the other hand to God as he takes the oath. And if he breaks his oath, he is not only committing a crime against the Constitution for which the Congress can impeach him – and should impeach him – but he is committing a sin against God.' At this point he raised his hand from an imaginary Bible, as if lifting it to God, and repeating softly said: 'A sin against God, for he has sworn on the Bible.'

Almost overnight, Kennedy managed to transfer the association with bigotry from his side to that of his opponent. Humphrey, the most tolerant of men, began to suffer from the label of intolerance. One of Kennedy's pollsters reported an old woman as saying not long before: 'I don't care about Humphrey, but I just don't want a

Catholic.' Now she quietly reported a change of mind. 'We have enough trouble in West Virginia, let alone to be called bigots.'

The most populous county of West Virginia had been initially polled as 64% for Humphrey, 36% for Kennedy. On primary day itself it went 52% to 48% for Kennedy. The final count over the whole state gave Kennedy 60% to 40%. It was a victory beyond all expectation.

The events at the Convention need not detain us long where the outcome looking back seems to have been certain. It was not till the beginning of July that Johnson made up his mind to compete. Stevenson received more than one tremendous reception from the delegates. But right to the end he spoke to those begging him to come forward in cryptic terms. On the Wednesday of the Convention, after the overwhelming demonstrations of the day before, he seemed to have decided that after all he must accept the widespread demand to enter the contest. But it was clear that he must be sure of his home base – Illinois. On enquiry of Mayor Daly of Chicago, he received the bitter news that he had no support there. That ended his chances and Kennedy was home.

One unexpected result emerged from the Convention. Lyndon Johnson was not only asked by Kennedy to run with him for Vice-President, but agreed to do so. 'It was always anticipated', said one of Kennedy's headquarters staff, 'that we'd offer Lyndon the nomination; what we never anticipated was that he'd accept. Kennedy had immediate trouble with some of his liberal activists over this invitation, but he knew perfectly well what he was about. Lyndon Johnson must be his 'Lord Constable for the Old South', leaving Kennedy himself free to concentrate on the big north-eastern industrial states. These calculations were on the whole successful.

One cannot fail to quote here a few words from his speech of acceptance. His face, we are told, was tired and haggard from a year of strain and a week of sleeplessness; his voice was high and sad:

The times are too grave, the challenge too urgent, the stakes too high to permit the customary passions of political debate. We are not here to curse the darkness, but to light the candle that can guide us through that darkness to a safe and sane future. As Winston Churchill said on taking office some twenty years ago: if we open a quarrel between the present and the past, we shall be in danger of losing the future. . . .

Then comes phrasing which was to prove historic: 'We stand today on the edge of a new frontier, a frontier of the 1960s, a frontier of unknown opportunities and perils, a frontier of unfulfilled hopes and threats.'

Such language will seem more or less meaningless to some, to others full of profound inspiration. The next phrases foreshadowed his whole attack. 'The new frontier of which I speak is not a set of promises – it is a set of challenges. It sums up not what I intend to offer the American people, but what I intend to ask of them.' This last thought was to be repeated on a still more famous occasion.

Now it was, or soon became, Kennedy *v.* Nixon. Theodore White, usually so well-balanced, waxes lyrical about the extraordinary achievement of Kennedy's election to the Presidency. 'Kennedy and his men' he says, 'had planned since the previous autumn a campaign that seemed utterly preposterous – to take the youngest Democratic candidate to offer himself in this century, of the minority Catholic faith, a man burdened by wealth [*sic*] and controversial family, relying on lieutenants scarcely more than boys and make him President.' Yet given Kennedy's dashing personality and powerful support, there seems nothing astonishing about his being chosen as the Democratic candidate. Now that he was facing Vice-President Nixon, a man of far greater experience than himself, the odds might be said to be slightly against him, but surely not by much.

White divides the campaign as *first*, the opening round with both candidates seeking their theme and purpose; *next*, the great television debates; and *lastly*, the final all-out efforts. For John Kennedy, round one began in euphoria, sagged swiftly almost to despair then rose to a point of cautious hope. While the Republicans were involved in their Convention at Chicago, Gallup Polls showed Kennedy as leading Nixon by 52% to 48%. But August was a bad month. The Kennedy campaign sank to 'a miserable low'. There was a special session of Congress. Kennedy was trapped in the rear row of the Senate feeling remarkably ineffective. A new Gallup Poll put Nixon ahead by 53% to 47%. He had cut an impressive figure at the Republican Convention. The word went round among Kennedy's supporters: 'He's in a bad mood.'

He had already strained his voice in the spring primary; Baptist ministers were beginning to preach against the Church of Rome. But once he was on the road again things seemed better, and on 12 September at Houston, Texas, he struck a decisive and lasting blow for victory. He had accepted an invitation from the Greater Houston Ministerial Association to discuss his religion. He would make an opening statement, then submit himself live to any questions they might care to ask. At the Ambassador Hotel, Los Angeles, over the weekend, he worked out his message with the Unitarian Ted Sorensen. 'We can win or lose the election in Houston on Monday night,' said Sorensen to a friend. The ministers had assembled in the pink-and-green-carpeted ballroom of the Rice Hotel in Houston by 8.30 pm. There were three hundred of them and three hundred spectators. Kennedy spoke briefly and in his most incisive fashion:

I believe in an America where the separation of Church and State is absolute: where no Catholic prelate would tell the President (should he be a Catholic) how to act, and no Protestant minister would tell his parishioners for whom to vote; where no church or church school is granted any public funds or political preference, and where no man is denied public office merely because his religion differs from the President who might appoint him or the people who might elect him. . . .
. . . That is the kind of America in which I believe. And it represents the kind of Presidency in which I believe: a great office that must be neither humbled by making it the instrument of any religious group, nor tarnished by arbitrarily withholding its occupancy from the members of any religious group. I believe in a President whose views on religion are his own private affair. . . .

The questions as they have come down to us do not look very formidable. One or two specimens must suffice. What would he feel as President about the persecution of Protestant missionaries in Roman Catholic countries of South America? 'I would use my influence as President of the United States to encourage the development of freedom all over the world.' The next question gave him a chance to make himself still more clear on the fundamental issue: would he ask Cardinal Cushing of Boston, his hierarchical superior, to forward his endorsement of the separation of Church and State to the Vatican? He replied: 'May I just say that as I do not accept the right of any, as I said, ecclesiastical official to tell me what I shall do in the sphere of my public responsibility . . . I do not propose also to ask Cardinal Cushing to ask the Vatican to take some action. I do not propose to interfere with their free right to do exactly what they want.' Would he accept Church direction in public life? He spoke most carefully in answer:

If my Church attempted to influence me in a way which was improper or which affected adversely my responsibilities as a public servant, sworn to uphold the Constitution, then I would reply to them that this was an improper action on their part, that it was one to which I could not subscribe, that I was opposed to it, and that it would be an unfortunate breach – an interference with the American political system. . . . I am confident there would be no such interference.

He made it plain that if he found any conflict between his conscience and the responsibility of the Presidency, he would resign that office. But he was sure that no such conflict would arise.

The answers he gave were a total success from the point of view of winning the election. Theologically he had cleared his position with expert advisers. The cases where a Catholic position might in fact be in contrast with the Protestant consensus were not pressed home to him. The crucial point was that he was under no obligation to take his orders from any religious quarter.

Then came the television debates between Kennedy and Nixon. Ten years earlier only 11% of American families enjoyed the pleasures of a television set. By 1960 the percentage had increased to 88%, a stupendous change. There were four debates: on 26 September, 7 October, 13 October and 21 October. When finally the figures for all four debates were assembled, the total audience exceeded all previous records; the average audience was not far short of seventy millions. Theodore White concludes that in retrospect the TV debates were the greatest opportunity ever presented for a genuine discussion of the real differences of philosophy and ideas between Kennedy and Nixon. But it was an opportunity missed. In other words nothing very much was clarified. For that reason it is hardly worth studying in detail the ebb and flow of the argument. The rival champions not only made their own statements, but they were intensively cross-examined by veteran correspondents. All the answers, however, had to be provided in dogmatic two-minute snatches. No deep light was thrown on either the issues or the candidates. It seems nevertheless to be accepted that the debates were a triumph for Kennedy and a disaster for Nixon. When they began Nixon was apparently in front. When they finished the positions were reversed. The Gallup Poll by that time recorded 49% for Kennedy, 46% for Nixon and 5% undecided. Of those who voted, 57% believed that the TV debates had influenced their decision. Six per cent, or over four million voters, ascribed their final decision on voting to the debates alone. Of these four million, one million voted for Nixon and three million for Kennedy. White suggests therefore that two million of the Kennedy margin came from television's impact. And yet Kennedy only won by 112,000 votes. He would seem to have been justified in stating after the election: 'It was TV more than anything else that turned the tide.'

It is not so well-known that those who only *heard* the debates on radio were evenly divided as to which of the candidates had been more successful. The Kennedy supremacy was entirely visual. Kennedy was, in fact, an exceptionally attractive man. Nixon in his own way was also good-looking. Yet for whatever reason, partly because he had recently been ill, partly because he had, we are told, a light, naturally transparent skin, he cut a sorry figure. 'The Vice-President', says White, 'by contrast with Kennedy appeared to be tense, almost frightened, and occasionally haggard-looking to the point of sickness. He sat, in the first debate at least, half-slouched, his "Lazy Shave" powder faintly streaked with sweat, his eyes exaggerated hollows of blackness, his jaw, jowls and face drooping with strain.' From that moment onwards the Kennedy camp thought that they were winning easily and no doubt most of the journalists encouraged them in that opinion. Yet in the end Kennedy only won by a whisker.

If one is going to agree with White that Kennedy achieved a majority of two million votes through television alone, a lot of votes must have been lost in some other way. In the last week or so there was undoubtedly a strong swing back to Nixon which the Kennedy team had not expected and did not appreciate at the time. Various explanations have been offered. The late intervention of Eisenhower, which should have been called on much earlier, was a substantial fillip to Nixon. A good many Americans, when confronted with Kennedy's picture of an exciting future and his call for effort and sacrifice, clearly drew back at the last moment.

On the night of 25 October Kennedy took a large step towards winning the Negro vote, more crucial than ever before in this election. Martin Luther King, the revered Negro leader, had been arrested and sentenced to four months hard labour. He had been snatched away secretly to the Georgia State penitentiary. Kennedy was advised by a young professor dealing with the Civil Rights section of his campaign to place a long-distance telephone call to Mrs Martin Luther King. He assured her of his interest and concern and, if necessary, his intervention. Bobby Kennedy telephoned a plea for King's release to the Georgia judge; King was released on bail pending appeal. The effect on many Negroes was electrifying. The father of Martin Luther King was a Baptist minister who had come out for Nixon a few weeks earlier on religious grounds. 'Because this man,' said the Reverend Mr King Sr, 'was willing to wipe the tears from my daughter[-in-law]'s eyes, I've got a suitcase of votes and I'm going to Mr Kennedy and dump them in his lap.' All over the country Negro leaders whose Protestant feelings had hitherto held them back from supporting Kennedy followed King's example.

'We have done everything that could be done,' said Jack Kennedy as election day dawned. He and Jackie voted in Boston; he then went to 'the Cape' to rest and wait, sometimes in Bobby's house, sometimes with Jackie in his own. He showed flashes of his well-known humour. He reported that Johnson, his running mate, had just rung him up to say: 'I hear that *you* are losing Ohio, but *we* are doing fine in Pennsylvania!' The Kennedy fortunes ebbed and flowed. At one moment Kennedy's aides were indignant because Nixon would not concede the victory. Kennedy, quick as always to put himself in the other fellow's place, was more generous. 'Why should he concede?' he asked. 'I would not if I were him.'

At another moment Bobby Kennedy said despondently: 'We are being clobbered,' and Kennedy, who understood the realities better than anyone, looked grim. The phrase 'cliff-hanger' began to be freely employed. From 10 pm the Kennedy lead shrank steadily. Kennedy reproached himself for giving insufficient attention to California. He feared that the western and midwestern states might defeat him yet. Illinois was crucial.

When he retired to bed at 4.20 am it looked as though he had won. It was not quite certain but nearly so. When he awoke about nine o'clock, Sorensen could inform him that he was President of the United States. He had won by 112,000 votes out of sixty-nine million.

'If you divide America into eight major geographical communities, Nixon carried five and Kennedy only three' (White). Nixon's were the block of five predominantly farm states, the eight states sprawling across the Rocky Mountains, the five border states, the six industrial mid-western states and the five Pacific states. Kennedy claimed New England, the most heavily Catholic section of the community (six states), ten states of the 'Old South' and five mid-Atlantic states. These three regions gave Kennedy just enough votes in just enough places to give him victory.

Sorensen mentions seven factors, each of which gave Kennedy on balance an advantage: television debates, the campaign tactics, the greater popularity of the Democrats, his running mate Lyndon Johnson, on balance the support of the Negroes, an impression of new leadership in foreign policy, and a recent increase in unemployment. But he is emphatic – and I myself accept his view, though many others did not – that Kennedy's religion told heavily against him. Not many Republicans switched to Kennedy, but shoals of Protestant Democrats reverted to Nixon. The achievement of being the first Catholic President is now taken for granted, but it needed someone who was rightly called 'the hell of a candidate' to pull it off at the time.

Benjamin Bradlee and his wife were asked for supper on the first evening following the victory. Bradlee was at that time covering Washington for *Newsweek* and is now Managing Editor of *The Washington Post*. He and his wife Tony had been neighbours of the Kennedys in Washington since 1958 and enjoyed considerable intimacy with them, Tony being a particular friend of Jackie's. In Bradlee's own words (*Conversations with Kennedy*, New York, 1975): 'The President Kennedy that I saw and heard in the flesh was a President off duty, a President trying to relax.' The portrait in his book, he says, is necessarily personal and one-dimensional, reflecting only what Kennedy said to him, not what he said to others. Some who were more intimate with Kennedy have found it difficult to recognize the Kennedy of these conversations.

'We arrived early,' writes Bradlee, 'Tony great with child, and were greeted by Jackie, in the same condition. When Kennedy came downstairs, before anybody could say a word, he flashed that smile and said: "Okay girls, you can take the pillows out!" Over dinner, he told how he had rung up Chicago's Mayor Daly, while Illinois was hanging in the balance, to ask how he was doing. 'Mr President,' Kennedy quoted Daly as saying, 'with a little bit of luck and the help of a few close friends, you are going to carry Illinois.' And it was Illinois which finally put him over the top.

Bradlee does not make the mistake of confusing these light-hearted conversations with serious business. He and his friend were told that same evening by Kennedy: 'Okay, I will give each one of you guys one appointment, one job to fill.' The friend suggested the replacement of Edgar Hoover, head of the FBI. Bradlee had the same idea for Allen Dulles, chief of the CIA. Next morning Bradlee learned that just about the first steps taken by Kennedy were to confirm Hoover and Dulles.

5

The search for excellence

Forming the government
The Imperial Presidency
What sort of man?

The first task was to form the government. Under the American system ten weeks would be available compared with twenty-four or forty-eight hours in Britain. The work was carried out sometimes in Palm Beach, sometimes in New York, sometimes in George-town. Quite apart from the time difference Kennedy's methods of selecting his administration, and in particular his Cabinet, must seem astonishing by British standards. It does not seem to have aroused special criticism in America. But nor did the result produce any special enthusiasm.

Hugh Sidey in his *Portrait of a President* (New York, 1975) reports the comments of a Democrat who had served in the administration of Roosevelt: 'They are a conservative bunch,' he observed about the new Cabinet men, 'too much for me. They seem like good organization men, modern men. They are not a very colourful group. I like the colourful boys.'

At a dinner party a Washington hostess leant close to Clark Clifford, a leading lawyer who was helping Kennedy make the selection, and confided: 'This Cabinet sure does not have much glamour.' Clifford said that that was the way they preferred it – 'I don't want any mercurial, flashy, brilliant men in there. I want men who can make things run right, men who can carry out the orders of the boss.' That may well have been part of what Kennedy wanted. It was certainly not all he wanted and not exactly how he wanted his administration looked on. There was great talk of the search for excellence or, as was later to be said sarcastically – 'for the brightest and the best'. The idea of making a good impression loomed large.

A symposium edited by Lester Tanzer called *The Kennedy Circle* appeared in 1961, before the Kennedy men could be judged on performance. It still stands up quite well and puts the Cabinet appointments in a wider perspective. It draws a sharp contrast between the men of the New Deal and those of the New Frontier. In New Deal days, 'a good idea was a good idea, period. But in Washington now, a good idea is one that works and the best idea is one that works fastest, with the least fuss, while irritating the fewest people.'

At that time, the early months of the New Frontier, pragmatism was the word. At a party on one of the first hundred nights, the wife of a government official circulating the living room was heard to ask each guest in turn: 'Are you pragmatic?' We are reminded that the word 'pragmatism' was literally invented at Harvard. William James proclaimed it to be the attitude of looking away from first things, principles, supposed necessities, and of looking towards last things, fruits, consequences, facts. Later, James put it more succinctly: 'meaning other than practical, there is for us none.' In the days of Mr Wilson's first government the phrase 'keeping one's options open' became famous or notorious. So did the expression 'no sacred cows'. But then and later Harold Wilson has never deviated far from an orthodox Labour position. It would be harder to name a social philosophy to which Kennedy ir 1961 could be held to be committed.

Arthur Schlesinger's fifth chapter in *A Thousand Days* (1965), 'Gathering of the Forces', is revealing. Schlesinger's older and perhaps deeper loyalty had been to Stevenson, but he had played no small part in mobilizing the liberals, particularly the Harvard liberals, in support of Kennedy. He was consulted a good deal (along with many others) while the Kennedy administration was being constructed. But he talks about a moment at which only agriculture and the post office 'were not tenanted'. In other words the leading posts had been filled. 'At this time,' he tells us, 'there was spreading unhappiness among the liberals over the failure of any of their particular favourites except Goldberg (Secretary of Labour) to make the Cabinet.' Schlesinger mentioned this discontent to the President-elect, who replied: 'Yes, I know; the liberals want visual reassurance, just like everybody else. But they shouldn't worry. What matters is the programme. We are going down the line on the programme.' Schlesinger suggested that what he had in mind was an administration of conservative men and liberal measures. He said: 'We will have to go along with this for a year or so, then I would like to bring in some new people.' He paused and added thoughtfully, 'I suppose it may be hard to get rid of these people once they are in.' Strange admission to be made at the very start by a reforming President, if that is how we should look on him.

If the policy jobs below the Cabinet are brought into the reckoning the appearance is slightly more progressive. But if this was really the Cabinet which fitted in with Kennedy's ideas it would be hard to apply the term liberal to him at this stage. The most important posts in his government were State (foreign affairs), Treasury and Defence. Here what can only be called the unpreparedness of Kennedy is staggering, in British eyes at least. 'State, Treasury and Defence', he told Schlesinger that December day, 'are giving me the most trouble. I would like to have some new faces here, but all I get are the same old names.' Even under American conditions, so different from British, it seems extraordinary that after aiming night and day at the Presidency for years, he should have had no ideas at all about whom he would wish to have as his main subordinates. When such overwhelming attention had been given to planning victory, so much indifference to the implications of victory seems incredible.

Kennedy was ruefully aware of his neglect of this area. As he remarked on one occasion, 'For the last four years I spent so much time getting to know people who could help me get elected President that I didn't have any time to get to know people who could help me, after I was elected, to be a good President.' In the event he paid most attention to the advice of Robert Lovett, a New York Republican banker, who had served in Roosevelt's war-time administration and in Truman's Cabinet as Secretary of Defence. He was perhaps the leading figure of the New York financial and legal community, which itself was the heart of the American 'establishment'. It had always looked on Kennedy with some suspicion, mostly because of his father, but also because John Kennedy's main associations were with Democratic politicians and academic intellectuals. Moreover, the speech made by Kennedy in

1957 attacking French policy in Algeria had created the impression that he was anti-NATO.

Now that he was President they were prepared to 'rally round'. 'And now that he was President he was prepared to receive them' (Schlesinger). This was part of his strategy of reassurance: he himself remarked that he must not seem to have too many Harvard liberals and Irish Catholics in vital positions. 'I can use a few smart Republicans. Anyway, we need a Secretary of the Treasury who can call a few of these people on Wall Street by their first names.'

Kennedy, according to Schlesinger, was captivated by Lovett. He was certainly prepared to offer him his choice of the three chief Cabinet portfolios – State, Defence and Treasury. Lovett declined them all but had much say in the selections arrived at. Lovett informed Kennedy that he had voted for Nixon, but Kennedy, we are told, was by now losing much of his interest in how people voted, let alone which party they were supposed to belong to.

As Secretary of the Treasury he appointed Douglas Dillon, who had been Under-Secretary of State for Economic Affairs in the Eisenhower administration. This led to plenty of protests among Democrats, particularly the liberals. He was generally regarded as a typical exponent of Republican economic policies. His standing with Wall Street, no doubt one reason for his selection, did not impress them. But Kennedy brushed aside these criticisms, remarking of Dillon: 'Oh! I don't care about those things. All I want to know is: is he able, and will he go along with the programme?'

Robert McNamara became his Secretary of Defence. He was nominally a Republican, though he had voted for Kennedy. He modestly said of his views: 'The Republicans think I am a Democrat and the Democrats think I am a Republican, and I don't get the benefits of either.' He was a superlatively efficient business executive, just a year older than Kennedy, who had been elected President of the Ford Motor Company the day after Kennedy had been elected President of the USA. Lovett put Kennedy on his trail. Kennedy's brother-in-law Sargent Shriver was sent down to interview him. After learning his reaction Kennedy authorized Shriver to offer McNamara an appointment either as Secretary of Defence or as Secretary of the Treasury (Dillon not having been appointed to the second position). He declined the first but came to Washington the next day to see Kennedy and put one question which meant a lot to him: Had Kennedy really written *Profiles in Courage*, or had it been ghosted? Kennedy assured him that he had indeed written it with help from Sorensen on the research. McNamara still held back, but came under Kennedy's spell and accepted the Defence portfolio after a second meeting.

Neither the Treasury nor Defence had given Kennedy much trouble. 'State' presented more perplexities. Adlai Stevenson had on paper the highest claims and expected to be offered the appointment. But it does not seem that Kennedy ever contemplated his having it. He told Stevenson that he (Stevenson) had taken up too many controversial positions. Someone was needed who would have less difficulty with Congress. Kennedy also, we are told by Schlesinger, questioned Stevenson's capacity for decision and was not sure how their personal relationship would work out. While he always tried to treat Stevenson well, he remained sceptical of his hold over the liberal fraternity.

Congressman Chester Bowles of Connecticut had been the first outstanding liberal to support Kennedy and in theory had continued as his adviser on foreign affairs. But the political objections to Stevenson applied to him also. He was too liberal for Congress and possibly for Kennedy. He was made Under-Secretary of State as a consolation prize. Lovett having declined, the choice now lay between Senator William Fulbright, David Bruce (the gifted and immensely experienced Ambassador in London) and Dean Rusk. Fulbright was out of favour in Jewish and Negro circles. Bruce was judged too old at sixty-eight, though fifteen years later he was going as strong as ever. So the lot fell to Dean Rusk. Before the war he had been a Rhodes Scholar and a young professor of Government. He had served with the army in the Far East, become Assistant Secretary for Far Eastern affairs in the State Department and now for nine years had been head of the Rockefeller Foundation. The more obviously brilliant McGeorge Bundy, Harvard's Dean of the Faculty, and Walter Rostow of the Massachusetts Institute of Technology were installed next door to the White House as Kennedy's on-the-spot foreign policy aides. There was some question as to whether Rusk would be able to hold these potential empire-builders in check and remain unmistakably in charge of foreign policy in a departmental sense. Rusk, a strong and quiet character without presence or glamour, had no doubt on that score.

Kennedy therefore for his three top Cabinet ministers had chosen two whom he had not known before, McNamara and Rusk, and two who were wholly Republican (Dillon) or partly Republican (McNamara). None of them would have any major standing with the public or present any obstacle to his complete supremacy in his own administration. If he wanted a real intimate in the Cabinet, he achieved his purpose decisively by making his brother Bobby Attorney-General. This was entirely his own doing; it was contrary, it would seem, to any advice that was offered him. Bobby had certainly not sought the position, but Kennedy was determined to have his brother in the Cabinet and this was the only post available. Bobby's legal experience and standing were exiguous, but his devotion to the President, his political skills as a campaign organizer and, for all his youth, his formidable personality were known to all.

Later on, Ben Bradlee was to ask Kennedy why he thought Bobby was great . . . 'and never mind the brother bit'. The President answered: 'First his high moral standards, strict personal ethics . . . then his terrific executive energy. . . . He has got compassion, a real sense of compassion. . . . His loyalty comes next. It wasn't the easiest thing for him to go to Joe McCarthy's funeral.' Bradlee adds that no explanation was offered as to why it was not the easiest thing, but in fact JFK was running for President and 'taking real heat for having been soft on McCarthy'.

A slightly different aspect of Bobby's loyalty is brought out in another story reported by Bradlee, which Kennedy had told him with relish. It appears that Bobby had heard Chester Bowles quoted as saying that he was not sure he was 'with' the administration in their handling of the early days of the Cuban missile crisis. When they next met, Bobby went over to Bowles, grabbed him by the coat collar and said: 'I want you to know something. You're with us in this all the way, right?' It had apparently been a tense moment.

The President was, however, quite ready to joke about the appointment: 'If I need somebody older, there is no need to go outside the family. I can always get my father.' 'I would like to tell my brother that you can't be elected President until you are thirty-five years of age.' 'I see nothing wrong with giving Bobby some legal experience as Attorney-General before he goes out to practise at the Bar.' This recalls reassuring remarks about his own youthfulness to a group of worried Democratic leaders prior to the 1960 campaign.

Bobby and his preternatural rapport with his brother were to become more and more significant. 'Bobby,' as Kenneth O'Donnell says, 'was the one man whom JFK trusted and depended on, in a time of pressure, more than anybody else.'

Thirteen years later, Susan Mary Alsop, a perceptive, well-informed commentator, could still recall the exhilaration of being in Washington in 1961 and 'smelling the air of Kennedy's administration'.... 'There was adrenalin everywhere and the sparkle in the eyes of the men of our generation impressed me even more than did the enthusiasm of the young men new to office, brilliant as these latter were' (*To Marietta from Paris, 1945–1960*, New York, 1975). She adds revealingly, 'that great public figure Averell Harriman summed it up for many of us when he said to me [later]: "When Kennedy was alive was the last time I felt young".'

To feel young was indeed the very essence of the New Frontier. Arthur Schlesinger has described better than anyone the excitement prevailing in governmental circles: 'The pace was frenetic. Every one came early and stayed late. Telephones rang incessantly. Meetings were continuous. The evenings too were lively and full. The glow of the White House was lighting up the whole city.'

The New Frontier went well beyond politics; for a time at least it was a complete way of life. The cult of excellence subsumed Pablo Casals playing in the White House; a dash round the book-shops to obtain Lord David Cecil's *Melbourne*, a favourite book of the President; a sudden desire to imitate his speed writing. But it involved also the President challenging his Press Secretary to a competition in 'push-ups' (press-ups) and his demand, at one point, that all his staff should shed five pounds in weight. We read of tennis before breakfast, endless touch football, and fifty-mile hikes (this last accomplished only by Bobby). We read of young and middle-aged high-jinks in and out of the various swimming pools, with some being thrown in, others falling in and still others plunging in fully clothed, out of sheer exuberance.

For my part, I can only compare it with the life at Charlton, near Oxford, in the last days of the first Earl of Birkenhead (F. E. Smith). Selected undergraduates would be expected to play golf before lunch and tennis all the afternoon with riding between tea and dinner. The conversation led by our host was as sparkling as any I have ever known, the mental brilliance escalating, or seeming to escalate, under the physical exhilaration.

But at that point in our lives we were not presuming to rule the country. The men of the New Frontier were claiming to do just that. Today it makes bizarre reading, but at that time it must have been 'very heaven'.

At this juncture it will serve us well to examine briefly the actual powers and limitations of the high office to which John Kennedy had been elected in 1960, and try to put it in some kind of perspective. The first essay I ever wrote in the school of 'Modern Greats' at Oxford was taken fifty years ago to H. A. L. Fisher, Warden of New College. I had been asked to draw a comparison between the British parliamentary and the American presidential systems. Fisher, an eminent historian, had written among many other books a life of Lord Bryce, one-time British Ambassador in Washington, and according to Fisher the most learned human being since Aristotle. Not surprisingly we spent much time discussing Bryce's *American Commonwealth* and *Modern Democracies*. I am glad that Arthur Schlesinger in his masterly book *The Imperial Presidency* (1974) should still quote Bryce extensively.

Every student has always been aware that the American Constitution is based on the separation of powers. An essential feature is the fact that neither the President nor his Cabinet is directly responsible to the legislature, because the President is independently elected and therefore has his mandate directly from the people. In Britain the responsibility to the House of Commons of the effective executive, in other words the Cabinet, is the very heart of the system. Every now and then some gifted writer in England, Dick Crossman or Humphry Berkeley for example, comes forward to argue that the executive power of the Prime Minister is now so great that we have got the equivalent of a presidential system. But there is no answering the question whether the strength of the Prime Minister in proportion to the size of our country is as great as that of an American President. In fact it varies a good deal. In my own governmental experience (six years under Mr Attlee outside the Cabinet, three years under Mr Wilson inside the Cabinet) I have seen the power or influence (the distinction is not important here) go up and go down. If a

Prime Minister does not physically weaken or run into serious trouble he will tend to become more and more powerful the longer he stays at No. 10. But the fundamental difference just mentioned between the two systems remains unaffected. That of the United States continues to be based on the separation, that of Britain on the unification of powers. That was true of Kennedy's time and is still true of our own.

That does not mean however that the constitutional position of the Presidency has always been exactly the same as it was when the Constitution was drawn up nearly two hundred years ago for a population of not much more than four millions. Schlesinger brings out the many vicissitudes through which has passed the President's relationship with Congress. On the whole the Presidency has gained in power substantially and at an increasing pace. (Whether the gain was also that of the nation is a separate issue.) But it was not an uninterrupted progress in one direction. Schlesinger for example writes in regard to the first half of the nineteenth century: 'Nearly every President who extended the reach of the White House provoked a reaction toward a more restrictive theory of the Presidency, even if the reaction never quite cut presidential power back to its earlier level.' During the Civil War Lincoln greatly expanded the presidential initiative. Later on Congress got their own back as best they could.

The revival of Presidential initiatives under Theodore Roosevelt and Woodrow Wilson produced a not surprising reaction. Franklin Roosevelt showed himself a most potent President as soon as he came to power. But he preferred, in Schlesinger's words, 'to base his actions on congressional legislation, rather than on executive prerogative'. In foreign affairs he allowed himself to be considerably hamstrung by Congress and gravely hampered in his desire to promote resistance to the Nazis. In fact from 1919 to 1938, Congress exercised a dominant influence over foreign policy with results that were admitted on all hands to be disastrous. The major revival of the presidential prerogative after Pearl Harbour can be attributed not only to the gravity of the war crisis, but to the recognized failure of Congress in foreign affairs. Modern technology, by making the world so much 'smaller' had worked in the same direction in demanding quicker and often, therefore, *executive* decisions in international and defence situations.

From 1945 to 1961 the Presidency continued inexorably to accumulate overall power at the expense of Congress. This however was not obviously true of domestic affairs, where Congress showed its old disposition to strike back at the over-magnified Presidency. In foreign affairs Congress abdicated increasingly. The Communist menace produced an American foreign policy that inevitably placed an unprecedented responsibility on the executive. The agreed task now was to prevent the non-Communist nations being destroyed from without or within by the Communists.

A vast expansion of international commitments was carried out under Eisenhower, who in ordinary circumstances because of his political beliefs would have minimized rather than exaggerated the Presidential function. Dulles, the Secretary of State, developed a diplomacy of 'brinkmanship' – a readiness to go to war at any moment rather than give way to the Communists. A foreign policy of this kind, which placed a great strain on the constitutional theory that the war-making power lay with Congress, had been carried a long way by the time Kennedy arrived. It remained for Kennedy to clothe it with the language of dynamic idealism calculated to arouse all Americans and if possible all freedom-lovers.

It is not difficult after Vietnam to say that such a policy was ill-starred from the beginning. 'Washington', in Schlesinger's words, 'had appointed itself the saviour of human freedom and endowed itself with world-wide responsibility and a world-wide charter' (Moscow had already done the same for the eastern bloc). Maybe the rôle was always beyond the capacity of any one country. But there were many of us in Britain, if I am to be candid, who still clung to the idea of collective security as the one hope of world peace, and who for a long time saw the United States as its only effective instrument. There was nothing ignoble about that part of the dream.

Such at any rate was the atmosphere when Kennedy became President. He had announced his intention to be a strong and active President – stronger and more active, it was understood, than any of his immediate predecessors. But on the home front his scope seemed to be severely limited. The fact that his own ideas on domestic policy were also limited and at least as conservative as liberal, made it perhaps less painful for him that his hands were tied. Certainly he had some excuse for relative inaction. He had been elected to the Presidency by the narrowest of margins. His majority in the House of Representatives was more nominal than real. The Southern Democrats were a highly conservative force. It was easy to believe that a majority did not exist for progressive legislation.

In international affairs Louis Heren of *The Times* concludes that his natural bent was 'romantic and aggressive'. Whether those are precisely the right adjectives, Kennedy was certainly determined to leave a glorious mark on world history in the interests of the United States and more widely of world peace. He arrived at a moment when such a rôle seemed to be not only the right and the duty of any President aspiring to greatness, but to lie within his grasp. And in that spirit we shall find him setting about his task.

Arthur Schlesinger is at great pains to insist that Kennedy did not enlarge the claim of the President to govern independently of Congress. 'Kennedy's Presidency', he writes, 'was too short to permit confident generalization; but his ironic and sceptical intelligence customarily kept the Presidency in healthy perspective.' That is written with the language of love. I am afraid that I do not find it convincing. It is true that on the domestic front Kennedy did not over-rule Congress: we shall in fact find him stultified by it. But in international affairs, his main interest, Kennedy had no intention of allowing Congress to defeat his purposes. We shall find the Bay of Pigs crisis seriously mishandled in the spring of 1961. We shall find the Cuban missiles crisis superbly handled in the autumn of 1962. Congress was equally impotent in each case. After the Bay of Pigs, the CIA were on paper brought under closer scrutiny, but the plans to assassinate certain foreign leaders were not interfered with.

Strictly speaking the world glamour that Kennedy gave to the Presidency did not involve a constitutional departure. But in practice as he proceeded on his path of glory, more and more was expected from him and more and more latitude was permitted. His choice of Cabinet members, particularly of Rusk as Secretary of State, was designed to provide him with undisputed sway within the executive branch of government. Robert Kennedy's account of the Cuban crisis indicates surprise that the two most crucial Cabinet members, McNamara and Rusk, cast the whole burden of decision-making on the President's shoulders. But

John Kennedy had brought that on himself and was the last man to complain.

The relationship between Kennedy and his Cabinet, as described for example by his brother, is one striking aspect of the 'Imperial Presidency'. Schlesinger however treats Johnson (followed by Nixon) as its real architect. Here he seems much less than fair, if an 'Imperial Presidency' is to be regarded as a damaging phrase. The truth is that Johnson inherited an 'Imperial Presidency' from Kennedy, though no doubt he and Nixon developed it further, the latter carrying it to a tragic climax.

When Harold Wilson paid his first prime ministerial visit to Johnson, I asked him on his return how he had got on. Very well indeed, he replied, but there was one thing which worried him. 'I tremble to think what would happen if Lyndon Johnson went round the bend. There's nothing to stop him blowing the world to pieces. Now if I went round the bend, I like to think that the Cabinet would pull me up in time.' As a member of his Cabinet I accepted the compliment, but couldn't help asking whether a fairly recent British Prime Minister had not in fact gone round the bend for a short while. Harold Wilson agreed but said, 'However, I am not him.' The point is that Kennedy had bequeathed to Johnson a style of Presidency beyond the capacity of any single human being to live up to.

Johnson voluntarily took on Kennedy's Cabinet – not the procedure of a man determined to have his own way at all costs. When Harold Wilson's Cabinet was formed in 1964, the great majority of its members had voted against him for the leadership and indeed had for years favoured the positions of his predecessor Hugh Gaitskell as opposed to his own. It took a long time for him to gain a normal supremacy, though he certainly achieved it in the end.

Schlesinger writes of Johnson overriding first in theory and then in practice the written and unwritten checks contained in the Constitution. There is plenty of room for constitutional argument there. Nixon went further along the same lines and later embarked on criminal procedures. Applying Harold Wilson's language, 'he went round the bend'. The time came when he destroyed not only his own reputation, but the moral and intellectual basis of the presidential claim to omnipotence. Initially under Johnson over Vietnam and still more obviously under Nixon, the idea that 'the President knows best' became discredited and risible.

Theodore White devotes a long section of his absorbing book (*Breach of Faith*, New York, 1975) about the fall of Nixon to asking the question 'Why?' For the psychological handicaps of Richard Nixon we can feel much sympathy. But they are not here our concern. On the political side, 'the most deceptive inherited social myth was of American power'. The virulence of that myth was fresh and rested on the fleeting dominance of American arms as they spread triumphant over the entire globe in 1945. White goes on to point out the internal implications, including the grant of autocratic powers to the President 'who must command the war effort'. But by the time Nixon came to power, Americans were confronted with a new reality: they were engaged in the first major war that they would not win. That realization had split the country at every level. Resentment at the waste and killing in Vietnam had spilled out into the street 'in sputtering violence and frightening bloodshed' (White). Johnson had had the tragedy of Vietnam to contend with directly. The problems confronting Nixon were not less ghastly. The 'Imperial Presidency' can be seen as at once a cause and a consequence of these traumatic years.

Arthur Schlesinger, the devoted champion of the Kennedys, has seldom been generous to Richard Nixon. But there are passages towards the end of *The Imperial Presidency* for which the latter should be thankful. 'If it had not been Watergate, it would surely have been something else, for Watergate was a symptom not a cause.' And again still more clearly, 'Nixon's Presidency was not an aberration but a culmination. It carried to reckless extremes a compulsion towards presidential power arising out of deep-running changes in the foundations of society.' In general terms we can accept that verdict. But Kennedy must be seen as a President who took over the controls in a period of rapid movement, accelerated the rate of progress (upwards or downwards) and must share the responsibility for the credit and blame to be allocated thereafter.

What sort of man was Kennedy by this time as he stood on the threshold of such tremendous responsibilities? Even his best friends could not claim (his war heroism and his books apart) that he could as yet point to actual achievements. His achievements must be, as millions felt sure they would be, in the immediate future.

For fifteen years he had been preoccupied with winning power.

Had he any notion of how he would use it now that at last he had won it? In retrospect can any serious meaning be attached to the concept of the New Frontier which raised so many expectations? To these questions conflicting answers have been and will no doubt continue to be given. A sardonic critic with considerable inside information, the novelist Gore Vidal, goes to one extreme. On his theory the father drove his sons to 'win, win, win'. But never at any point, says Vidal, 'did he pause to ask himself or them just what it was they were supposed to win'. For years Jack Kennedy was driven by his father and then by himself to be first in politics, which meant to be the President. But once that goal had been achieved, 'he had no future, no place else to go'. Gore Vidal recalls the exchange between Kennedy and the famous journalist James Reston, who asked the newly elected President what his philosophy was. 'What vision did he have of the good life?' Mr Reston got a blank stare for answer. Kennedy apologists we are told used this exchange as proof of their man's essentially pragmatic nature. If the President were given a specific problem he would solve it through intelligence and expertise. A philosophy 'was simply no use to a man of action'. Gore Vidal goes on to become still more unkind about President Kennedy. But can we find any truth in what he has already told us?

Another still better-placed observer told Louis Heren at the end of 1961 that the trouble with the Kennedy administration was 'they had no fire in their bellies'. They were not like the old New Dealers. 'They don't want to do good. They just want to do something.' Action for the sake of action. For a crushing reply we turn back to the massive works of Schlesinger and Sorensen; we receive a partial but not complete refutation. Schlesinger's long chapter in *A Thousand Days* entitled 'Kennedy On The Eve' is a fine piece of eloquent writing. He ladles out the epithets. Kennedy was reticent, patrician, bookish, urbane but additionally the Irishness in him came out in many ways – 'in the quizzical wit, the eruptions of boisterous humour, the relish for politics, the love of language, the romantic sense of history, the admiration for physical daring, the toughness, the joy of living, the view of life as comedy and as tragedy'.

In some sense at least all this was no doubt true. We accept also from Schlesinger that Kennedy was Irish, Catholic, New England, Harvard, Palm Beach, Democrat and so on, but that no classification contained him. This, one may say in passing, is true of any man with claims to greatness, and we are judging Kennedy by that standard. Schlesinger however becomes more and more lyrical and vaguer as he proceeds. By the time, we are told, that Kennedy's sense of wholeness and freedom gave him an extraordinary appeal not only to his own generation but even more to those who came after, 'the children of turbulence', the eulogy has begun to lose its practical bearing. Sorensen sets about his task with even more intimate knowledge and equal enthusiasm. He tells us that the most formal statement of Kennedy's political credo was in his 1960 address to the Liberal Party of New York:

I believe in human dignity as the source of national purpose, in human liberty as the source of national action, in the human heart as the source of national compassion and in the human mind as the source of our invention and our ideas. . . . Liberalism . . . faith in man's ability . . . reason and judgment . . . is our best and only hope in the world today.

He has some more quotations to offer which do not advance us much further. But when asked which kind of President he hoped to be, liberal or conservative, Kennedy replied: 'I hope to be responsible.' A politician must regard that as a complete 'non-answer'. Sorensen tells us that as senator, candidate and President his tests were: can it work? can it help? and often but not always – can it pass?

In other words at the time he became President he was about as uncommitted in political and social doctrines as any democratic leader in the history of politics. But we have not yet grappled with the more scathing part of the critics' argument. No one, friend or foe, has questioned his enormous appeal to ever-widening audiences. Victor Lasky in an unpleasant but comprehensive book published while Kennedy was still alive (*J.F.K.: The Man and the Myth*, 1966) quoted an analysis in *The Saturday Evening Post* which accepted 'Kennedy's greatest political asset is an intangible and indefinable charm. A warmth which makes voters feel instinctively that whatever they believe in he believes in too.' But Lasky went on to argue that 'the Kennedy personality far from possessing the warmth in question was actually cold, self-interested and calculating'.

Here a deadlock is reached as always in a discussion of the

ultimate sincerity of a great demagogue – Roosevelt, Kennedy or whoever it may be. Or if the word 'demagogue' is disliked, we will refer instead to a statesman with immense appeal to the masses. Certainly by the time he was elected President, and still more by the date of his death, President Kennedy had established a tremendous rapport with the multitude. We noticed earlier his shyness, though the charm was always present, in his first speech under David Powers' tuition. But Sorensen describes the gradual disappearance of this shyness. 'The youthful aspirant for Congress who had reluctantly toured taverns and textile mills in search of Massachusetts voters – who even as a Presidential hopeful felt he might impose upon, or be rejected by, each new group of voters – became in time the President who welcomed every opportunity to get away from his desk and get back to the people.' Millions in America and later elsewhere were utterly convinced that his feeling for them was genuine, not synthetic. The testimony of those who knew him best is unanimous to the same effect. No doubt his ever-widening love of humanity and flair for showing it were exploited like his war record for political purposes on a vast scale. If democracy is to work at all, can it be otherwise?

On personal grounds there was indeed an immense amount 'going for him' as he assumed his solemn office. But no little mystery attached to the policies to be expected.

6

Pride and downfall

The Inauguration
The euphoria
The Bay of Pigs

It was 19 January 1961, the day before the Inauguration. Jack Kennedy set out from his Georgetown home to visit Eisenhower. The latter summoned a helicopter to the White House lawn by pressing a button. 'I'm showing my friend here', he said half-seriously, 'how to get out in a hurry.' They went through a carefully-prepared list of the main problems. Eisenhower dwelt on the perils of the Laos situation: 'This is one of the problems that I'm leaving you that I am not happy about. We may have to fight.' 'How can he stare disaster in the face so unconcernedly?' asked Kennedy, wonderingly, of the aide as they drove away. He would learn soon enough that this was one of the occupational acquisitions of leadership. Eight inches of snow descended on Washington. The evening was given up to an immense Frank Sinatra gala and after that a party given by Joe Kennedy. His son reached home by 3.30 am.

The day of days began in a way that certainly delighted Jack's mother. He went alone to an early Mass in a church in Washington and found her there, to his complete surprise, sitting in another part of the church. 'I had not urged him to go', said Mrs Kennedy later. 'The fact that he did go on his own and did think it was important to start his administration with Mass in the morning gave me a wonderfully happy feeling.' The episode is further evidence that Jack Kennedy's religion was genuine but private, in fact one of the least public things about him. At 10.40 am Sam Rayburn, Speaker of the House of Representatives, and Senator

John Sparkman, Chairman of the Congressional Inauguration Committee, picked up the Kennedys and escorted them to pay a call on the Eisenhowers. Coffee followed and a pleasant little talk. Then the two illustrious men, the old President and the new, drove the mile from the White House to the Capitol through the cheering crowds. Eisenhower talked reassuringly about the prospects of averting war with the Russians if one stood sufficiently firm.

Senator Sparkman introduced the President. 'We are here today to inaugurate the thirty-fourth President of this great Union.' Kennedy stepped forward and delivered his message, coatless. 'It came with the Boston accent, with the left hand doubled into the fist and the right forefinger hammering the rostrum.'

At the time of delivery it bade fair to go down to history as one of the most effective inaugurals ever delivered. In later years it did not stand up altogether well to scrutiny; it cased to rate with the inaugurals of Lincoln and the best of Roosevelt.

Foreign affairs had always interested President Kennedy far more than domestic. They occupied far more of his time and energy as President. 'The big difference' he said early in his term, 'was between a Bill being defeated and the country being wiped out.' The threat not just of national defeat but of world destruction never left him. Though nothing, not even that spectre, could impair his love of life or joy in office.

Certainly it was world affairs which dominated his inaugural address. Domestic issues were simply left over. The veteran Speaker Rayburn said of it that evening, 'That speech was better than anything Franklin Roosevelt ever said at his best – it was better than Lincoln. I think – I really think – he is a man of destiny.' Over-excited perhaps. But many old hands paid similar tributes.

The rich and striking phraseology, the sheer artistry of the rhetoric, the youth and glamour, the communicated depth of feeling – these factors alone made it seem like a speech to be ranked among the greatest. To analyse the content of such an oration may well be to lose sight of its historical significance. Yet the task must be briefly attempted. No speech could have been better calculated to arouse enthusiasm in the United States and in many other countries. But for what purpose? With what end in view was the enthusiasm being aroused?

Sorensen, who rendered his usual discreet and invaluable assistance in the preparation of the speech, denies that it can be summarized. It was already a compact summary of the President's hopes and resolves, yet one or two main themes can be extracted. The speech was in the first place an appeal to Americans to be true to their highest traditions – and those traditions are presented as traditions of freedom – freedom, liberty, human rights. The changes were rung on the words but not on the underlying concepts except insofar as the idea of revolution is added. 'We observe today not a victory of party but a celebration of freedom.' The world was very different from when their forebears prescribed the same solemn oath that he was taking. 'And yet the same revolutionary belief for which our forebears fought is still at issue round the globe. The belief that the rights of man come not from the generosity of the state but from the hand of God.' They dared not forget they were the heirs of that first revolution.

He issued the tremendous, proud (some would say over-proud) declaration:

Let the word go forth from this time and place, to friend and foe alike, that the torch has been passed to a new generation of Americans, born in this century, tempered by war, disciplined by a hard and bitter peace, proud of our ancient heritage, and unwilling to witness or permit the slow undoing of those human rights to which this nation has always been committed, and to which we are committed today at home and around the world.

In the next paragraph he spelt out a new universal commitment in still clearer terms:

Let every nation know, whether it wishes us well or ill, that we shall pay any price, bear any burden, meet any hardship, support any friend, oppose any foe to assure the survival and the success of liberty.

There followed pledges of loyalty to allies, of assistance to impoverished nations, of a new alliance for progress with Latin America and inflexible support for the United Nations. Next came the passages which had needed the most delicate drafting. He turned 'to those nations who would make themselves our adversary'. To them he offered 'not a pledge but a request: that both sides begin anew the quest for peace'.

Kennedy's speech cannot simply be labelled a reply to Khrushchev. It was too personal, too original, too utterly an individual effort to rank as a mere reply to anybody, but it would hardly have taken its actual form if Khrushchev had not spoken a few days earlier in tones of aggressive over-confidence. 'Comrades,' said the Soviet Premier, 'we live at a splendid time: Communism has become the invincible force of our country. Through their struggles and their labour Communists, the working class, will attain the great goals of Communism on earth.' Quoting Vietnam, Algeria and Cuba as promising examples, he named Asia, Africa and Latin America as the most important centres of revolutionary struggle against imperialism.

It has been argued by Schlesinger in later years, though not in his *A Thousand Days*, that Khrushchev's belligerence was meant 'less as a provocation to the United States than as an element in a complex manoeuvre aimed at China'. Kennedy and his advisers at the time, including Schlesinger, could be forgiven for not reading this significance into the speech. Kennedy deliberately set out to counter Khrushchev's claim that Communism was indeed the wave of the future. His references to the American Revolution were not accidental. He was insisting that the Americans were not static or backward-looking, that in their own revolution they had a source of inspiration which was far superior physically and morally to anything that the Communists could offer.

Yet given his premise that this was an hour of 'maximum danger', a phrase that Schlesinger was later to describe as 'hyperbolic', he could hardly have taken more trouble to avoid provocative language and to point to peaceful solutions. 'Let us', he cried, 'never negotiate out of fear but let us never fear to negotiate.' He condemned the arms race and left no one in any doubt that in his view a nuclear war would end civilization, but American defences were to be strengthened in a large way. 'We dare not tempt them with weakness. For only when our arms are sufficient beyond doubt can we be certain beyond doubt that they will never be employed.' The words were mild enough but the message was not likely to be missed in the Kremlin. In fourteen minutes it was all over and he had left his indelible footprint.

That night he visited all five of the inaugural balls, winding up after midnight at the house of his friend Joe Alsop the famous columnist. At one of the balls he said what no doubt he felt: 'I think this is an ideal way to spend an evening and I hope that we can all meet here again tomorrow to do it all over again. . . . I don't know a better way to spend an evening – you looking at us and we looking at you.' He had a magnificent power of sharing and enhancing the happiness of others, which does not mean that the immense problems ahead were out of his mind for long. But on the whole he exulted in their challenge.

A few words are unavoidable here about the context of the inaugural speech in American foreign policy. Also about Kennedy's general approach to Communism, although we shall be returning to the latter topic repeatedly. In his *The Imperial Presidency* discussed at some length in the previous chapter, Arthur Schlesinger is a good deal more critical than in his *A Thousand Days* about the ideas behind the speech, though he does not say so explicitly. He writes about the years leading up to 1961:

> The new American approach to world affairs, the obsession with crises, the illusion of 'world leadership', the obligations of duty so cunningly intertwined with the opportunities of power, carried forward the process, begun during the Second World War, of elevating 'national security' into a supreme value. No sensible person would reject national security, realistically construed, as a self-evident necessity of State. But, under the stimulus of the Cold War, a mystique of national security, increasingly defined in short-run military terms, emerged as the decisive criterion of right and wrong.

Looking back, an idea not far removed from this was prominent in the inaugural address. Be that as it may, Schlesinger insists that the obsession with security compelled and licensed 'the increasing centralization of foreign policy in the Presidency and everything, therefore, undermined the constitutional separation of powers'.

Kennedy, as explained already, was determined to be a strong and active President. In the House of Representatives, the Democratic Party had won 21 fewer seats than two years earlier. It still held on paper a majority of 262 to 174, but bearing in mind the conservative nature of the Southern Democrats, this majority was far more nominal than real. In domestic affairs he was beleaguered by his weak position in Congress. In foreign affairs he was impelled by circumstances and temperament to assume a vigorous initiative.

There is a temptation to which some of his admirers have succumbed to treat his outlook as having reached its full maturity by the time of his Inauguration; in fact he had gained much in knowledge and understanding between early 1961 and autumn 1963. At no time, however, did he set out to drive the partisans of Communism from the ends of the earth. Victory in the traditional sense would not be feasible in the foreseeable future; but he sought unremittingly to halt the external expansion of the Soviet system. He was ready to agree with Khrushchev that the third world provided the immediate battlefield.

We are told that of all Churchillian phrases, his favourite was this one: 'We arm to parley'. Certainly during his Presidency he did plenty of arming. The first policy directive which he laid down for the new Secretary of Defence McNamara says a good deal about his priorities: 'Under no circumstances should we allow a pre-determined arbitrary financial limit to establish either strategy or force levels.' In three years, Kennedy built up the most powerful military force in human history. It was the largest and swiftest build-up in peacetime America at a cost of some seventeen billion dollars in additional appropriations.

That part of his programme is sometimes referred to as 'the Arrows' held in one of his hands. In the other was 'the Olive Branch' exhibited, it is claimed, in his attitude to disarmament generally, to the United Nations, to co-operation in Space, to foreign aid and the Peace Corps. In his dealings with Khrushchev, he was struggling with varying success, but genuine sincerity, to pursue what has been called in another connection 'a double line'.

All who knew him are agreed that Jack Kennedy had a special horror of nuclear war, although he could discuss it calmly enough at the conference table. Many times he said to O'Donnell in private, for example after his meeting with Khrushchev in Vienna and often later during the crisis periods in Berlin and Cuba, 'I keep thinking of the children, not my kids or yours, but the children all over the world.' Yet he was in no conceivable sense a pacifist or in any ordinary sense an appeaser.

At this point in time, there were few signs of encouragement in the world picture. It was true that already in December of the previous year Khrushchev had dropped hints that he would welcome a meeting with Kennedy. He sent him a cordial message on his Inauguration and liberated two captured American fliers – a gesture that encouraged Kennedy considerably.

But the overriding signs were ominous. In his first State of the Union message at the end of January, Kennedy spoke still more gravely than in his inaugural. 'Each day the crises multiply. Each day their solution grows more difficult. Each day we draw nearer the hour of maximum danger . . . I feel I must inform the Congress that . . . in each of the principal areas of crisis, the tide of events has been running out and time has not been our friend.' And this final prediction no less gloomy than the rest: 'There will be further set-backs before the tide is turned.' The speech was criticized in the press as unnecessarily pessimistic. But in fact he had rather underestimated the perils that would present themselves in the ensuing few months. A unique second State of the Union address would be required in the spring and still worse dangers would present themselves in the summer.

In the first four months of 1961 the situation was most tense in Laos. Eisenhower in his parting message to Kennedy said that the Laos situation contained the possibilities of all-out war.

It was the top priority when Kennedy met Macmillan at Key West, Florida, on 26 March, the first of seven such meetings, four of them in 1961. The two men had not met previously. The encounter was significant for Kennedy but much more so for Macmillan, who flew from the West Indies. He had looked forward to it with considerable apprehension. It is true that there was a kind of family connection. Macmillan's wife Dorothy was the aunt of the Marquis of Hartington, the young heir to the Duke of Devonshire who had married Kennedy's sister and had been killed in action in France. The link, though not very close, was much closer than any that had ever existed between an American President and a British Prime Minister. On the other hand the gap in years was unusually large between Kennedy (forty-three) and Macmillan (sixty-seven). The disparity was admittedly still greater between Kennedy on the one side and de Gaulle and Adenauer on the other, but that was not much consolation to Macmillan.

From Macmillan's standpoint the recollection of Kennedy's father was not reassuring. In retrospect he was the most unpopular American Ambassador who had ever served in Britain. He was still remembered in that country as having warned President Roosevelt that in backing Britain to the hilt he would be 'left holding the bag in a war in which the Allies expect to be beaten'. Would the new President have been reared in anti-British sentiments in the home? Macmillan is said to have asked a columnist friend: 'How am I ever going to get along with that cocky young Irishman?'

More fundamentally the British could not but be aware that a new phase of American foreign policy was upon them. There had been an explicitly avowed friendship deriving from the war years

79

between Macmillan and Eisenhower. But Kennedy, whatever else he might prove to be, was obviously not going to be another Eisenhower. In the easy-going days of the latter, Britain had enjoyed great freedom to cultivate influence within the Anglo-American alliance even apart from a Macmillan-Eisenhower friendship. Kennedy was above all determined to reassert American leadership in the world and to do so clearly and forcefully. It was possible on the face of it that Britain's rôle would be diminished. Nor was this all. Macmillan was greatly disturbed about the trend of American policy in Southeast Asia and not at all happy about giving the Americans a blank cheque in Laos. All in all there were good reasons for anxiety.

Macmillan, in one of his personae a far-sighted businessman, had given intensive thought to his prospective relationship with the new President. He had not rushed in after the election. He had 'played it cool' and waited till the President sent for Harold Caccia, the very efficient British Ambassador. Macmillan heard with satisfaction that Kennedy would like to see him in February or March and gladly accepted the proposal. Even before that he had written to the Foreign Secretary Sir Alec Douglas-Home, 'I have for some time been thinking how we would handle the new American President if it should be a Kennedy.' There had been a long comradeship of nearly twenty years with Eisenhower; there was nothing of the kind available here. 'We must therefore, I think, make our contacts in the realm of ideas. I must somehow convince him that I am worth consulting, not as an old friend (as Eisenhower felt) but as a man who, although of advancing years, has young and fresh thoughts.' Macmillan, rightly on the whole, felt able to make this latter claim of himself, although his Labour opponents would certainly not have conceded it.

Now that a meeting was due to take place he cleared his own mind in his usual systematic fashion. 'I am preparing a letter', he noted, 'to be sent to him after the weekend. This *must* interest him and put out one or two exciting ideas – yet it must not be pompous or lecturing or *too* radical.' The letter eventually went off. The biographer of Kennedy need not dwell on it but must at least underline the recognition by the shrewd Macmillan that 'exciting ideas' were a necessary ingredient in any diet which would attract Kennedy. Another of Macmillan's notes a few days later is revealing from a Conservative Prime Minister: 'Jock Witney [the

American Ambassador] called for a talk. He seemed to think that the new President's appointments were "conservative" – therefore reassuring to him but, as I did not say, correspondingly depressing to me.' According to one British opinion Douglas Dillon, the new Treasury Secretary, was 'to the right of Montagu Norman'. The latter, so long Governor of the Bank of England, was a synonym for financial restrictionism.

When the moment arrived all seemed to go well; certainly Macmillan thought so: 'Before our conversation had gone on for many minutes I felt a deep sense of relief. Although we had never met and belonged to such different generations we seemed immediately to talk as old friends. From all the accounts I heard I was not surprised that I should take a vast liking to him. It was encouraging to find that he seemed to feel something of the same.' All the evidence proves that Kennedy came to feel a considerable attachment to Macmillan. Macmillan's combination of deeply serious and knowledgeable statesmanship with rather elaborate jokiness appealed to Kennedy. 'I'd fly over Cuba,' said Macmillan, 'if they shoot me down you can have your incident.' Kennedy repeated that remark and others with appreciation. It is not so clear that his advisers shared his admiration or had any particular desire to foster the relationship.

Anyone who studies these matters should pay very close attention to Dr David Nunnerley's book *President Kennedy and Britain* (1972). He describes Lord Harlech (in 1961 soon to be British Ambassador in Washington) as his most willing and tireless source of information. And who could be better equipped for the rôle? The list of other persons interviewed is highly impressive. Dr Nunnerley states categorically that Kennedy came away from their first meeting disappointed with Macmillan. Macmillan, however, had given him most of what he asked for. Kennedy considered Laos a test not only of Soviet intentions but also of the value of the Anglo-American alliance. Macmillan advised very strongly against any military action but finally agreed 'with deepest despondency' to back up the President subject to Cabinet approval with limited supporting action.

Macmillan recalled afterwards that the American President had been flanked by an impressive display of 'top brass' from the Pentagon who explained at length their plan for strong action in Southeast Asia. Kennedy asked to be left alone with Macmillan, to whom he turned with the question: 'What do you think of all that?' 'I don't think much of it,' replied Macmillan. 'Nor do I,' said Kennedy. Macmillan went on to warn Kennedy from British experience of the dangers of becoming more and more involved in such an area – one step would lead to another and so on, *ad infinitum*.

Kennedy suggested that Britain had been very successful in Malaya, but Macmillan pointed out the sharp difference between the two situations. In Malaya the British had been still in control of the government, the police and the secret service. That, however, and various other possibilities would be ruled out for the Americans in Southeast Asia as imperialistic. Kennedy listened as carefully as always.

At this same meeting with Macmillan the question of a successor to Harold Caccia, the British Ambassador, was discussed. Macmillan noted: 'Kennedy was emphatic for David Ormsby Gore. "He is my brother's most intimate friend" (and, of course, "my brother" is thought by many to be the Grey Eminence).' Macmillan, who may or may not have had the idea in mind, was happy to make the appointment when the time came (autumn 1961). 'No Ambassador,' he records, 'has ever served us so well in Washington.' Few would cavil at that verdict, although it would be quickly pointed out by David Ormsby Gore (now Lord Harlech) himself that he brought to his task unique advantages. As Macmillan puts it, he had access to the White House such as no Ambassador has had before or since. There were so many personal factors at work. Lord Hartington, Kennedy's deceased brother-in-law, already referred to more than once, had been the cousin and best friend of David Ormsby Gore. Kathleen Kennedy was a very close friend of the Ormsby Gores and godmother to their eldest child. Whenever Jack Kennedy was in London he would see David Ormsby Gore. When in America Ormsby Gore would stay regularly with the Kennedys. And, incidentally, David Ormsby Gore was a nephew of Harold Macmillan in the sense that his mother's sister was married to the Duke of Devonshire whose sister was married to Macmillan.

Kennedy, as Macmillan saw him, moved in three worlds – the political world, the smart world and the intellectual world. David Ormsby Gore could keep pace with him in all three. He was a popular and rising politician; he was thoroughly at home at dances and parties of all kinds. He could play a graceful part at seminars led by Arthur Schlesinger of Harvard or Isaiah Berlin of Oxford.

Kennedy and Macmillan separated. But after a thorough tour of the West Indies, the latter visited the President again, this time in Washington before returning to England. Macmillan was much impressed by the President's quiet confidence and great courtesy. He listened well, did not talk too much and encouraged others on both sides to speak. 'I opened,' says Macmillan, 'on the general theme of the Soviet advance in recent years and the need to organize the unity of the Free World. I emphasized the strength of the Six in Europe and the dangers of France – under de Gaulle – of Europe moving into a "Third Force" – still more dangerous, perhaps, after de Gaulle's death and the rise of a post-Adenauer Germany.' Difficulties with the French, in other words with de Gaulle, loomed large in the discussion. Macmillan ventilated various ideas which met with a sympathetic response from Kennedy. But another of Macmillan's canny reservations must be quoted: 'All this was satisfactory and yet I could not help feeling that he spoke about all these things in a rather detached way. Perhaps because it is his character to be ready to listen to anything. What he decides is another matter.' The references to Kennedy's entourage carry another small barb: 'He has surrounded himself with a large retinue of highly intelligent men, young and old. All this great army of advisers is engaged on studying all the more or less insoluble problems which the modern world presents to its baffled inhabitants. . . . So far, apart from various messages to Congress and some excellent press conferences, nothing much has happened.' The New Frontier was being cut down to size.

But we must retrace our steps a little to pick up the threads of the Laos issue.

The French held back from offering support but Kennedy's statement at a press conference on 23 March 1961 lacked nothing in bluntness. 'We strongly and unreservedly support the goal of a neutral and independent Laos; if there is to be a peaceful solution there must be cessation of the present armed attacks by externally supported Communists. . . .' Whether it was due to Kennedy's words or fleet dispositions in the China Sea, or other factors, the Russians began to exhibit a new readiness for compromise. By the beginning of May some kind of truce had been arranged on the ground.

On 28 March, influenced no doubt by Laos and not by Laos alone, Kennedy had come before Congress with a new tough and, it was claimed, highly sophisticated defence policy. In his inaugural and his State of the Union addresses he had paved the way. Now he left the world in no doubt whatever about the far-reaching steps being taken both quantitatively and qualitatively to increase the American defences. Some of the language was of a general character whose significance, however, was unmistakable. 'Our strategic arms and defences must be adequate to deter any deliberate nuclear attack on the United States or our Allies. The strength and deployment of our forces in combination with those of our Allies should be sufficiently powerful and mobile to prevent the steady erosion of the free world through limited wars.'

Nothing, however, expressed his personal interest more than a new emphasis on guerrilla warfare. 'We need a greater ability to deal with guerrilla forces, insurrections and subversions. . . . We must be ready now to deal with any size of force including small externally supported bands of men, and we must help train local forces to be equally effective.' Kennedy himself plunged into a study of works on guerrilla warfare including those of Che Guevara and Mao Tse-tung. Suddenly the concept of guerrilla warfare became a policy, almost an infatuation. It was still the hour of euphoria – Schlesinger's 'golden interlude'; it would not last very long.

No fiasco was ever more of a fiasco than the adventure of the Bay of Pigs in Cuba. No expedition was ever a greater failure than that organized by the United States authorities which sent 1,400 Cuban exiles to invade their homeland with the idea of overthrowing Castro. Early on Monday, 17 April 1961, they landed. Early on Wednesday, 19 April, they surrendered and were marched off to Castro's prisons. Twenty months later their release was secured. But at the time one cannot gainsay the summary of Hugh Sidey: 'Jack Kennedy with the military power to destroy the world did nothing.' The setback had no redeeming features except the wisdom which comes from an analysis of folly.

During the election Kennedy had drawn attention sharply to the Communist threat ninety miles from the coast of Florida and denounced Eisenhower's lack of action. But in fact under Eisenhower a lot more was going on than he supposed. The original plans envisaged guerrilla infiltration. But these were being scrapped in favour of a beach-head assault by a small conventional force with support from artillery and the air. The project was mentioned to the President-elect on 17 November, and on 29 November, spelt out in greater detail. On that day he received a detailed briefing on the CIA's new military conception. Kennedy told Dulles, the head of the CIA, to carry the work forward. He himself saw it as 'a contingency plan'. He did not yet realize how contingency planning, in Schlesinger's phrase, 'could generate its own momentum and create its own realities'.

Schlesinger was very much involved in all the planning, although his reservations look well on the record. On 11 March he was summoned to a meeting with the President in the Cabinet Room. 'Top brass' was present in large supply. By now the contingency had become a reality. Having created the Cuban brigade as a possible option, the CIA were presenting its use against Cuba as a necessity. Kennedy tentatively agreed that among various alternatives, the simplest thing might be to let the Cubans go where they wanted to go – to Cuba. In order to minimize the political risk he directed that a more liberal and representative exile organization should be formed as soon as possible. In other words, his feet were set on the slippery slope.

Schlesinger noted after the meeting of 29 March: 'The final decision will have to be made on 4 April . . . the CIA representatives dominated the discussion.' The Pentagon Joint Chiefs of Staff gave an impression of whole-hearted support. On 4 April came a climactic meeting at which Senator Fulbright strongly opposed the plan. So did Schlesinger himself in memoranda of 5 April and 10 April. The President became what has charitably been called 'a prisoner of events'. On 6 April Schlesinger noted, 'We seem now destined to go ahead on a quasi-minimum basis.' And on 7 April, it was apparent that 'he had made his decision and is not likely now to reverse it'. And so it proved. The principal condition on which Kennedy insisted before approving the plan was to rule out any direct overt participation of American armed forces in Cuba.

Early in the morning of Monday, 17 April, the Cuban exile brigade achieved tactical surprise in their place of landing, fought ably and bravely while their ammunition lasted and inflicted heavy losses on a Castro force which soon numbered up to 20,000 men. But their ammunition did not last very long. A ten days' supply was on the freighter *Rio Escondido* but that freighter was sunk off-shore by Castro's tiny air force, along with another supply-laden freighter, the *Houston*. Two other freighters, the *Atlantico* and the *Caribe*, fled south.

That night, Tuesday, in the Cabinet room, the CIA and the Joint Chiefs of Staff begged Kennedy to reverse his public pledge and openly introduce American air and naval power to back the brigade on the beach. Kennedy would not go back on his word. He finally agreed, however, that unmarked navy jets should protect the anti-Castro forces of B–26s when they provided air cover the next morning for the supply boats. But yet again everything went wrong. The B–26s arrived too early and were soon disposed of or frightened off. Without ammunition the exiles were quickly rounded up. In short, while the lack of ammunition led directly to disaster, Castro's control of the air led directly to the lack of ammunition. The plan had been to destroy Castro's air force on the ground before the battle began, but the first strike on the Saturday had been a failure. The second strike was cancelled by the President on the Sunday in view of mounting world antagonism.

Kennedy was sick at heart over the political and diplomatic calamity, but still more over the fate of the invading exiles killed or captured, and of their leaders in Florida. After the midnight meeting of the Cabinet on the Tuesday, he sent Schlesinger and Berle to pacify them. The former had never seen angrier men. He and Berle brought them back to Kennedy in Washington. The President expressed, with superb sincerity and dignity, his share in their grievous sorrow. He was in every way at his best. The exile leaders were deeply moved.

The excuse is put forward for Kennedy that he had only been in office for seventy-seven days. He could not know which of his inherited advisers were competent and which were not. Again, it was understandable that he would 'trust his luck to the limit'. Everything since 1956 had always gone right for him.

With hindsight it is easy to see that what he had approved was militarily and diplomatically unwise. But at the time he was mis-informed on more points than one, most flagrantly on the prospect of a Cuban rising to support the exiles against Castro. Kennedy insisted in public on taking the full responsibility. In private he was more outspoken in resentment. 'My God!' he said, 'can you imagine being President and leaving behind someone like all those people here?' But it was himself whom he blamed fundamentally. 'How could I', he kept asking himself, 'have been so off-base? All my life I have known better than to depend on the experts. How could I have been so stupid as to let them go ahead?' He vowed that he would never again be over-awed by professional military advisers.

Macmillan's comments, however unpalatable, must be recorded. 'There was a plan for a big invasion to include American troops. It seems that the President vetoed this and gave his approval to the simple landing of some partisans. The agencies operated the full invasion plan, but without American troops, hoping no doubt to force the President's hand. He stood firm, hence the fiasco.' This is not dissimilar to Kennedy's own view of what went wrong as interpreted by O'Donnell. The whole project had only made sense to the President on the assumption that there were plans for a co-ordinated rising in Cuba. After the calamity had come about he was much shocked to discover that no such plans had existed. He reached the embittering conclusion that the Chiefs of Staff and the CIA had assumed that when it came to the crunch the President would order the navy jets and the marines into action. As he said one day to Dave Powers: 'They couldn't believe that a new President like me wouldn't panic and try to save his own face. Well, they had me figured all wrong.'

7

A year of Krushchev

Paris, Vienna and after

By May 1961 President Kennedy was feeling positively buoyant. Amazing though it may seem his popularity poll had jumped to 83% *after* the Bay of Pigs. 'My God,' said Kennedy, 'it is as bad as Eisenhower.' He loved to be popular though that was by no means his main criterion of success. Laos was, for the time being at least, a stalemate. So two crises had been survived. And now on 12 May came a surprising but welcome message from Krushchev which accepted the suggestion of a meeting in Vienna in early June.

The original idea of a meeting had come from Khrushchev, after the election and before the Inauguration. Kennedy was attracted by the idea but after an extended discussion of Soviet problems with all available advisers it was decided to aim at an informal rather than at a summit meeting. Not that Kennedy objected in principle to the latter. 'It is far better to meet at the summit than at the brink,' he said. But on balance it was felt that an official summit meeting between the two leaders would be a mistake. It would arouse expectations that could not be fulfilled and inject considerations of personal prestige and face-saving. Conversely they were agreed that an informal meeting would be useful to the President in helping him to gain first-hand experience of Khrushchev. Also in this way he could make clearer than had been done previously, or could be done by letter, the vital interests for which the United States would fight.

Moreover, Kennedy believed fervently in the power of personal communication in general and was highly confident of his own talents on that plane. As yet he had never met anyone who was totally impervious to his form of reasoning or quite unaffected by his charm. Ambassador Thompson carried back to Moscow a presidential letter of 22 February suggesting a rendezvous in the late spring at Vienna or Stockholm. On 9 March Khrushchev gave him the impression that he was pleased at the prospect of a meeting though in no way inclined to yield on issues. But even by this time the hopes for better relations were beginning to fade. The Russians were creating new difficulties at Geneva in regard to the Test Ban proposals. They were proposing a Troika Plan which would produce a Soviet veto on the test-verification process. There was no immediate hope of agreement there. Then came the Bay of Pigs fiasco. Kennedy put the idea of a meeting with Khrushchev out of his mind for the moment. He had no intention of leading from weakness. However, here it was Khrushchev who was coming forward and saying he would like to meet him. Khrushchev reciprocated Kennedy's hopes expressed earlier for better relations; he specifically welcomed Laos, disarmament and Berlin as leading topics. To this day nobody is sure about what his real purpose was.

It may be surmised that after the Bay of Pigs he thought that Kennedy would be easy meat. In other words he calculated on getting the better of Kennedy around the conference table, just as Kennedy calculated on getting the better of him. Or he may just have wanted to resume the campaign for driving the West out of Berlin. In his speech of 6 January he had described the Allied position there as particularly vulnerable. He had announced that if the Allies 'did not come to their senses' he would sign a peace treaty with East Berlin. This, as he saw it, would destroy the Allied legal position in West Berlin, which depended on the 1945 Agreement. Their legal position once undermined, the extrusion should not prove too difficult. Kennedy had all along wanted to meet Khrushchev for the reasons indicated. But by now he was keener than ever. Any impression of feebleness deriving from the Bay of Pigs affair should be eradicated as quickly as possible. Khrushchev must be made aware forthwith that he would not be dealing with a weakling. Kennedy intended in effect to propose a standstill in the Cold War and an understanding that neither nuclear power should take any steps to threaten world peace.

It is noteworthy that he went ahead with his second State of the

Union message on 24 May. His language was uncompromising enough. 'These', he said, 'are extraordinary times and we face an extraordinary challenge. Our strength as well as our convictions have imposed upon this nation the rôle of leader in freedom's cause.' He ticked off two billion dollars' worth of new recommendations and repeated that 'this is a most serious time in the life of our country and in the life of freedom around the globe'. There was some understandable concern that the message might anger Khrushchev at the wrong moment. Kennedy refused to be deflected. If Khrushchev was going to be offended by the billions more asked for the defence of freedom, then that was the way it would have to be. We can forgive Khrushchev for seeing it otherwise.

This second State of the Union message was historic for another reason. In the presidential campaign of 1960 John Kennedy had laid much emphasis on the American failure to keep abreast with the Russians in the Space competition. He was too much absorbed in other matters when he reached the White House to give this topic his full attention. But on 12 April, Moscow announced that Cosmonaut Yuri Gagarin had completed an orbital flight round the earth in less than two hours. Kennedy was faced with the decision of whether to try to overtake the Russians or permanently play second fiddle. After prolonged and heart-searching discussions with every kind of expert, he included in his State of the Union message a dramatic pledge to land a man on the moon and return him safely to earth before the decade was out.

Congress supported him by a nearly unanimous vote. The successful plunge of Commander Shephard into Space, though not into orbit, a few weeks earlier was helpful. The Space budget was increased by 50% in that year. The following year it exceeded all the pre-1960 Space budgets combined. The language used by Kennedy to defend his decision could be described as either sublime or ridiculous, according to the mind of the listener:

In a very real sense, it will not be one man going to the moon, it will be an entire nation, for all of us must work to put him there. . . . We go into space because whatever mankind must undertake, free men must fully share.

'But why', some say, 'the moon?' And they may well ask 'why climb the highest mountain? Why thirty-five years ago fly the Atlantic?' . . . Many years ago the great British explorer George Mallory, who was to die on Mount Everest, was asked why did he want to climb it, and he said: 'Because it is there.' Well, Space is there and the moon and the planets are there and new hopes for knowledge and peace are there.

Sense or nonsense, who shall say? That at any rate was John Kennedy's decision and collectively it has been supported by the American nation.

First on 31 May 1961 came the visit to de Gaulle in Paris. He had been charmed and encouraged by de Gaulle's message when he was elected President – 'Welcome, dear partner', and other elegant phrases. He was anxious to take the first opportunity of meeting him.

John Kennedy had a success on all levels, but it was Jacqueline who won every heart. At the final press conference Kennedy, graceful as always, paid her a self-deprecating tribute. 'I do not think', he began, 'it altogether inappropriate to introduce myself to this audience. I am the man who accompanied Jacqueline Kennedy to Paris and I have enjoyed it.' 'Now', said de Gaulle, as he bade him farewell, 'I have more confidence in your country.' Kennedy on his side felt that overall the talks had been satisfactory.

At the end of the first meeting they found themselves in full agreement on the need for unflinching resolve in Berlin. On Laos de Gaulle told Kennedy that France would not commit troops unless there was an all-out war. In that case, of course, France would be at the side of the United States with her armies. That was all that could be expected from de Gaulle at that juncture. So far, therefore, so good. But on the second day de Gaulle left Kennedy in no doubt that regarding NATO there was a fundamental difference between them. France had now regained her health and spirit. She could not live under the shadow of NATO much longer. She must have her own nuclear force. She, in fact, intended to develop it, come what might.

Kennedy kept repeating that France had no need of her own nuclear weapons. They would add nothing to her protection. It would be far more helpful to the European cause if the European nations strengthened their own conventional armaments. But de Gaulle would yield nothing. On this issue agreement was clearly impossible. Kennedy repeated that America would go to war if Europe were attacked. De Gaulle accepted John Kennedy's personal word for it, without altering his stated position. They parted on terms of personal cordiality. De Gaulle wrote a long-hand letter to Jackie which set the seal on her triumph.

The talks in Paris were a happy outing compared with those with the Russians in Vienna. There was some pleasant if heavy-footed banter in the opening stages. Touching the two star-shaped medals on Khrushchev's chest, Kennedy asked what they were for. Khrushchev replied that they were Lenin peace medals. 'I hope you keep them,' said Kennedy with, we are told, a chuckle. At one moment when Kennedy was lighting a cigar, his lighted match slipped away and landed behind Khrushchev's chair. 'Are you trying to set me on fire?' demanded Khrushchev. Kennedy assured him that he wasn't. 'Ah!' laughed Khrushchev, 'a Capitalist, not an Incendiary.' And so on and so forth. Harmless badinage which might have led somewhere. But in fact it didn't.

The talks went on for something like eleven hours, in addition to social jollifications. The disagreements were not on the face of it numerous. On Laos, which earlier in the year had seemed so perilous, Khrushchev was ready to agree on a neutralist solution. But the longer they talked, the more strongly it came home to Kennedy that Khrushchev was not ready to move an inch towards a meeting of minds. He seemed convinced that there was no reason why he should. Given a little time and Communism would sweep to inevitable victory.

The crisis came, as expected, over Berlin: the symbol and focal point of the global conflict. Kennedy and Khrushchev would both have said that they wanted to preserve the status quo. But for Kennedy the status quo meant the existing balance of international force. For Khrushchev it meant the uninterrupted progress, as he hoped, of the Communist Revolution across the world. He announced what he described as an irrevocable decision.

The Soviet Union would sign a peace treaty in December which would turn the whole of Berlin into East German territory. If, after that, the Western powers attempted to enforce their existing occupation rights (indeed, if they did not withdraw their troops before the deadline), the Western powers would be squeezed out of Berlin and West Berlin would be squeezed into the Eastern orbit. If the West did not give way to the ultimatum, there would be war. Kennedy fought every inch of the way. He postponed the ending of the talks, but there came a moment when Khrushchev made his intentions brutally plain. 'In that case,' said Kennedy as a final word, 'it will be a cold winter.'

Kennedy told a friend in the press that 'sombre' would be a good word for the meeting. Schlesinger informs us that the experience deeply disturbed him. Here for the first time was a leader with whom he could not exchange ideas, who seemed impervious to reasoned argument and, most depressing of all, was apparently indifferent to the prospect of the obliteration of mankind.

O'Donnell, loyally and rather indignantly, disputes a statement made by Reston in *The New York Times* which was widely repeated. Kennedy was described by Reston as 'shaken and angry'. O'Donnell agrees that he was angry but not that he was in any way shaken. 'If he felt any panic he kept it well concealed.'

'Tense and tired' (Schlesinger) seems a fair description of him as he flew to London. Macmillan reports the visit in his usual objective fashion. 'The arrival', he says, 'of the Kennedys in London on 4 June was a cause of widespread interest and even excitement. The young President with his lovely wife and the whole glamour which surrounded them both caused something of a sensation.' Next morning he was at pains to provide the President with the right psychological situation. Schlesinger presents him as showing an instinctive understanding. ' "Let's not have a meeting", he is reported as saying with a weary wave of the hand, "Why not have a peaceful drink and chat by ourselves?" ' Macmillan records the extent of his own intuition. 'It was clear', he says, 'that as soon as the President arrived he wanted no kind of formal meeting with advisers and experts; he wanted a private talk, and this lasted from 10.30 am to 1 pm.'

The greater part of the talk consisted of Kennedy giving his impressions of de Gaulle and Khrushchev. 'Naturally he was full of Khrushchev and he was obviously much concerned and even surprised by the almost brutal frankness of the Soviet leader. . . . de Gaulle was very avuncular, very gracious, very oracular and very unyielding.'

Macmillan records his own disappointment: 'Little progress with the French and none with the Russians.' The only compensation, and it was a large one, was the further deepening of his relationship with Kennedy. 'I find my friendship beginning to grow into something like that which I got with Eisenhower after a few months at Algiers.' Macmillan observes that Eisenhower, trained as a soldier, did not find it easy to *discuss* a problem. 'Kennedy, with an entirely different mental background, is quick, well-informed, subtle; but proceeds more by asking questions than by answering them.' Once again there is the implication that this, the most powerful individual in the world, was still very uncertain as to how to proceed. The penalty, it may be said, of being the youngest man to be elected President of the United States.

In later years Macmillan recalled the air of utter exhaustion with which Kennedy arrived at Downing Street. Kennedy seemed to have made at least three miscalculations: he had overestimated the effect of his charm, which meant nothing to a man like Khrushchev; he had underestimated the coherence of Khrushchev's Marxism and the difficulty of arguing with him without much more knowledge of Marxism than possessed by Kennedy or his advisers. (Macmillan compared it afterwards to arguing with a mediaeval schoolman without a training in that discipline.) And he overestimated Khrushchev's decency. He was himself so nice in a Western educated way that he was not prepared for the degree of evil to be found in a man who had helped to liquidate so many of his fellow-humans. In some respects he was naive.

O'Donnell is anxious to demonstrate that Kennedy and Khrushchev 'gained an understanding and a respect for each other during the talks that served the United States and Russia well in the later crisis periods'. He quotes a letter that Khrushchev wrote to Kennedy soon afterwards, enclosing a model of an American whaler. 'It is also', he wrote, 'a pleasure for Nina Petrovna and myself to fulfil Mrs Kennedy's wish and to send to you and your family little Pushinka, (a direct offspring of the well-known cosmos traveller Strelka, which made a trip in a cosmic ship on 19 August 1969, and successfully returned to earth).' We are told that the little dog Pushinka made herself at home in the White House and became a pampered member of the family.

But the meeting between Kennedy and Khrushchev cannot be described as successful.

The confrontation with Khrushchev undoubtedly had a lasting effect on Kennedy. It certainly did not in any way intimidate him. Whether it led him to over-react is a matter for argument. He had already in his first defence statement in March set out a large expansion of the defence budget. In the State of the Union message of 24 May he had gone much further. Now, on 25 July, he entered into a stronger than ever commitment in front of the nation and the world overseas. 'West Berlin has now become', he said, 'the great testing place of Western courage and will, a focal point where our solemn commitments and Soviet ambitions now meet in basic confrontation. We cannot and will not permit the Communists to drive us out of Berlin either gradually or by force.'

He announced new and powerful steps to expand the defences immediately, among them a request to Congress for the current fiscal year of an additional $3,247,000,000 of appropriations for the Armed Forces, and a substantial increase in the strength of the army, navy and air force. 'To fulfil these manpower needs, I am ordering that our draft calls be doubled and tripled in the coming months: I am asking the Congress for authority to order to active duty certain ready reserve units and individual reservists, and to extend tours of duty. . . .' High among the other items was a major new programme for civil defence.

He indicated a readiness for negotiations if they were desired. For this purpose he had to over-rule Dean Acheson and other hard-line advisers. And he had plenty of trouble in producing any semblance of Western unity. In Sorensen's words, quoted without dissent by Nunnerley, 'The French were against all negotiations. The British were against war without risking negotiations: and the Germans, as their autumn elections drew nearer, were against both these positions and seemingly against everything else.' What Kennedy finally enunciated was vague enough. 'We will, at all times, be ready to talk, if talk will help.' But he did not fail to add: 'We will be ready to resist with force if force is used upon us.'

Kennedy was due to meet Macmillan at Bermuda on 21 December 1961. But two days earlier he suffered a shattering blow. On that day he had been visiting his father at Palm Beach. Joe Kennedy saw him off at the airport, returned to his house with Caroline and played for half an hour with his grandchildren, who were assembled for Christmas. Then he played nine holes at the nearby Palm Beach Golf Club with his favourite niece, Ann Gargan, complaining that he didn't feel too well but putting it down to a cold. But now tragedy struck. On the sixteenth fairway he was compelled to sit down; he complained that he felt really ill. He was driven home by Ann. His instruction as he went upstairs, 'Don't call any doctors', was over-ruled. He was taken to St Mary's

Hospital and received the last rites of the Catholic Church. Jack Kennedy received the same news in a telephone call from Bobby. He put down the receiver, 'his face taut' (Whalen). 'Dad's gotten sick,' he said to one of his staff. He returned to Florida at once, on board the presidential jet, accompanied by Bobby and his sister Jean. The family gathered from California and Boston, in addition to Washington.

Joe Kennedy had suffered a severe thrombosis, a blood clot in an artery of the brain. His right side was paralysed and he was unable to speak. As Whalen puts it: 'Long a figure of boundless energy and roaring authority, in spite of unremitting efforts to recover his health and strength, from now on he was mute and crippled and massively frustrated.' Hearing the grievous news Macmillan at once suggested coming to Palm Beach or Washington, instead of Bermuda. But on the day after the stroke, Joe Kennedy showed some improvement and appeared to recognize his children. The President therefore went through with the original arrangements.

Macmillan noted afterwards that he felt that Kennedy and he had 'become even closer friends than before'. But the following distinction is hardly a compliment:

There is a marked contrast between President Kennedy 'in action' on a specific problem (e.g. the Congo, West Berlin, Ghana), and his attitude to larger issues (the nuclear war, the struggle between East and West, Capitalism and Communism, etc.). In the first, he is an extraordinarily quick and effective operator – a born 'politician' [not in a pejorative sense]. On the wider issues he seems rather lost.

Khrushchev had already increased his defence budget by a third since Vienna (Kennedy had announced one large expansion just *before* Vienna). Not surprisingly perhaps, Khrushchev announced that this further vast increase on the American side was belligerent. Some militant response from him was awaited. Khrushchev's response on 13 August was to set up the Berlin Wall and stop all movement from East Berlin to the West.

The Allied reply proved difficult to organize. Sorensen says that efforts in that direction proceeded uncertainly for a year. Whatever may be said of de Gaulle and Adenauer, Kennedy and Macmillan had excuses for not being altogether in line. In the United States, as Nunnerley points out, Kennedy's action had geared American opinion to an acceptance of the imminence of a crisis in Berlin, and this was simply not so in Britain. Seventy-one per cent of an American sample expressed a willingness to fight for Berlin, whereas the corresponding figure for Britain was forty-six per cent, and for France no more than nine per cent. The American administration lacked full confidence that their policy would be backed by their Allies, although there was an underlying belief that Britain, more conciliatory though she was towards Russia, 'would be all right on the night'.

At least the Americans made one unmistakable gesture of strength and resolution. Fifteen hundred American troops were sent racing along the Autobahn on 20 August to vindicate the right of access into Berlin. It is said that on that day, more than on any other, the President felt that the American people were entering the danger zone. Operationally it was a triumphant success. Vice-President Johnson and General Clay, former military governor of the American Zone, were despatched to Berlin to welcome the column on behalf of the President. The President was determined that the whole world should be aware of the full American commitment.

The escalation went on steadily. Nuclear testing was resumed by the Russians under ground on 30 August. After consultation with Macmillan Kennedy issued an appeal that further tests should be halted, but after the third Russian blast he felt that he had no option but to issue his prepared statement. 'In view of the continued testing by the Soviet government, I have today ordered the resumption of nuclear tests, in the laboratory and under ground, with no fallout.' Bobby Kennedy said later, 'We felt war was very possible then.' Bad news kept coming in. The Russians were strongly opposed to Secretary-General Hammarskjöld and were threatening to quit the UN organization. Now came the dreadful news that Hammarskjöld had been killed when his plane crashed over the Congo. The whole United Nations was in a state of ferment. Kennedy before the General Assembly paid generous tribute to Hammarskjöld, ending with a moving plea: 'Ladies and gentlemen of this Assembly, the decision is ours. Never have the nations of the world had so much to lose, or so much to gain. Together we shall save our planet, or together we shall perish in its flames. Save it we can – and save it we must – and then shall we earn the eternal thanks of mankind and, as peacemakers, the eternal blessing of God.' But the effect of his words remained quite unpredictable.

When things were just about at their nadir the Russians, as mysterious as ever, began to show signs of desiring a compromise. In talks with Dean Rusk at the United Nations Gromyko indicated a wish for discussions rather than the use of force, at that point at least. It was felt on the American side that the tension over Berlin was just beginning to dissolve. Not long after Kennedy invited Gromyko for further explorations. At this point Kennedy and his aides had gained the impression that the Soviet was more anxious to talk about Berlin than was the United States. Kennedy played 'hard to get'; he informed Gromyko that the Soviet Union had made no acceptable proposals for any possible bargain. Until it did, the United States was not interested in negotiations. He rounded off the proceedings by giving Gromyko a Russian poem to read called *The Swan, The Pike and the Crayfish*. The three of them failed to draw a cart for lack of co-operation:

> ... The swan makes upward for a cloud,
> The crayfish falls behind, the pike the river uses;
> To judge of each one's merits lies beyond my will;
> I know the cart remains there, still.

Gromyko roared with laughter. 'Yes', he said, acknowledging the hit, 'but those are animals. We are talking about people.' No one could question the trouble that Kennedy took over relationships that might matter.

There were unpleasant developments still to come. The Russians resumed testing in the atmosphere in October, forcing the Americans to follow, though this was not in fact possible until the spring. Yet the worst seemed to be over for the time being at least. The Russian line had softened for no obvious reason, unless we find it in the immense increase in the armed might of America and the clear determination that these weapons would, in the last resort, be used.

But that was by no means the whole of American policy. Deputy Secretary of Defence Roswell Gilpatric had spelt out the American military superiority in sheer physical terms in an address to the Business Council in Hot Springs, Virginia, in October. 'Our confidence', he said, 'in our ability to deter Communist action, or resist Communist blackmail, is based upon a sober appreciation of the relative military power of the two sides. The fact is that this nation has a nuclear retaliatory force of such lethal power that any enemy move which brought it into play would be an act of self-destruction on his part.' Kennedy was asked a little later why he did not speak out as unequivocally as Gilpatric had done. He replied in words that go close to the heart of his statesmanship: 'I don't want to get up against Khrushchev like we were last year.' He took both fists and brought them together as if they were two heads smashing against each other. 'I want him to be able to get off the hook in this thing. I don't want to force him into anything. When I get up and say those things it sounds too belligerent.'

In reporting to the Queen, Macmillan made allowances for the President's distress, as a result of his father's tragic condition. He recognized his deep attachment, but he could not help opining that 'the President's own health was not good. He is very restless owing to his back. He finds it difficult to sit in the same position for any length of time – it is really rather sad that so young a man should be so afflicted, but he is very brave and does not show it except, as I say, by his unwillingness to talk for any length of time without a break.'

What follows is somewhat diluted praise – 'he is a very sensitive man, very easily pleased and very easily offended.' But the final words are altogether favourable: 'he is a most agreeable guest and carries the weight of his great office with simplicity and dignity.' He suggested that the Queen might write him an occasional letter. 'The President is fond of writing letters and, I think, of receiving them.' What is more surprising in his notes of the Conference is a passage like this one:

I got the feeling that the President is getting impatient with Adenauer, and really angry with de Gaulle. He does *not* intend to risk war about Berlin, although outwardly and publicly he talks big.

No doubt President Kennedy was determined to avoid provocation.

But did Macmillan seriously misunderstand him in supposing that he was not ready 'to risk war about Berlin'? The answer seems to be 'yes' and 'no'. The testimony of O'Donnell must be taken seriously, although it does not follow that Kennedy revealed to him (or to anyone) the whole of his mind, or that his attitude never varied. On the way back from the Vienna confrontation in the summer he had called O'Donnell into his cabin in the aeroplane and unburdened himself with exceptional frankness. He did not usually reveal 'his deep feelings' or spell out all the factors which he was weighing up before a decision. On this occasion he dwelt at length on the disproportion between cause and effect in allowing a dispute over 'questionable' West German rights to Berlin to start a nuclear world war. So O'Donnell tells the story. 'Before I back Khrushchev against the wall,' he went on, 'and put him to a final test, the freedom of all of Western Europe will have to be at stake.'

Later he came to feel that Adenauer was blocking American and British efforts to work out a peaceful settlement of the Berlin problem. In regard to which Kennedy commented: 'Well if they, the Germans, think we are rushing into a war over Berlin except as a last desperate move to save the NATO Alliance, they've got another think coming.' All of which sounds rather close to his attitude as diagnosed by Macmillan. But, as O'Donnell points out, 'Kennedy honoured our commitment in West Berlin as one that could never be broken.' In practice, therefore, he was entitled to receive the homage of that city when he made his great declaration during his visit in June 1963, 'Ich bin ein Berliner.'

It is as convenient here as anywhere to try to estimate the influence of Macmillan and Britain on Kennedy and American policy.

One of Nunnerley's conclusions provides a minimum statement. 'As in Laos, so over the Berlin and Cuban crises and over the issue of an American resumption of atmospheric tests, the British Government in urging restraint strengthened Kennedy's hand in overcoming the wilder ideas of some members of his Administration.'

Beyond that, who can say? There was a first-class working relationship between the leaders of the two nations and an unprecedented personal friendship between the President and the British Ambassador. Macmillan's position suffered, however, in American eyes from what they regarded as 'an exaggerated belief in the possibilities of negotiation with the Soviet Union', and from various attitudes towards Southeast Asia, Berlin and so on, which seemed to flow therefrom. Conversely the American administration suffered in British eyes from a seeming inability to restrain the elements 'spoiling for a confrontation with the Soviet Union'. But certain fundamental attitudes were held in common. To mention four only: the refusal to be intimidated by Soviet threats; the acceptance of the need to negotiate with the Russians as with any opponent; the genuine belief in the cause of a united Europe; and the determination to bring about a Nuclear Test Ban Treaty, if humanly possible.

Macmillan and Kennedy, on behalf of their respective countries, could fairly be described as partners. The fact that the junior partner in power was the senior partner in age and experience was something of a balancing factor. But this is not how American historians tell the story. And who knows precisely where the truth lies?

Whatever Macmillan may have supposed – wrongly, one would think – about Kennedy's not being ready to risk war for Berlin, the latter seemed to have achieved his purpose for the time being. December 1961 passed without a peace treaty being signed between the Soviet Union and East Germany. Khrushchev and Kennedy did not meet again after the encounter of June 1961. In fairness to Khrushchev this was Kennedy's decision, not his. A unique private correspondence established between the two men was a kind of substitute for personal meetings. The arguments, however, over Laos, nuclear testing, Vietnam and Berlin were more or less the same as those in the published document. Khrushchev had some nice things to say about Kennedy. He told Salinger and others that he had acquired a healthy respect as well as a personal liking for Kennedy, despite their differences. (For the estimate of Kennedy given in his Memoirs, see page 131). One can detect in these remarks of Khrushchev a modest element of sincerity.

Kennedy had by now no illusions about him. He found him neither comic nor lovable. He regarded him as a clever, tough, shrewd adversary. By the time the correspondence started the Russians had already begun nuclear testing in the atmosphere without any hint of warning. They professed great indignation when the Americans followed reluctantly in the spring of 1962. The combination of aggressiveness and deceitfulness which they exhibited over the Cuban missiles provides an excuse for arguing that the Khrushchev–Kennedy correspondence was a Russian device for fooling the Americans. But the best opinion seems to favour the opposite view. The correspondence certainly played its part in averting calamity at the moment of supreme crisis. The crucial exchanges at that time would have been less likely without the foregoing correspondence; the steady movement from then on towards the Test Ban Treaty of 1963 owed something at least to the personal relationship achieved between Khrushchev and Kennedy.

8

Domestic pressures: The economy and Civil Rights

John Kennedy's main interest as President was always international affairs. It is thus perhaps ironic that although he confessed little understanding of economics his economic record was a genuine success story, and that while Civil Rights was not initially for him a pressing concern, he found himself caught up in the popular civil rights movement of the '60s and eventually earned the sympathy and respect of the young liberals and blacks who were urgently requesting legislation.

Sorensen can be relied upon to put Kennedy's economic record in its most favourable light. But some of the facts that he records with gusto cannot be explained away even by the most captious critic. 'During the four years following John Kennedy's Inauguration, the United States experienced the longest and strongest economic expansion in this nation's modern history. The output of goods and services increased more in four years than in the previous eight.' The post-war trend of recurring recessions had been broken, the recession which was 'due' in 1963 had been skipped and nearly every indicator of the economy was at a record level. Sorensen refers to Kennedy's presiding over a new era in fiscal and economic policy. And expansion was not by any means the whole story.

Kennedy was just as successful in the fight against inflation as in that against recession. He had become convinced that the new balance of payments problem made continued inflation intolerable. He decided that the time had come for a major assault on the ever elusive problem of constantly rising prices in a free and expanding economy. It is a simple fact that prices remained stable in the Kennedy administration to a degree unmatched in the tenure of his predecessor or during the same period by any other industrial country.

This combination of rapid expansion and stable prices was not achieved by accident. It was the product of enlightened and firm presidential policies. Yet Sorensen is the first to explain to us that Kennedy, when he became President, was still an economic novice. 'Kennedy had little formal background in economics. . . . Young Jack Kennedy probably didn't learn much economics in high school, or for that matter anywhere else. . . . He had little interest in his father's business and had no taste for economic theory.' We are told moreover that he never mastered the technical mysteries of debt management and money supply. It seems that in his pre-presidential days he found it difficult to remember the difference between fiscal policy dealing with budget and taxes, and monetary policy dealing with money and credit. He used to remind himself that the name of the man most in charge of monetary policy, the Chairman of the Federal Reserve Board, had the surname Martin, which began with an 'm' as in 'monetary'. One is reminded inevitably of Sir Alec Home's admission that he needed match-sticks to work out economic problems. But that pleasantry undoubtedly did Sir Alec a lot of harm. It is not clear that Kennedy's little joke became public knowledge.

Somehow one must reconcile his economic ignorance with his indubitable economic victories. It is claimed that he surrounded himself with the most knowledgeable group of articulate economists in US history (Sorensen). Walter Heller and other members of the Council of Economic Advisers have often been referred to approvingly. Kennedy was apparently embarrassed when referred to publicly as 'a good Keynesian economist'. But Sorensen has no doubt 'that John Kennedy, after two years as President, had learned far more economics than most men in either public or academic life'. And no one questioned his native ability to absorb information and ask the right questions.

In his first State of the Union address in January 1961 he spelt out his assessment of the economic situation in gloomy terms. 'The present state of our economy is disturbing. We take office in the wake of seven months of recession, three-and-a-half years of slack, seven years of diminished economic growth and nine years of falling farm income.' He said that, except for a brief period in 1958, insured unemployment was at the highest peak in American history. 'In short, the American economy is in trouble. The most resourceful industrialized country on earth ranks among the last in the ranks of economic growth.'

He gave the assurance that his administration did not intend to stand helplessly by. 'I will propose', he said, 'to the Congress within the next fourteen days measures aimed at ensuring a prompt recovery and paving the way for increased long-range growth.' He was as good as his word. Some of his measures would require congressional action, but the need was to get more money into the economy fast. Nearly 800 million dollars represented extended jobless benefits for nearly three million unemployed, 200 million dollars in additional welfare payments to 750,000 children and their parents, and more than 400 million dollars in aid to over a thousand distressed areas. These were leading features but by no means the whole of his recovery programme. The effect was immediate. Prompt action provided not only an initial impetus to recovery, but grounds for the basic consumer and the business man to spend and invest with confidence.

Arthur Schlesinger brings out more clearly than Sorensen the conflicting schools of thought among those advising the President. When Hubert Humphrey introduced him to Walter Heller, the economist who was to render him conspicuous service, during the campaign in October, Kennedy's first question to Heller, as it had been to so many others, was: 'Do you really think we can make good on that promise of a 5% rate of growth?' And this commitment and the problem of fulfilling it never left his mind. But the equation contained more factors than appeared to the economists around him. He asked one Washington economist, Robert Nathan, the usual question about how to obtain the 5% growth rate. Nathan replied that he could get that rate all right, but the price would be a deficit of five billion dollars a year for the next ten years. The President said that would be splendid, if Nathan would organize the political backing.

The systematic creation of annual deficits was the one thing which the political situation short of a depression precluded his doing. 'I don't want to be tagged as a big spender early in this administration,' he said. 'If I do, I won't get my programmes through later on.' He had to cope with a conservative-minded Congress and, more generally, defeat the idea that the Democrats were the party of big spending and inflation. Schlesinger insists that Kennedy 'was unquestionably the first Keynesian President'. Nevertheless he opposed an increased deficit in 1961. His objections were political and not intellectual. His problem throughout was not doctrine but politics. In June Walter Lippmann, doyen of columnists, said with some plausibility that Kennedy was carrying on in all its essentials the Eisenhower economic philosophy – the philosophy, in other words, of the balanced budget.

The Keynesian economists led by Heller were vigorously demanding a tax cut. So far from achieving this in 1961 they suddenly found themselves fighting to keep taxes from being increased. The occasion was the Berlin crisis of 1961. A special 'Berlin Surtax' had for a time a great appeal. It was with no little difficulty that the President was persuaded to turn it down.

By the end of 1961 the gross national product was moving ahead well and the fear of recession receding. The fight against recession and the fight against inflation were carried on simultaneously. His battle with 'Big Steel' represented the chief crisis in the war on inflation. Though of course it was only one episode, it represented the most direct and dangerous challenge by a powerful private interest group to the President's anti-inflation efforts. It came to a head in April 1962.

On Tuesday 10 April the President received in his office Roger Blough, the United States Steel Chairman. Seated on the sofa next to the President's rocking chair, he handed him a press release announcing a $6 per ton price increase. The President felt stunned. 'He felt', said Sorensen, 'that his whole fight against inflation was being reduced to tatters.' If the steel industry could make a mockery of his plea for self-restraint, then every industry and every union in the country would thereafter feel free to defy him.

He felt not only stunned but duped. Blough knew perfectly well that the President's powers and prestige had been used in the attempt to persuade the steel workers to exercise wage restraint in the interests of price stability. Now the employers were out to sabotage the whole understanding. The question of good faith was involved, the President was to say later. In his coldest manner he told Blough: 'I think you are making a mistake.'

Mrs Lincoln, his personal secretary, recalls his fury when he came out to her office after Blough had left him. He walked up and down the length of the office. 'This is uncalled for,' he said, 'it's a double-cross on the part of US Steel.' A little more pacing back and forth and he seemed to collect himself. 'I'll see you in the morning. I'm going over to the pool before I eat supper.' That evening, at a reception of the Congressional leaders and their wives, no one would have guessed what he had just been through or was about to embark on. Accompanied by Jackie in a beautiful white dress, he was smiling and shaking hands with everyone. But next day he was in fighting mood.

To Ben Bradlee he spoke out starkly. 'It's the way it was done. It looks like such a double-cross. I think Steel made a deal with Nixon not to raise prices until after the election. Then came the recession and they didn't want to raise prices. Then when we pulled out of the recession they said: "Let Kennedy squeeze the unions first, before we raise prices".'

Bradlee asked him about his alleged vindictiveness against the steel companies. Kennedy said he'd heard all about that but asked, 'What would you have us do? We can go at this thing forty different ways. The point is, I can't make a charge and then walk away. That's when they say "We beat 'em". We can't just walk away and lie down. We're going to tuck it to 'em and screw 'em.'

Next day he electrified his press conference by a display of presidential anger beyond any anticipation. He referred to 'this serious hour in our nation's history when we are confronted with grave crises in Berlin and Southeast Asia' . . . The national energies were being devoted to economic recovery and stability. Reservists were being asked to leave their homes and families for months on end and servicemen to risk their lives. Four had been killed in the last two days in Vietnam. Union members were being asked to hold down their wages requests. Restraint and sacrifice were being asked of every citizen. At such a time, declared Kennedy, 'the American people will find it hard, as I do, to accept a situation in which a tiny handful of steel executives, whose pursuit of private power and profit exceeds their sense of public responsibility, can show such utter contempt for the interests of 185 million Americans'.

He became blunter still. 'I asked each American to consider what he could do for his country, and I asked the steel companies. In the last twenty-four hours we had their answer.' Now all the stops were pulled out to mobilize public opinion. For the seventy-two hours after Blough's visit the President was absorbed in the struggle. Then the United States Steel Corporation caved in. They rescinded the steel price increase.

'Oh,' cried the great poet Robert Frost, 'didn't he do a good one? Didn't he show the Irish all right?' But it was statesmanship, Irish or otherwise, which had triumphed. And, magnanimous as always in victory, he promptly turned his attention to the task of peace-making.

One unfortunate verbalism was remembered. The President in a moment of extreme exasperation had quoted his father as saying that the steel men were always 'sons of bitches'. This was later extended by hostile rumour to cover all businessmen. Kennedy, in a press conference, pointed out that this was 'obviously an error', because his father was a 'businessman himself'. His father was critical of the steel men: 'He formed an opinion which he imparted to me and which I found appropriate that evening. But he confined it, and I would confine it. . . . I felt at that time that we had not been treated altogether with frankness, and therefore I thought that his view had merit. But that's past, that's past. Now we are working together, I hope.'

His correction however was ignored and the legend that he was anti-business was unhappily strengthened. Relations between Democratic administration and business always meant more suspicion on the part of business than praise. The President was aware of this, but tried, unsuccessfully on this occasion, to keep the suspicion within limits. It was long remembered, fairly or unfairly, that he had said that businessmen were S.O.B.s. But Kennedy never gave up trying to convince the world of business that whatever they might suppose to the contrary, he wished them well.

In general he achieved a remarkable degree of price stability without imposing direct controls. Legislation was not altogether ruled out. The Department of Justice, Anti-Trust Division, was particularly successful against price-fixers in a record number of prosecutions. But the bulk of the effort lay in an unprecedented ceaseless use of the 'jawbone method' of keeping wages and prices down. This consisted in warnings to labour and management, presidential messages, press conferences and speeches, talks to conventions and private conferences. Two new techniques in particular were introduced. The President's advisory committee on labour management policy with members drawn from unions, business and the public was really effective, unlike its predecessors. Secondly, there was the enunciation of national wage/price guide-lines promulgated with presidential approval by his council of economic advisers. Whatever may be said about the limitation of such methods in Britain in later years, Kennedy made them work effectively in the United States during his period.

Kennedy stressed during the campaign that his would not be a businessman's administration, nor a labour administration, nor a farmer's administration, but an administration representing and seeking to serve all Americans. The trades unions collaborated with the government more closely than ever before. They were consulted on policy and politics; they were treated with special honour. His relations with labour were by no means without their tensions. Broadly, however, he satisfied them by treating them not with favouritism, but with dignity and equality. It all sounds so easy in the midst of our contemporary dilemmas.

Now back to the pursuit of expansion. In the spring of 1962 there was a sharp decline in the stock market giving rise to a general fear among the President's advisers that this decline might expand and become universal. There was a renewed drive among the economists for an expansionist programme. The only practical way to stimulate the economy seemed to be a tax cut. Professor Galbraith alone stood out. Tax-cutting was reactionary Keynesian-ism, providing the things the country least needed at the expense of the things it most needed. 'I am not sure', he said, 'what the ad-vantage is in having a few more dollars to spend if the air is too dirty to breathe, the water too polluted to drink, the commuters are losing out on the struggle to get in and out of the cities, the streets are filthy and the schools so bad that the young, perhaps wisely, stay away and hoodlums roll citizens for some of the dollars they saved in taxes.'

Galbraith insisted that the real expansion should take place in the area of public needs – schools, colleges, hospitals, foreign policy. Schlesinger considers that if political conditions had permitted, the President would have preferred such a policy of social spending to meet the public needs. But political conditions in his judgment simply did not permit it. The President said in mid-July that the real choice was between trying for a tax cut and failing and not try-ing at all. The Treasury under Dillon represented throughout the conservative financial attitude usually found in treasuries, but gradually Heller and Dillon drew together. On 13 August the President announced a decision against a tax cut in 1962. But at the same time he promised a comprehensive tax reduction bill for 1963. The edgy competition between Dillon and Heller became by 1963 a fruitful partnership.

In the autumn of 1962 the administration, in Schlesinger's words, 'quietly committed itself to a radical principle – the deliberate creation of budgetary deficits at a time when there was no economic emergency. But the price of securing the acceptance of this revolutionary trend included the decision to create the deficits through tax reduction rather than through social spending.' Kennedy still considered the expenditure route politically impossible. In the event the tax reduction bill made slow progress through Congress. By the time Kennedy died in November 1963 it was fairly certain that it would pass into law in the ensuing year.

There were other aspects of Kennedy's economic policy. Schlesinger hazards the suggestion that of all the problems he faced as President, he was least at home with the balance of payments. On the other hand his initiative in trying to secure world-wide reduction of tariffs won him general acclaim. It was the expansion in the national income coupled with price stability that leaves so lasting an impression.

He himself was not, however, complacent. Nancy Clinch in *The Kennedy Neurosis* can be relied upon to put the unpleasant or less satisfactory side. She insists that Kennedy's overall policies followed generally conservative lines. 'Domestically,' she adds, 'although Kennedy made progressive sounds, he spent meagre amounts to bring a long-delayed cure to the deep cancers of poverty, pollution and of discrimination of many types in the social body.' One wonders what President Kennedy if he were alive today, would make of such an unbridled onslaught. We are told by Schlesinger that 'the brilliant and indignant' book by Michael Harrington, *The Other America* (1962), brought home to Kennedy the overwhelming need for a broad war against poverty itself. Here perhaps was the unifying theme which would pull a host of social programmes together and rally the nation behind a generous cause. We must take it on trust that if he had lived, he would indeed have embarked on a far-reaching programme of this kind. The record supports the critics who said that in his three years of rule he did much for the creation, but little for the more just distribution of wealth.

In the spring of 1961 the most pressing social issue facing the new President was undoubtedly Civil Rights, and in this sphere Kennedy was eventually to win many liberal plaudits. After his assassination, Coretta, widow of Martin Luther King, said, 'Nothing had ever affected me as deeply as President Kennedy's death. Martin and I were personally in a dark abyss of sorrow for this gallant, compassionate and wise young man – a true statesman.'

On the day of the assassination little Martin, aged six, said to his father: 'Daddy, President Kennedy was your best friend, wasn't he?' 'In a way', says Mrs King, 'he was.' It would be ungenerous and unhistorical to try to whittle down that tribute, paid from that source.

Kennedy was, however, a slow starter in this field. In the late fifties, civil rights advocates regarded him as sympathetic, but only mildly so. Martin Luther King, who breakfasted with him in New York a month before the 1960 Convention, later said that he displayed at that time 'a definite concern, but . . . not what I would call a "depthed" understanding'. According to Schlesinger, most civil rights leaders preferred Humphrey or Stevenson for the Democratic nomination.

Sorensen analyses Kennedy's attitude somewhat bluntly. 'When Kennedy talked privately about Negroes at all before the 1960 election, it was usually about winning Negro votes. To him Negroes were no different from anyone else.' But Sorensen continues in a significant passage: 'Politics', he says, 'helped to deepen his concern.' The Negroes became an important element in his constituency, that is, in the American public he was trying to win, and his feelings for them mounted accordingly.

In his debates with Nixon during the 1960 election he was already proclaiming the handicaps of what he called 'the Negro baby born in America today'. Kennedy had certainly not attained the passionate grasp of the question which was his before he died. But by the time he was elected the root of the matter was in him. Certainly the black leaders, as we have seen, felt so.

The Democratic platform in the election contained a civil rights plank of unmistakable strength. The Republican programme was also much more advanced than hitherto. Both documents were far more responsive to the civil rights movement than either the Republican administration or the Democratic Congress had been a few months earlier. Kennedy was persuaded that in the circumstances he had to take steps to make his stand on civil rights legislation unmistakably clear. He indicated that he was appointing a two-man committee to prepare a comprehensive civil rights bill for introduction at the beginning of the next session. He promised to seek its enactment 'early' in 1961. During the campaign he placed less emphasis on legislation than upon the responsibility of the President to provide a moral tone and moral leadership in this field. But his commitment to early legislation was unequivocal.

In the light of these assurances, his actual record in 1961 and indeed in 1962 is open to criticism. In 1961 when it came to the point, he introduced no civil rights legislation, and in 1962 very little. The 'official' black leaders like Martin Luther King understood his difficulties and appreciated the argument that he would never get such legislation through Congress. They recognized that his heart was in the right place. He demonstrated his sympathies by various executive activities. He appointed Negroes to. high positions. The civil rights division of the Justice Department initiated thirteen voting rights cases. The pace of school desegregation was speeded up. But the younger blacks were not prepared to wait indefinitely. On 4 May 'Freedom Riders' set off in integrated buses (carrying whites and blacks together) to smash segregation in the South. Two days later, though still apparently unaware of their expedition, Bobby Kennedy spoke out strongly in his first major speech as Attorney-General at the University of Georgia. His conclusion left no doubt about his attitude: 'Our position is clear. We are upholding the law. . . . In this case – in all cases – I say to you today that if the orders of the Court are circumvented, the Department of Justice will act. We will not stand by or be aloof. We will move.'

From then on, 'the Kennedys' were cursed or blessed as a unity in the struggle against segregation. It fell to Bobby Kennedy's lot to bring to bear the executive pressures with mounting passion. But he spoke and acted at all times in full harmony with the President. The climax was reached when Martin Luther King held a mass rally for the Freedom Riders in the First Baptist Church, Montgomery, Alabama. Twelve hundred whites and blacks were jammed into the church while a crowd of several thousand with murder in their hearts surrounded it. Bobby Kennedy had arranged for six hundred Deputy Federal Marshals to be available for the protection of the Freedom Riders and their sympathizers. But they were in danger of being overwhelmed.

After intense telephone conversations with Governor Paterson of Alabama, Bobby Kennedy induced the latter to do his clear duty and provide the protection necessary. When it was all over no blood had been shed and it had not been necessary to send in regular troops. 'As such things go, the Freedom Riders were counted a success' (William Manchester, *The Glory and the Dream*, 1975). The work of desegregation went on, though large areas of segregation remained to be tackled.

9

The Cuba crisis: the world stood still

On Tuesday 16 October President Kennedy dined with Joseph Alsop. They found themselves talking about the odds for and against any particular event in history taking place. The President was silent for a while, then he said: 'Of course, if you simply consider mathematical chances, the odds are even on an H-bomb war within ten years.' Arthur Schlesinger reflects as he tells the story:' Perhaps,' he added to himself, 'within ten days.' Kennedy regarded the Test Ban Treaty the following year as his most satisfying achievement. I personally, along with countless others, look upon his handling of the Cuban missile crisis as his supreme contribution to world peace and security.

Before its occurrence the distinct possibility of a nuclear war blotting out civilization was at the back of many millions of minds all over the world. After it was over the anxiety inevitably continued, but the underlying terror had passed away. No one who salutes the achievement can fail to give the overwhelming credit to the President.

Kennedy had, as Harold Macmillan would later say, earned his place in history by this one act alone. 'He had been engaged in a personal as well as national contest for world leadership and he had won. He had reassured those nations fearing we would use too much strength and those fearing we would use none at all. Cuba had been the site of his greatest failure and now of his greatest success' (Sorensen).

Nor had the tremendous result been achieved by a single stroke of genius. The crisis is spoken of as lasting thirteen days. This reckons it from the Tuesday mentioned above, when the grim news of the offensive missiles first reached Kennedy, to Sunday 28 October when Khrushchev's answer reached the American government and it was realized that he had given in. For those who were in the know, and they were at first very few, the world was walking on the brink of a precipice throughout the whole of that period. Strength and restraint and flexibility had to be exhibited in equal proportions, and there could be no certainty until the end that, however wise or brilliant or heroic the American policy, the Soviet leaders would be sane enough to refrain from producing catastrophe.

The Cuba crisis did not blow up out of a clear sky or take the President entirely by surprise. Over a hundred voyages to Cuban ports by Communist vessels in July and August had caused him to pay close attention to the aerial photography and other reports on Cuba. But West Berlin and the possibility of a new Soviet move in that area were still a first preoccupation. By the middle of September there were countless assertions by Cuban refugees and others that Soviet offensive missiles had been seen on the island. The President's experts treated these with a certain reserve, but by 13 September he felt the need to issue an explicit warning: 'If', he said, 'at any time the Communist build-up in Cuba were to endanger or interfere with our security in any way ... or if Cuba should ever ... become an offensive military base of significant capacity for the Soviet Union, then this country will do whatever must be done to protect its own security and that of its allies.'

At this point American concern was by no means appreciated by Kennedy's European allies. But the Organization of American States agreed to lend its authority to the United States aerial surveillance of Cuba, and on Sunday 14 October information was brought back whose alarming character could not be doubted. By Monday evening the long rolls of film had been analysed. The first rude beginnings of a Soviet medium range missile base were laid bare. The next morning, McGeorge Bundy broke the news to the President as he read his morning papers.

Kennedy had been campaigning with O'Donnell. They had agreed to discount the assertions being made about offensive missiles in Cuba as Republican propaganda. But now, shown the photographs, Kennedy recognized at once with expert help that the Soviet missiles were there, that their range and purpose were offensive and that they would soon be operating. He came out of his office and said to O'Donnell: 'You still think that fuss about Cuba is unimportant?'

'Absolutely,' I said. 'The voters won't give a damn about Cuba. You're wasting your time talking about it.' 'You really think it doesn't amount to much?', he said. 'Not as a campaign issue,' I said.

He beckoned to me to follow him into his office. 'I want to show you something,' he said.

The President held a magnifying glass over one of the prints. 'You're an old Air Force bombardier,' he said to O'Donnell. 'You ought to know what this is. It's the beginning of a launching site for a medium range ballistic missile.' O'Donnell found himself getting pale. 'I don't believe it,' he said. 'You'd better believe it,' said the President. He told O'Donnell to organize a meeting in the Cabinet room. Not a word was to be said to anybody what it was all about. Other appointments were to be adhered to. An appearance must be maintained of business as usual.

A meeting of the fifteen or so most significant personalities was rapidly organized. The group with slight alterations remained in daily session until the crisis was resolved. It included Secretary of State Dean Rusk, the Secretary of Defence Robert McNamara, General Maxwell Taylor (Chairman of the Joint Chiefs of Staff), the Director or Acting-Director of the CIA, the Attorney-General Robert Kennedy and the Treasury Secretary Douglas Dillon, plus presidential advisers.

At the first meeting on the Tuesday morning, the choice seemed to lie between an air strike and acquiescence. Since the President ruled out acquiescence from the start the air strike seemed at first the only course available. From the outset the military authorities were sympathetic to such a strike. There should be no half-measures – it should be a major strike requiring perhaps 500 sorties. Here was a heaven-sent opportunity to get rid of the Castro regime forever and re-establish the security of the hemisphere.

But the disadvantages and the attendant perils of this course were pointed out quickly. Russians manning the missile sites would inevitably be killed. No one could guess the reaction of the Soviet Union, but it would be bound to be drastic. The possibility of nuclear war could not be excluded. Thousands of innocent Cubans would also be slaughtered. The long-term effect on the United States reputation in Latin America would be disastrous. A Soviet move against Berlin was likely.

During the afternoon and evening of that first day the idea of a 'quarantine' or blockade began to be discussed. It would be designed to stop the further entry of offensive weapons into Cuba and indeed could force the removal of the missiles present. On Wednesday Secretary of Defence McNamara became its strongest advocate. By the end of that day the majority of the executive committee were tending towards it. The Air Force did not give in easily. On the Thursday morning General Curtis LeMay argued strongly for an air strike as soon as possible. 'How will the Russians respond?' the President asked him. LeMay said the Russians would do nothing. Kennedy was frankly incredulous. After the meeting he said, 'Can you imagine LeMay saying a thing like that? These brass hats have one great advantage in their favour. If we listen to them and do what they want us to do none of us will be alive later to tell them that they were wrong.'

In the conference room he never forgot his sense of humour. General David M. Shoup, Commandant of the Marine Corps, summed up everyone's feelings: 'You are in a pretty bad fix, Mr President.' The President answered quickly, 'You are in it with me.' Everyone laughed and for the moment at least relaxed.

That Thursday afternoon the President received the Soviet Foreign Minister, Andrei Gromyko. Gromyko, seated on the sofa next to the President's rocking chair, carried on the deception that there were no offensive weapons in Cuba. The President knew there were and Gromyko knew there were, but he had no idea the President knew there were. Gromyko waxed tough about Berlin and then turned to Cuba, not apologetically but aggressively. He complained of what he called US interference with a small nation that posed no threat. He proceeded to indulge in a downright lie:

As to Soviet assistance to Cuba, I have been instructed to make it clear, as the Soviet government has already done, that such assistance pursues solely the purpose of contributing to the defence capabilities of Cuba and to the development of its peaceful economy. . . .

Training by Soviet specialists of Cuban nationals in handling defensive armaments was by no means offensive. If it were otherwise, the Soviet government would have never become involved in rendering such assistance.

The President contented himself with sending for and reading his September warning against offensive missiles in Cuba. His self-control and sense of irony were never more in evidence. 'I told him', said the President later, 'that there had better not be any ballistic missiles in Cuba. And he told me that such a thought had never entered Khrushchev's mind. It was incredible to sit there and watch the lies coming out of his mouth.'

In the evening of that same day, Thursday 18 October, the President at a meeting with the executive committee came down positively in favour of the blockade. If it worked the Russians could retreat with dignity, but if it failed the option of military action remained open. He directed that preparations be made to put the weapons blockade into effect on Monday morning.

So runs the general account. Bobby Kennedy in his *Thirteen Days* (New York, 1969) gives a less definite impression. The President, after asking a number of probing questions was 'not at all satisfied'. He sent them back to their deliberations. Next day, Friday, he left Washington as arranged for a weekend of election-eering in Ohio and Illinois. In Springfield, Illinois, he paused to lay flowers on Lincoln's tomb.

The second stage of the crisis ran from the Friday morning till the Monday evening. The service champions of a strike as against a blockade were not done with yet. But McNamara and, still more effectively it would seem, Robert Kennedy argued against it, not only on physical but moral grounds. With the memory of Pearl Harbour, and all the responsibility they would have to bear in the world afterwards, the President of the United States could not possibly order such an operation; 'a sneak attack would constitute a betrayal of our heritage and our ideals.' This speech of Robert Kennedy is said to have been the turning point. The President returned earlier than arranged from his tour.

He played the part of an invalid quite seriously in Chicago. 'I have a temperature and a cold,' he announced to Salinger, his press secretary. 'Tell the Press I am returning to Washington on the advice of Dr Burkley. We better make sure that all of us are saying the same thing.' He reached for a telephone message pad and wrote on it: 'Slight upper respiratory. 1½ degree temperature. Weather raw and rainy. Recommended return to Washington. Cancelled schedule.'

But the argument in the executive committee still proceeded. The military, with some civilian support, still argued for the strike. A straw vote indicated eleven for the quarantine, six for the strike. Now the President made it plain that his mind was made up. He would not embark at that time on military action. That could come later if necessary but in other ways he would take the most uncompromising action to force Khrushchev to remove the missiles. Stevenson made a brave and solitary plea for the simultaneous removal of the American missiles from Turkey as a conciliatory gesture. Bobby Kennedy was furious with him afterwards. 'He is not strong enough, or tough enough to be representing us at the UN at a time like this,' he said.

But the President, no great devotee of Stevenson as a rule, was more generous. 'I think Adlai', he said, 'showed plenty of strength and courage presenting that viewpoint at the risk of being called an appeaser. It was an argument that needed to be stated, but nobody else had the guts to do it. I admire him for saying what he said.' But he had satisfied himself that he could not make the concession which Stevenson pleaded for. He issued orders on the Saturday to get everything ready for the quarantine after a conference with the military leaders on the Sunday.

On the Sunday afternoon the President, in O'Donnell's words, 'betrayed the only sign of nervousness that we saw him show during the entire thirteen-day period of the missile crisis'. He telephoned Jackie and asked her to come to the White House that evening from the country so that he and his family could be together if there was a sudden emergency. A surprise nuclear attack on Washington was being prepared against, and an underground shelter at an unspecified location outside the city had been arranged for the President, his family and certain others. Later during the crisis the President asked Jackie to move out of Washington so that she could be closer to their assigned underground shelter. But she refused to leave him alone in the White House.

That evening, during his regular swim in the pool with Dave Powers, he reverted to language that he had used to Kenny O'Donnell on the way back from the Vienna meetings with Khrushchev. 'Dave,' he said, 'if we were only thinking of ourselves it would be easy. But I keep thinking about the children whose lives would be wiped out.' Later Dave Powers found him sitting in a chair with Caroline on his lap, reading to her from a story-book. 'I watched him sitting there with Caroline,' said David Powers, 'I thought of what he had been saying to me in the pool, about how worried he was about the children everywhere in the world and, you know, I got the strangest feeling. I handed him the papers and got out of there as fast as I could. I was all choked up.'

Now everything at home and abroad, most urgently at the United Nations, had to be prepared for the President's broadcast on Monday. Sorensen, the supreme speech writer, had already been hard at work on the draft. He had shown an early version to the President when the latter returned to Washington on the Saturday, but all sorts of amendments were made or suggested. An approach had to be made to the Organization of American States. The leading Allies had to be informed, as did former Presidents Hoover, Truman and Eisenhower. The British received their first indication on the Saturday, 20 October. At Sunday noon, Kennedy called David Ormsby Gore to the White House and outlined the alternatives. Ormsby Gore expressed a strong support for the quarantine and, with his knowledge of Macmillan, assured the President of a sympathetic British reaction. Later that day Kennedy telephoned to Macmillan explaining that he had had to make the first decision on his responsibility, but from now on he expected to keep in the closest touch.

Macmillan replied on Monday that Britain would give all the support it could in the Security Council. The President, we are told by Schlesinger, detected 'an element of reserve' in Macmillan's tone. Kennedy tried to remove any apprehension on his part that this might be a special American obsession with Cuba, and sought to convince him that this was a major showdown with Khrushchev. Thereafter, in Schlesinger's words, 'Macmillan did not falter and his counsel and support proved constant throughout the week.'

The President had a rather sour meeting with some twenty congressional leaders at 5 pm on the Monday. Most of them wanted much more drastic action. He hurried over to his rooms to change clothes for his 7 pm broadcast, muttering to Sorensen as he went: 'If they want this job they can have it – it's no great joy to me.' But he quickly recovered his 'cool'. In a few minutes, sitting alone except for Sorensen in the Cabinet Room, he was delivering the most momentous speech of his life. It did not set out to rival the eloquence of his first inaugural address, but the issues at stake were still more far-reaching. The whole future of the planet could be described not unreasonably as at stake. True to his nature, he limited the drama when the situation itself was most dramatic. 'Good evening, my fellow citizens.' He left no one in any doubt about the facts. 'The urgent transformation of Cuba into an important strategic base by the presence of these large, long-range and clearly offensive weapons of sudden mass destruction constitutes an explicit threat to the peace and security of all the Americas.'

He set out the nature of the blockade, which would be termed a 'quarantine'. He explained that 'at this time' the United States would not deny 'the necessities of life as the Soviets attempted to do in their blockade of 1948' ... but 'all ships of any kind bound for Cuba from whatever nation or port will, if found to contain cargoes of offensive weapons, be turned back'. Should these offensive military preparations continue, he went on, 'thus increasing the threat to the Hemisphere, further action will be justified. I have directed the armed forces to prepare for any eventualities.' At the time the paragraph that follows was considered to be the toughest:

It shall be the policy of this nation to regard any nuclear missile launched from Cuba against any nation in the Western Hemisphere as an attack by the Soviet Union on the United States, requiring a full retaliatory response upon the Soviet Union.

But the President strained every nerve to make it possible for Khrushchev to withdraw without total loss of prestige.

I call upon Chairman Khrushchev to halt and eliminate this clandestine, reckless and provocative threat to world peace.... He has an opportunity now to move the world back from the abyss of destruction – by returning to his government's own words that it had no need to station missiles outside its own territory, and withdrawing these weapons from Cuba.

As soon as the broadcast was over Salinger held his usual press conference, this time of record dimensions. There was no doubt about the extreme concern. To the question 'Is the President getting out of Washington?' he replied, 'He plans to stay here at least for the foreseeable future.' There were other questions of similar import. When the briefing came to an end Salinger sent one by one for the White House reporters who would accompany the President if Washington had to be evacuated. He told them that they were never to be more than fifteen minutes away from the White House and were to let him know where to reach them every minute of the night and day. This time it was 'for real'.

In Britain the quality press were at first not very cordial. *The Guardian* (23 October 1961) was markedly critical in tone:

In the United Nations the Americans have taken the initiative themselves. In this at least, and in their consultation with other governments beforehand, they have acted wisely. But even a limited military action will be hard to justify. In the end the United States may find that it has done its cause, its friends, and its own true interests little good.

The Daily Telegraph (23 October 1961), while more sympathetic with the 'President's refusal to condone a military build-up at his back door', declared: 'He has surprised more than his enemies by the announcement which he made last night.' Further on in the leader there is evident the same scepticism about the reasons for the President's actions as was later to be present elsewhere in the British press. 'He has, it seems been moved by evidence, provided by Cuba itself, that the island is being transformed into a rocket and submarine base. The outside world cannot, of course, assess the full validity of such evidence. . . .'

The Times (25 October 1961), adopted a similar approach:

In judging whether President Kennedy is right in militarily blockading Cuba, almost everything depends on the accuracy of the evidence that the Russians are in fact building missile bases on the island. . . . Once the evidence is accepted as true, it has to be recognized that the President had urgently to face an ugly and disturbing change in Russian policy in Cuba.

There was an outbreak of letters in the British papers during the week, some of them condemning Kennedy's action outright and calling attention to the anti-Russian bases placed around the confines of Europe. A large number of letters acclaimed Kennedy's right judgment but showed *more* concern over the question of disarmament than the actual decision. British journalists, notably *The Times* correspondent in Washington (for whose assessment see page 129) seemed to assume that the President had 'dramatically emphasized his determination to act alone to defend the United

States and Allied interests'.... But this opinion was firmly repudiated in Westminster: 'The Government', said *The Times* on 25 October, 'are anxious to remove the impression that President Kennedy and his administration are determined to act alone.... Officials in Whitehall are emphasizing that there is close and constant consultation on all issues.'

In the United States the week was hectic. The presentation by Adlai Stevenson at the United Nations was superb. We are primarily concerned with the President's own words and deeds. Tuesday brought the good news that the Latin American nations in the OAS had approved the blockade. There was no reaction yet from Khrushchev. Kennedy had half feared an immediate counterstroke. But later in the day there were reports from the navy that at least twenty-five Soviet ships of various descriptions and a few Russian submarines, possibly nuclear-armed, were heading towards Cuba; later still the news came through of Khrushchev's angry reaction. He warned Kennedy bluntly that he had no intention of observing the blockade; that the captains of Russian vessels bound for Cuba had been instructed not to obey orders to stop from the United States Navy and that any interference with Soviet ships would force him 'to take measures which we deem necessary and adequate to protect our rights'. So it looked as if the show-down had come.

A visit by Bobby Kennedy to the Russian Ambassador brought no reassurance. As he left Bobby Kennedy asked if the Soviet ships were going to go through to Cuba. The Ambassador replied that those had been their instructions and he knew of no changes. Returning to the White House somewhere around half past ten, Bobby found the President meeting the British Ambassador David Ormsby Gore (whom he trusted implicitly). Ormsby Gore made the helpful suggestion that the line of interception for the quarantine should be brought nearer to Cuba to give the Russians more time 'to analyse their position'. The President at once reduced the distance in accordance with Ormsby Gore's suggestion, but hopes were low.

Next morning the executive group awaited a climax that could not be long delayed. The blockade was to go into force at 10 am. The first Soviet ships would approach the boundary line half an hour later. O'Donnell leaves us in no doubt about the atmosphere of mingled pessimism and resolution in the Cabinet Room: 'All of us in the room assumed from the firm and definite tone of Khrushchev's threat that the Soviet ships would refuse to stop, that our navy ships and planes from the carrier *Essex*, which was standing near the line, would be forced to open fire, and the Russians would then respond with missiles from Cuba, or long-range ICBMs from Eastern Europe, or perhaps by seizing West Berlin.'

The American nuclear missiles were on a ready alert, including those based on Britain. They were aimed at the Soviet Union. Other awesome preparations had been made. If shooting started at the blockade line it was assumed that a nuclear war would quickly follow. Everything depended on what Khrushchev would do within the next two hours.

A report came through that a Russian submarine had moved into position between two of their ships. 'I think these few minutes', says Bobby Kennedy, 'were the time of greatest concern for the President. Was the world on the brink of a holocaust?' Was there anything that could have been done or left undone? John Kennedy's hand went up to his face and covered his mouth. 'He opened and closed his fist. His face seemed drawn, his eyes pained, almost grey. We stared at each other across the table. For a few fleeting seconds it was almost as though no one else was there and he was no longer the President.'

The group had not long to wait. A messenger came into the room and handed a note to the Director of the CIA who read it quickly and said: 'Mr President, we have a preliminary report that some of the Russian ships are stopping.' It was soon confirmed that twenty Russian ships had stopped before reaching the blockade line: some had turned round and were heading back towards Europe. Dean Rusk, sitting next to the President, said quietly: 'We're eyeball to eyeball and I think the other fellow just blinked.' Later Kennedy and others concluded that the real crisis was faced and overcome when the Russian ships began to turn back. Certainly the relief was profound. But soon it began to seem premature. The tensions continued and indeed escalated during the next three days. Work continued on the missile sites in Cuba and what else could that represent but an aggressive intention?

No one in view of recent deceptions could have any respect for Soviet good faith. Each hour the situation grew steadily more serious. In Bobby Kennedy's words, 'The feeling grew that this cup was not going to pass and that direct military confrontation between the two great nuclear powers was inevitable.'

In Florida the American army prepared for the invasion of Cuba. In Washington 'the pressure to attack mounted as each passing moment brought the installation closer to operation' (Schlesinger). Then on Friday came a glimpse of hope. A member of the Soviet Embassy staff in Washington, generally supposed to be their Intelligence Chief, approached the ABC television writer who covered the State Department and asked him to sound out Rusk on a possible compromise. In London similar moves were taking place. To quote Macmillan: 'When you begin to weaken your first step is to send along your footman.' But everything hung on Khrushchev's answer. It took the form of a long emotional personal letter which reached the President at six o'clock that evening.

The Soviet leader seemed genuinely anxious to avoid a confrontation if possible. 'If the United States would give assurances that it would not invade Cuba, nor permit others to do so, and if it would recall its fleet from the quarantine, this would immediately change everything.'

It was not only the diplomatic proposition but the tone of the letter which made a deep impression. Khrushchev obviously intended it to be received like his other personal letters to Kennedy as an expression of his feelings rather than an official communication. O'Donnell for one was deeply moved by Khrushchev's anguished fear that he had provoked Kennedy into a fighting mood and a readiness for war. 'Khrushchev pleaded with Kennedy not to lose his "self-control" and begged him not to let "the two of us pull on the ends of the rope in which you have tied the knot of war, because the more the two of us pull, the tighter the knot will be tied. . . . Let us not only relax the forces pulling on the ends of the rope, let us take measures to untie that knot. We are ready for this".'

Most of the President's advisers had their first good night's sleep for ten long days. Bobby Kennedy does not admit that he himself was more than slightly optimistic, or the President more than 'hopeful for the first time that our efforts might possibly be successful'.

But Saturday was a bad morning in Washington. A new and totally different Khrushchev message had been broadcast from Moscow. The Soviet Union now made the withdrawal of American missiles from Turkey a condition of the withdrawal of their own missiles from Cuba, so it was easy to believe that Khrushchev had sent him an earlier letter without consultation. Whether that was so or not the friendliness had altogether vanished. Word came that an American intelligence plane was missing over Cuba – presumably shot down by the Russians. The bases were on the point of becoming operational. In self-defence the Americans must act quickly or it would soon be too late. It was strongly argued that a military response by the United States had now become inevitable. Once that prospect began, he could hardly stop short of a full scale invasion of Cuba. But the President's cool statemanship was never more in evidence. No collection of top brass, however formidable, could push him around this time.

Again and again he emphasized that the implications of every step must be fully weighed. What would be the next move and the move after that? NATO was supporting the United States, but were these truly completely aware of the dangers for them? We had to realize that we were deciding for the United States, the Soviet Union, NATO – and really for all mankind.

For the moment deadlock prevailed. Appropriately it was broken by Bobby Kennedy, not only the President's brother, but his dearest friend and his closest ally. He had played the leading part when the President was absent from the executive meetings, though there was no actual chairman. On Saturday afternoon he produced the simple yet brilliant suggestion that the first conciliatory letter from Khrushchev should be replied to, and the second menacing one ignored. The President now wrote to Khrushchev: 'I have read your letter of 26 October with great care and welcome the statement of your desire to seek a proper solution.' As soon as work stopped on the missile bases and the offensive weapons were rendered inoperable under UN supervision, he would be ready to negotiate a settlement along the lines Khrushchev had proposed. It seemed to offer the last chance of peace.

That evening Bobby Kennedy handed a copy of the reply to the Soviet Ambassador. The latter raised the question of the removal of the American missiles from Turkey. This particular issue caused the President much uneasiness. The missiles in Turkey were no good by this time to the United States. He was under the impression that steps had already been taken which would lead to their removal, but this in fact had not been done. Bobby Kennedy told the Ambassador that the President had ordered the removal some time ago. It was to be expected that within a short time after the crisis was over, the missiles would have gone, though a decision by NATO would be necessary. There could, however, be no *quid pro quo* or any arrangement made under threat or pressure. He went on to emphasize the President's desire to have friendly relations between their two countries.

But there was nothing soft about the totality of the message. The Ambassador was informed that unless assurances were received in twenty-four hours the United States would take military action by Tuesday. That night in Washington there was no question of yielding, but gloom in high circles was general. Robert Kennedy reported to the President while Dave Powers went on eating and drinking with apparent unconcern. 'God, Dave!' said the President, 'the way you are eating up all that chicken and drinking up all my wine anybody would think it was your last meal.' 'The way Bobby's been talking,' said Dave, 'I thought it *was* my last meal.'

The meeting that night, says Kenny O'Donnell, was 'the most depressing hour that any of us spent in the White House during the President's time there'. 'We agreed that our chance of receiving any reply from Khrushchev the next day was a long shot at best.' The President took the preliminary steps to arrange for an air strike and a possible invasion of Cuba.

He had been much concerned earlier that day to find out if Major Anderson, the U2 pilot shot down over Cuba, had a wife and family. When he learnt that he had two sons, five and three years old, he had turned to Dave Powers with a stricken look on his face. 'He had a boy about the same age as John,' he said. Now when the evening meeting was adjourned the President stayed behind at his desk writing on a pad of yellow paper. O'Donnell asked him what he was writing. 'A letter to Mrs Anderson,' he replied. In a matter of this kind there can never have been a President, except Abraham Lincoln, or a statesman anywhere who was quite so sensitive.

Before turning off his light and getting into bed he said to Dave Powers, 'We'll be going to the ten o'clock Mass at St Stephen's, Dave, and we'll have plenty of hard praying to do so don't be late.' But by Sunday morning the appropriate prayers were those of thankfulness rather than petition. Khrushchev's answer had begun to come in at nine o'clock in the morning. He had given in. 'Work would stop on the sites; the arms which you describe as offensive would be crated and returned to the Soviet Union; negotiations would start at the United Nations.'

It had been the closest of close run things. The President said a few weeks later: 'If we had invaded Cuba I am sure the Soviets would have acted. They would have had to, just as we would have had to. I think there are certain major compulsions on any major power.' His relief on that Sunday 28 October was immense. As he went off to church he said to Dave Powers: 'I feel like a new man. Do you realize that we had an air strike all arranged for Tuesday? Thank God it's all over.' Later he said, 'This is the night to go to the theatre like Abraham Lincoln.' Bearing in mind that it was at the theatre that Lincoln was assassinated, one assumes that this was another example of his famous irony. In victory he remained magnanimous and prudent. Somebody suggested that he should appear on television to announce the victory over the Soviet aggressors. 'There will be none of that,' he said sharply. 'I want no crowing and not a word of gloating from anybody in this government.'

Khrushchev had been assisted to escape from the crisis without complete loss of face. To humiliate him further would be unthinkable. Kennedy issued a brief statement praising Khrushchev's 'statesmanlike decision' to stop building bases in Cuba and agreeing to dismantle offensive weapons as an 'important and constructive contribution to peace'.

Considerable argument broke out in England as to whether the British rôle had been one of humiliating impotence. Macmillan was in the difficult position of wishing to assert that the British part had been significant without disclosing at that time private conversations, and without seeming to detract in the slightest extent from Kennedy's triumph. In the last volume of his memoirs he gives a full and fascinating account of the exchanges that took place between him and the President. Sometimes the President rang him as many as three times in a day. One can hardly suppose that these were courtesy calls. It is obvious that Kennedy put a high premium on Macmillan's advice. The latter mentions one conversation in particular which took place on Wednesday 24 October: 'Had I', says Macmillan, 'been able to make use of it in Parliament, it would certainly have dispelled the accusation that there was no special relationship.' President: 'We are going to have to make the judgment as to whether we are going to invade Cuba, taking our chances, or whether we hold off and use Cuba as a sort of hostage in the matter of Berlin. That's really the choice we now have. What's your judgment?' PM: 'Well, I would like to think about that.' The same kind of relationship was revealed in a whole string of discussions, particularly when U Thant began to make proposals of doubtful advantage.

No one can say whether Kennedy would have acted differently if he had not taken part in these exchanges with Macmillan. But if consultation is to mean anything at all, the British government through Macmillan, not forgetting the key figure of Ormsby Gore in Washington, was consulted intensively throughout the week. In Macmillan's eyes one supreme merit of the President's handling throughout was his firm resistance to the pressure from his own generals for military action. On the last Saturday Macmillan records that the President and his advisers were still struggling to find some peaceful alternative. It may well be, although Macmillan does not claim this explicitly, that the British influence just about tipped the scale in favour of what proved to be for once a real peace with honour.

There is another way, much less favourable to Kennedy, of looking at those thirteen days. It has been expounded by various American writers, but by no one perhaps more cogently than by Louis Heren, then in charge of the Washington bureau of *The Times*. In his book about President Johnson, *No Hail, No Farewell* (London 1970), he provides a considered and concise judgment of President Kennedy's statesmanship. It would be unfair to call him anti-Kennedy. However he certainly does not subscribe to the Kennedy legend, remarking that 'he was not the great President claimed by his many friends if only because his administration had been too short'. He describes him as making 'many mistakes'. He acknowledges that Kennedy would probably 'have done better at home than Johnson or his brother', but records his conviction that 'unlike in his domestic affairs he was aggressive and romantic abroad'. 'I for one', says Heren, 'resented the Cuban crisis. The world was taken to the nuclear brink although Khrushchev was prepared to remove the missiles from Cuba if Kennedy took American missiles out of Turkey.' Heren calls this an 'obvious solution' rejected for no given reason. He implies that electoral considerations were rather high in Kennedy's outlook.

Heren asserts that 'there was no consultation with the NATO Allies who were closer to the brink than the United States'. He appears to be referring here to the period before Kennedy's broadcast. It is not clear whether at the time he wrote his book he knew how closely Macmillan was consulted thereafter. However he remains anxious to be fair. This at least he concedes: 'The Kennedy charisma was a great gift. As the world saw him he emerged from the Cuban crisis as a cool leader whose calculated boldness had saved the world from incineration.'

There is yet another angle to be mentioned. This one derived from Schlesinger. Once again the wisdom of *A Thousand Days* has been developed in *The Imperial Presidency*. The missile crisis in his view was unique in the post-war years in that it really combined all those pressures of threat, secrecy and timing that the foreign policy establishment had claimed as characteristic of decisions (generally) in the nuclear age. Kennedy's action should have been celebrated as an exception, but was instead enshrined as a rule. The missile crisis was superbly handled but Schlesinger sorrowfully concludes that the very brilliance of Kennedy's performance strengthened 'the imperial conception of the Presidency', of the President acting on his own apart from Congress; and it was this attitude that brought the United States so low in Vietnam.

Why did Khrushchev try it on? He himself provides a definite answer in his book *Khrushchev Remembers* (1974). He writes, 'We stationed our armed forces on Cuban soil for one purpose only – to maintain the independence of the Cuban people and to prevent the invasion by a mercenary expeditionary force which the United States was then preparing to launch. We had no intention of starting a war ourselves.' By the same token he treats the outcome of the episode as a Soviet triumph. 'We behaved with dignity and forced the US to demobilize and to recognize Cuba – not *de jure*, but *de facto*. Cuba still exists today as a result of the correct policy conducted by the Soviet Union when it rebuffed the United States. I'm proud of what we did. Looking back on the episode I feel pride in my people, in the policies we conducted and in the victories we won on the diplomatic front.' There has been little disposition among dispassionate historians to accept this version.

Robin Edmonds was Minister at the British Embassy in Moscow from 1969 to 1971. His book *Soviet Foreign Policy 1962–1973* (1975) is expert and seemingly judicial. He does not take seriously the Khrushchev 'defensive' apologia. The risks for Khrushchev and the rest of the world were so high that Khrushchev must have reckoned that there was a prize to be won far more valuable than the security of Cuba. The prize, in Edmond's view, was nothing less than to establish a strategic balance with the United States. This would make possible an accommodation between the Soviet Union and the United States right across the board. The ultimate reason for Khrushchev's failure, not forgetting the skill and courage of Kennedy and his advisers, was that in 1962 the Soviet Union was still far from achieving parity with the US in effective armaments. Edmonds refers to Khrushchev's error as one of Himalayan proportions. Khrushchev survived it for two years, but the defeat which it led to made sure of his downfall. In the words of a British statesman, they reckoned that he 'mucked it up'.

Incidentally, Edmonds rejects by and large the explanation that Khrushchev underestimated Kennedy's character after the episode of the Bay of Pigs and their meeting in Vienna. But, as we have seen, according to Schlesinger, one of three American eye-witnesses mentioned by Edmonds, Kennedy arrived in London after the Vienna Conference 'tense and tired ... for all the poise and command he displayed in the talks, the experience deeply disturbed him'. This is confirmed by Macmillan's recollection.

Khrushchev remembers that after his last meeting with Kennedy in Vienna the latter looked not only nervous but deeply upset. 'Looking at him I couldn't help feeling a bit sorry and somewhat upset myself. I hadn't meant to upset him.' One may take that or leave it as one chooses; the various accounts are not very far apart. Khrushchev concludes a considered estimate of John Kennedy in this way: 'I would like to pay my respects to Kennedy, my former opposite number in the serious conflict which arose between our countries. He showed great flexibility and together we avoided disaster. When he was assassinated, I felt sincere regret. I went straight to the US Embassy and expressed my condolences.' Earlier he refers to Kennedy as a man who understood the situation correctly and who genuinely did not want war.

In the spring of that year Salinger visited Khrushchev in Moscow as a personal representative of President Kennedy. 'The Premier', he records (*With Kennedy*, New York, 1966) 'was the most mercurial man I had ever met. His mood could change in an instant from blustery anger to gentle humour.' Many instances are given of the latter. After a long monologue on recent Russian successes with chemical fertilizers he suddenly stopped talking, glanced at Salinger impatiently and said: 'I don't know why I waste my time explaining all this to you. You don't know anything about agriculture.' Salinger had to admit that he didn't. Khrushchev smiled. 'That's all right; Stalin didn't either.' Most of the time he was very friendly about Kennedy. 'Your President', he said, 'has accomplished much and shown himself to be a big statesman. Please convey to him that I want to be his friend.' But at other moments he was defiant and menacing. 'It is unwise to threaten us with war and unwise to attempt to keep us from signing a peace treaty with Germany with threats of war. . . . I repeat we do not recognize and cannot recognize the right of the Western powers to keep their troops in West Berlin.'

Nothing, however, that Khrushchev said in the spring could have prepared Kennedy for the aggression of the autumn.

10
The First Lady

Jacqueline Kennedy was the most talked about, criticized and admired First Lady since Eleanor Roosevelt. A young woman in her thirties, she could not compare with a great international personality like Eleanor Roosevelt, but in some noticeable respects she resembled her. Like Eleanor she did as she pleased, was always herself and could not be pigeon-holed. She behaved in public with dignity and a great sense of style. More often than not described as 'regal', she was considered at first to be too superior, her interests too rarefied, to make a good wife for a President; in the event she contributed immeasurably more to the cultural life of American society than her predecessors in spite of – or because of – being many years younger than any of them.

'There is more to her', said Eleanor Roosevelt, no mean judge of character, 'than meets the eye.' She was indeed a rare person, doubtless owing her complex personality to her mixed ancestry – Irish on her mother's side, French on her father's.

The early months of her marriage to John Kennedy proved irksome to her. Theirs had been a somewhat chequered courtship, ('spasmodic' was how she described it), due partly to his campaigning activities and partly to her discouragement at the idea of his being 'mad enough to intend to become President'. She later confessed that 'it was like being married to a whirlwind'. He was completely absorbed by politics, always travelling, whilst she, too intelligent for self-pity, resumed her studies, taking a course in American history at Georgetown University.

In appearance she was youthful, of slightly above average height, svelte, poised, graceful, dark, with striking features, a flawless complexion, large compelling brown eyes, firm but well-shaped mouth, a wide-open friendly smile, and soft-spoken. In public she was elegant and aloof; in private casual, impish and irreverent. Always considerate of employees, she had the rare talent of extending cordiality to them without inducing familiarity.

Jacqueline Kennedy had no love for campaigning, still less for political discussion. But once the campaigning was over she soon learned to function as a politician's wife and to play her public part. Brought up as a Republican, she deftly explained her new allegiance by saying 'You have to be a Republican to realize how nice it is to be a Democrat'. In the White House husband and wife drew closer together. They were able to spend more time with one another. He found with her and the children a happiness he had not known before, became more relaxed, less demanding.

The rôle of First Lady eminently befitted Jacqueline Kennedy, providing her with a stage on which she shone as a gracious hostess, accomplished public figure and a charming person. In large gatherings she outshone everybody, exercising an elusive, magnetic attraction, witty and sophisticated. She obviously enjoyed the attention she so easily compelled.

In many respects she had much in common with the President, whilst in other ways they were complementary. Both were physically attractive, wore a natural air of self-assurance, were quick in movement. She held herself erect, but he, owing to his back injury, had at times a somewhat hunched look. Both were athletic, good swimmers. She however preferred water-skiing, while he was a sailing enthusiast. She took up golf to please him but abandoned the favourite Kennedy sport of touch football after sustaining a broken ankle at her first attempt. 'It's touch,' commented one visitor, 'but it's murder.' She excelled at horsemanship, her equestrian skill acquired through her father's devoted tuition being of a high order.

Both made a cult of excellence. They were unremittingly hard workers, highly-organized, sharing a strong appreciation of the value of time. He possessed the Kennedy family sense of urgency to the full. He seemed somehow to sense that his time was brief. He spent his minutes with care and liked to have his appointments bunched tightly together, with little waiting time in between. She too parcelled her time, planned well ahead, had a total mastery of detail, endless detail, although rarely holding herself to a schedule. Like him she conveyed the impression of having all the time in the world, but whereas he was unfailingly punctual, Jacqueline Kennedy was often said to be late. He was punctilious about social obligations, but if Jacqueline, on occasion, did not wish to participate in an activity, she could seldom be prevailed upon to do so if it did not harm her husband. He loved people; she regally ignored crowds unless nudged by her husband. Nevertheless she was a great political asset to him, especially on his visits abroad, a fact of which he was fully aware and did not hesitate to acknowledge.

Both were highly intelligent. He applied his intelligence to the concrete, she inclined to the aesthetic. Both were fond of reading, particularly historical books.

Paul Fay Jr, John Kennedy's war-time naval comrade and friend for twenty-one years, in his book *The Pleasure of his Company* (1973), recounts a charming incident illustrating John Kennedy's pride in Jacqueline's accomplishments. Contemplating with them both the proposed purchase of a small Greek metal statuette a few inches in height, supposedly some 2000 years old, Fay doubted whether it was genuine and suggested that the President 'was being taken'. 'Ask Jackie,' said Jack. 'I looked sceptical,' Fay continues, 'I had not thought of Jacqueline as an authority on classical statuettes. "Ask Jackie", Jack continued, "any question you can think of dealing with Roman and Greek history, and she will give you the answers ... then ask her about the authenticity of the figurine".' Fay protested his ignorance.

Jack took over. With obvious pride he started quizzing Jacqueline, using a book on Greek history as his source for questions. At first she hesitated. 'Jack, this is ridiculous ... how are my answers going to prove how old that Grecian statue is?' Jack persisted and Jacqueline began answering. It was an amazing performance ... she answered every question with ease.

They both had keen, retentive memories; he deliberately cultivated a prodigious memory for names and faces. Both were considered witty – his wit the exuberant, sometimes earthy kind, hers subtle, teasing, satirical.

Jacqueline was a devotee of art and music and extremely

knowledgeable in both fields. John Kennedy 'could never dig all that cultural jazz'. Although he recognized and respected artistic excellence, he lacked a real appreciation of it. Nevertheless he believed it important that he should lend his prestige to distinction in creation and performance, convinced that the health of the arts was vitally related to the health of society. His musical taste was for gaudy musicals – 'horse operas'. His favourite 'party piece', doubtfully rendered, was said to be 'Won't You Come Home, Bill Bailey?', whilst Jacqueline maintained that the only tune he recognized was 'Hail to the Chief', the American presidential theme song, in spite of occasionally making his entrance too soon with the ruffles and flourishes. He found her 'arty' friends somewhat uncongenial. 'The White House,' he joked, 'is becoming a sort of eating-place for artists. But *they* never ask *us* out.'

But this presentation of Kennedy as a philistine could be misleading. At the time of the Inauguration the combination of the revered poet Robert Frost on the rostrum and W. H. Auden, Alexis Léger, Paul Tillich, Jacques Maritain, Robert Lowell, John Hersey, John Steinbeck, Allen Tate and fifty other writers, composers and painters in the audience seemed, in Schlesinger's words, 'to prefigure a new Augustan age of poetry and power'. And Kennedy laboured persistently to sustain the expectation.

In 1961 he invited August Heckscher (the President's special consultant on the arts) to conduct an inquiry into the resources, possibilities and limitations of national policy in relation to the arts. 'Obviously governments', he told Heckscher, 'can at best play only a marginal rôle in our cultural affairs. But I would like to think that it is making its full contribution in this rôle.'

Schlesinger stresses John Kennedy's growing interest in architecture, which showed itself markedly in his attitude to the physical appearance of Washington. In all this he responded visibly to Jackie's influence.

Their tastes in food were diverse. He was a 'meat, potatoes, fish chowder and sea-foods man'. She understood the art of *haute cuisine*, loved fine French food and was a gourmet.

Before his marriage John Kennedy was known as a sloppy dresser, recorded as having appeared at a public meeting with odd socks and even in brown 'loafers' with his tuxedo. He retrieved his reputation later, however, becoming known as a 'three–suits-a-day' man, even when no public function was scheduled, finally being awarded the accolade of 'America's best-dressed man'.

Clothes were always of vital importance to Jacqueline. As the youngest and the most glamorous First Lady to occupy the White House for generations, she became a natural trend-setter, fostering a novel, elegant, deceptive simplicity in dress and general *tenue*. Her father, himself a dashing master of style, had early inculcated in her the art of dressing. Always well-groomed, she had a dramatic ability to appear suitably at her best on all public occasions, evoking admiration and envy. 'She could be in a barn', wrote a woman reporter, 'leaning on a pitchfork, blowing the hair out of her eyes, and she'd look like Miss America.' She brought all her immense resources of ambition, energy and enthusiasm to the time-consuming planning of her wardrobe, ordering clothes, employing 'scouts' – friends and professionals – to be on the look-out for gowns, fabrics and ideas in the *haute couture* collections which would be to her taste, and always kept track of what the *grands couturiers* in Paris, Rome and London were featuring. She was much criticized for extravagance in dress, but was never ostentatious in appearance.

There was indeed one important field of conflict between the President and the First Lady which persisted throughout the White House régime – that of expenditure, not only in her personal affairs but in the general running of the White House. In spite of his wealthy background John Kennedy had been brought up strictly and was a keen economizer. Jacqueline too knew well how to economize effectively when it came to the point, but could be erratic when control clashed with her personal desires. Clothes were her blind spot, but so too were paintings, house furnishings and antiques. Confronted so young with an organization of the magnitude of the executive mansion, it was understandable that at first the significance and scope of the budgeting eluded her grasp.

'How much', she asked the Chief Usher on her second day in the White House, 'is our total operating budget?' 'Five hundred thousand dollars a year, but that does not include your personal expenditure.' 'Well, just remember this. I want you to run this place just like you'd run it for the chinchiest [meanest] President who ever got elected.' The President and Mrs Kennedy were horror-struck at the size of the first month's bills and from then on the 'battle of the budget' was joined, a matter of increasing concern to the President even in moments of supreme constitutional crisis.

'From now on,' he thundered, 'please see that I get a complete list of all the cheques written and exactly what they're for.'

Nevertheless it is fair to say that their relationship, particularly after he achieved the Presidency, grew in strength. Jacqueline considered her rôle at the White House to be firstly that of good wife and mother to the two children, and only secondly that of First Lady. She was at all times solicitous for his welfare and general comfort, watched over his diet, studied his tastes and did all she could to ensure that his family life should be as relaxing and enjoyable as possible, and did not hesitate to subordinate her own inclinations where she recognized that his interests were paramount. She carefully husbanded the hours they were able to spend together and guarded the family home on the second floor as if it were a sanctuary.

They escaped together for short or long weekends to Hyannis Port on Cape Cod and to Jackie's family's summer home in Newport, Rhode Island; sometimes for a brief respite to Camp David, the official presidential retreat in the Maryland Hills, or to Glenora, an estate rented in Virginia. In 1963 they built a home of their own in the same part of the country. During these family weekends the President walked and swam, played with his children in the sands, read intensively for pleasure or went sailing, a pursuit he always loved.

Jacqueline liked to come up with little surprises for her husband – gifts that would amuse him. She had re-upholstered, for example, the old North Carolina porch rocker, which he had used for some years in the Senate, had had the frame stained and the cane back padded with foam rubber and covered with oatmeal-coloured monk's cloth. This was to match the new, more elegant surroundings of the White House at the time of its restoration, a fact which the Press seized on with the headline: 'JFK is Rocked by Wife's Thoughtfulness'.

Whilst the early years of their marriage were marred by his illnesses, she had her own health problems too; there was an early miscarriage and later a still-birth before the birth of their first child Caroline in 1957, followed by that of John Jr in November 1960. They were conscientious, loving parents, always accessible to the two children, who grew to be unusually spirited and original, casting their spell over the White House. Jacqueline had an innate understanding of children, her own and other people's equally. A glance, a smile drew them to her wherever she went. Between placid cleanliness and healthy childhood play she was on the side of play, and could often be seen frolicking with her own two in their playground at the White House.

She was determined that they should lead as normal lives as possible and guarded their privacy with an almost fierce intensity. She herself carefully planned and directed all the publicity that the children received. When away from the White House on a trip it was her invariable practice to leave behind pre-addressed postcards for each of them, one for every day she would be gone, on which cancelled foreign stamps would be appropriately glued. At such times John Kennedy would re-arrange his timetable to be able to give them more time himself. Many stories are told of their mischievous behaviour, of his delight in their escapades, of his devotion, of his tolerance when they unwittingly intruded on high-level meetings.

'With John Jr', recounts Paul Fay, 'there was always a personality struggle to determine who was going to give orders, John or his father.' The President never failed to take huge delight in his son's bubbling, uninhibited personality, and when they were together was unable to keep his hands off him. Kennedy loved to taunt and tease John and would watch with great pleasure his son's youthful responses, not infrequently getting as good as he gave. Saturday morning at 'the Cape' was, in John Kennedy's phrase, 'time for father and son to get to know each other'. The favourite pastime then was a shopping spree at the local toyshop with father throwing himself as zestfully as the children into the choice of purchases.

Another endearing practice throughout his term as President was to allow Caroline each morning to accompany him from the family living quarters in the East Wing along the terrace to his office in the West Wing, 'Buttons' holding 'silly Daddy's' hand – a poignant memory still lingering in the minds of entourage and staff.

In Jacqueline Kennedy's relations with other members of the Kennedy 'clan' there was a gulf. 'Just watching them', she remarked on one occasion, 'wore me out.' Their unceasing competitiveness, the constant one-upmanship, sense of urgency, general air of merriment, exchange of banter and bouquets, exasperated her. She found their addiction to parlour games like Monopoly and charades boring, and displayed a general reluctance to join in their activities. They on their part understandably found difficulty in relating to her. 'You'll have a hard job', one of her sisters-in-law was heard to remark, 'getting to the bottom of *that* barrel.'

Her relations with her mother-in-law, Rose Kennedy, with whom in many ways she had much in common, were never more than cordial. Both had a deep appreciation for *haute couture* and aimed always at perfect grooming. They could at times be prevailed upon by the family to give impromptu dress shows of their latest Paris purchases. However they rarely sat down together to chat about the children. Jacqueline, in a much-quoted comment, is supposed to have criticized Rose for being too selfish, for thinking only of herself. Warmth and spontaneity were lacking on both sides. Rose Kennedy, now in her middle eighties, maintains a personal relationship with each of her twenty-eight grandchildren. Jacqueline Kennedy expresses her heartfelt admiration.

With her father-in-law Joe Kennedy, 'the Ambassador', however, she got along exceptionally well. They talked together for hours, teased each other unmercifully, were as playful as two children, sailed together in the *Marlin* at Hyannis Port. 'Love him, just love him,' she would remark when his name was mentioned. She really had a great fondness for him and, after he fell ill, suggested that he should be brought to the White House to live, adding 'you know how I feel about him – it's more than admiration.' She had somehow from the first penetrated the dour, gruff outward shell, the aggressive exterior, and contacted the natural charm which lay beneath, discovered the delightful sense of humour, warm and gentle, rarely revealed outside the family circle.

If it is true, and it is, that no President ever worked so hard at his job as John Kennedy, then it is equally true that no First Lady ever accomplished so much in so little time as Jacqueline Kennedy.

'She's planning', said Mamie Eisenhower to the Chief Usher, in her most disapproving tone, 'to re-do every room in this house. You've got *quite* a project ahead of you. There certainly are going to be some changes around here.' Mrs Eisenhower had just completed her final task in the White House – that of accompanying her successor Jacqueline on an introductory trip around the executive mansion described by Thomas Jefferson as 'big enough for two emperors and the Grand Lama'.

Ever since Abigail Adams, wife of the second President, had

complained bitterly of its barn-like, unfurnished vastness, successive Presidents' wives had literally thrown up their hands in despair, bequeathing a conglomeration of styles and periods, of makeshift arrangements, random art, faded furnishings, potted palms and tawdry glitter. Confronted with such a challenge Jacqueline resolved to restore the mansion as a truly historic house, to make it her special project. 'Everything in the White House', she said, 'must have a reason for being there. It would be sacrilege to redecorate it – a word I hate. It must be restored and that has nothing to do with decoration; that is a question of scholarship.'

A master of exacting detail, she set about the mammoth task in truly professional style, appointing a Fine Arts Committee of carefully-chosen experts to advise and guide her. It was also the function of the latter to locate authentic furnishings of museum quality and significance reflecting the history of the Presidency from the period of Thomas Jefferson (1801–9) the first President to spend a full term there, and to raise funds. Legislation was then procurred designating the White House a national museum, thus enabling it to receive gifts. Jacqueline Kennedy appreciated from the outset that there was little hope of an official appropriation for the kind of grand-scale restoration she had in mind and that it would be necessary to rely on private sources.

She studied meticulously the old records of early plans and decorations at the White House and thought out her own ideas step by step, taking care that every move should be approved beforehand by the Committee. She had a subtle, ingenious way of getting things accomplished. With the Chief Usher in tow she roamed the mansion and explored the basement storage rooms. She uncovered and resuscitated long-banished 'treasures' and items of particular historic interest, such as Woodrow Wilson's wheelchair, the armchair used by Ulysses S. Grant and the famous James Monroe pier table. She threw out the horrors, the 'Mamie' pink of the upstairs rooms, the Grand Rapids furniture, the heavy Victorian mirrors and, of course, the potted palms.

Art collecting dominated the first year. Jacqueline Kennedy kept two personal art 'scouts' busy locating particular items. She had a remarkable memory for pictures she had once seen and liked and could be very patient and persistent when it came to obtaining them. Crates of paintings were always arriving and being returned for framing or re-touching. Galleries and museums all over the country, including the Smithsonian and the Boston Museum of Fine Arts, offered the loan of their treasures for the State Rooms. Some magnificent Cézanne landscapes, originally bequeathed to the White House, which had found their way to the National Gallery of Art, were tracked down and reclaimed.

Gifts and offers of help of one sort or another poured in from all over the United States. Lists of prospective donors who might have appropriate period furniture or who might be willing to donate funds were carefully screened, donations being specifically designated as being subject to deduction from tax.

Many of the acquisitions were authentic pieces from the period of a particular President, or from a President's private home, such as President Monroe's priceless Bellangé chairs. Sometimes the gifts were small – a piece of velvet of the right period to cover two chairs used by Lincoln; sometimes impressive, such as the $165,000 painting donated by Walter Annenberg.

Jacqueline Kennedy was in command at every stage of the restoration. No detail from chandeliers to ash trays escaped her attention. The State Rooms when completed were classic examples of elegant grandeur. Every item, every picture, piece of furniture, lampshade and vase had been individually selected, appraised and put into place. The household staff stood aghast, silent with awe at the changes.

The White House began rapidly to acquire the status of a museum. Jacqueline's efforts, her manifest expertise and persistent quest for quality and historic significance impressed the public and brought her much acclaim. John Kennedy supported and encouraged her whole-heartedly throughout. He applauded as the inherited furniture was carted away and watched progress with mounting pride in his wife, conceding her an ever-increasing respect.

In February 1962, Jacqueline Kennedy took the whole nation on a televised tour of the State Rooms and proudly showed the public the results of her labours. Moving slowly, at ease, from room to room, without a script, she described in her low voice the changes which had been made and what she had sought to achieve, giving the history of many of the newly-collected paintings, heirlooms and *objèts d'art*, and saying how they had been acquired. It was a personal triumph, a memorable occasion. 'It's terrific!' said the President. 'Terrific! Can we show it in 1964?'

A White House Historical Association was created and a curator appointed. A guide book, issued in accordance with Mrs Kennedy's precise indications, was a one-dollar best-seller, raising still more funds to meet the cost of restoration. The public flocked in their thousands on visiting days.

Jacqueline Kennedy, to her everlasting credit, systematically, painstakingly, with steely determination, consummate artistry, verve and skill, and a strong sense of history, had succeeded in transforming the leading family's residence from a mausoleum, a hotel lobby, into a national show-place. In so doing she created a lasting memorial to her vision, enterprise and culture.

I I
Mission to the world

After Cuba
Irish rhapsody
Alliance for progress

The Cuba missiles confrontation was hailed as a turning point at the time. For once the label is justified. Khrushchev, as Sorensen says, 'had looked down the gun barrel of nuclear war and decided that that course was suicidal'. In retrospect, the Soviet aggression over Cuban missiles can be regarded as their last fling – for the time at least. Its failure, says Schlesinger, struck from Soviet hands the weapon of nuclear blackmail and forced the Russians to re-examine the whole strategic position. Their conclusions cannot have been encouraging. The rearmament introduced by Kennedy from 1961 onwards, on top of developments already in train, had altered the whole military balance to their detriment. The third world had resisted their blandishments. On the other hand, their fears insofar as they contained any rationality, should have been allayed by the extraordinary restraint exercised by Kennedy during the crisis and in the hour of triumph.

But the effect on Kennedy had been hardly less profound. In the last resort, if driven to desperation, the Russian Samson retained the power to pull down the pillars of the world temple. Berlin, Laos and now Cuba – any of these crises could have escalated into a vast catastrophe. 'That', said the President, in a characteristic understatement, 'is rather unhealthy in the nuclear age.' He had pulled it off this time in a situation that favoured him, but another time elsewhere, who could say? He turned his attention to the idea of a Test Ban with renewed earnestness.

Schlesinger, in his final summation of Kennedy's life's achievements, lists first of all 'the new hope for peace on earth, the elimination of nuclear testing in the atmosphere and the abolition of nuclear diplomacy'. Even if we allow for the overwhelming sympathy aroused by the assassination, the British leaders and the British people have accepted some such estimate. On the most fundamental level the last year of the Kennedy Presidency can be treated as a year of far-reaching achievement. But in one large area he encountered failure though not, on any fair-minded estimate, through any fault of his own.

The concept of a unified democratic Europe as part of a free-trading Atlantic community had become a basic element of Kennedy's world strategy. It had acquired the title of 'The Grand Design'. Macmillan had worked out a different though overlapping scheme of his own under this same title. Within three months of the Cuban victory, de Gaulle had vetoed the entry into Europe and strangled the Grand Design at, or indeed before, birth. De Gaulle made no secret of his determination to prevent American leadership of Europe. He gloried in his power at that moment to put not only the British, but the Americans in their places. However adroitly Kennedy had played his hand, de Gaulle for certain limited purposes held the ace of trumps.

The internal tensions among the Western Allies must be sketched in briefly before we return to West-East relationships. The British side of the story has been told authoritatively by Harold Macmillan in his last volume of memoirs. His desire and that of his colleagues to enter Europe had become by now an almost frantic preoccupation. But hardly less urgent in the inner circles of the British government was the conviction that a new independent nuclear deterrent must be secured at all costs.

On 15 December Macmillan visited de Gaulle at Château Rambouillet; on 19 December he went into conference with President Kennedy at Nassau. The former meeting was to be devoted to entering Europe; the latter to obtaining a new nuclear deterrent. Macmillan described the first visit as 'unfruitful and depressing'. It left him in no doubt that 'de Gaulle would, if he dared' use some means, overt or covert, to prevent British entry'. Nevertheless, he had by no means abandoned hope when he made his way to Nassau and found himself engaged in more strenuous arguments with Kennedy than ever before or afterwards.

It was admittedly embarrassing to Kennedy that the American

missile Skybolt, earmarked both for the United States and Britain, should be turning out such a failure that it would soon be rejected for US purposes. Kennedy, however, had not been warned quite how seriously the British would take it when the news at last filtered through to them. All concerned on the British side were in fact furious with anger, suppressed or otherwise, and deeply concerned about the prospective gap in their own defences. By all accounts Macmillan's performance at Nassau was as eloquent and effective as anything in his entire career; he came away with the promise of Polaris nuclear submarines as a substitute for Skybolt. He may be said to have prevailed, or Kennedy to have shown a generous sympathy for an ally who had just proved his loyalty and capacity.

But the strings attached to the use of Polaris landed Macmillan in no small criticism at home. He did not feel very much a victor when he recorded 'three hard days' hard negotiation – nearly four days in reality. The Americans pushed us very hard and may have out-smarted us altogether. It is very hard to judge.'

The French had no reasonable grounds for criticism. But that did not in any way deter de Gaulle. He chose to treat the whole Nassau episode as a perfect example of Anglo-American contempt for European interests. Not to mention American contempt for British interests. He turned down with disdain the offer of some Polaris submarines for France. He manufactured out of Nassau a new excuse for rejecting the British application to join the European Community and for driving right off the map the Grand Design.

Meanwhile, a certain groping towards a Test Ban treaty was observable. As we read the accounts of Schlesinger and Sorensen and compare them with that of Harold Macmillan, we find not unnaturally more emphasis on the initiative of the President in the one and on that of the Prime Minister in the other. But by and large the collaboration between the two leaders emerges as hardly capable of improvement.

The pursuit of a Test Ban treaty was not, of course, novel. But until the coming of Kennedy the enthusiasm of the British far exceeded that of the Americans. Kennedy's emergence went a long way, although not quite all the way, to produce a unity of outlook. As David Nunnerley puts it: 'With Kennedy sharing Macmillan's conviction as to the desirability of a Test Ban agreement, there was none of the vacillation and hesitation which had characterized his predecessor's policy and which, in the British view, had made the task of securing positive results all but impossible.'

When a three-nation conference opened on 21 March 1961 Britain and America jointly put forward what *The Times* called 'sweeping concessions designed to meet Russian objections'. But at the time of the Cuba crisis, the usual state of deadlock continued.

To Macmillan's eternal credit he wrote to Khrushchev at the very height of this same crisis suggesting that the resolution of the traumatic difficulties would pave the way to a Test Ban agreement. 'This', he said, and it must have needed audacity to say it, 'is an opportunity which we should seize.'

Once the crisis was over Kennedy, supported by Macmillan, began pressing again for a treaty. There were indications that Khrushchev was favourably impressed by the general tone of Kennedy's utterances. The latter had certainly strained every nerve to avoid and discourage any talk of victory. Khrushchev wrote to Macmillan and later in December to Kennedy. 'It seems to me', he wrote to Kennedy, 'that the time has now come to put an end once and for all to nuclear tests. The moment for this is very appropriate.' When the Disarmament Conference was re-convened in February, an air of optimism prevailed. But soon the familiar impasse displayed itself. The Americans had come a long way, but they still could not accept the Russian offer of only three on-site inspections. Seven or eight was the lowest figure they could swallow. It seemed probable that the British would have accepted the Russian offer as a compromise if they had been on their own. But it was judged impossible to desert the Americans on so vital a matter.

Macmillan records a total breakdown on 8 March of the discussions at Geneva. He was not putting all the blame on the Russians. He was considering 'what action I might take if the Americans (as I fear) are stubborn or frightened of the internal or political pressure'. A long and powerful despatch to the President occupies eight pages in his memoirs. He feels entitled to describe it as the basis on which the Test Ban was founded. It does not figure in the records of Sorensen and Schlesinger. Be that as it may, a joint letter went from Kennedy and Macmillan. Khrushchev's reply was rude and declamatory. But it contained a passage in which he grudgingly accepted the idea of emissaries coming from the West to Moscow early in July, which the Western leaders were quick to exploit. On this basis the negotiations could at least begin.

In the meanwhile Kennedy was far from inactive. On 10 June he delivered at the American University in Washington DC one of the great speeches of our era. Ted Sorensen, as always, was deeply concerned with its preparation; it is not immodest of him to say of it that 'it was the first presidential speech in eighteen years to succeed in reaching beyond the Cold War'. Its concrete proposal was a ban on atmospheric testing but its full purpose was very much wider. He proposed, he said, in the open air on the university campus, to deal with what he called the most important topic on earth, 'world peace'. He had no intention of imposing a Pan-American philosophy on the world:

... If we cannot now end our differences, at least we can help make the world safe for diversity. For in the final analysis our most basic common link is the fact that we all inhabit this planet. We all breathe the same air. We all cherish our children's future. And we are all mortal.

And to the logic of this analysis he added what to many Americans would seem a staggering conclusion: that the whole attitude towards the Cold War must be reconsidered. 'We must', he said, 'have a relaxation of tension without relaxing our guard.' He went on to widen and deepen the message in that speech and those which followed it in the late summer and autumn.

In the United States it seems that the effect of the deeply pondered announcement of 10 June was blanketed by the President's speech next day on the still more topical issue of Civil Rights. (Macmillan mentions the 10 June speech but only in passing.) There seems no doubt however of its impact on Khrushchev. He described it later to Harriman, then leading the American negotiations in Moscow, as 'the greatest speech by any American President since Roosevelt'.

Kennedy dashed off on a flying visit to Europe, West Germany, Ireland, England and Italy, where he was received most cordially by the Pope; all were taken in his stride. His reception in Berlin was historic, finishing with the never-to-be-forgotten words 'Today in the world of freedom, the proudest boast is "Ich bin ein Berliner"'.

Kenneth O'Donnell recalls, rather to one's surprise, that there were even bigger crowds in Naples than Berlin and an even more overwhelming explosion of hero worship. Everywhere he went he radiated youthful charm and proclaimed invaluable support for the Western Alliance.

No one outside the Kremlin will ever know whether the Test Ban treaty would have been signed without the tremendous oration of 10 June coming just at this time.

Once, however, Khrushchev had accepted the Western negotiators, a treaty was always more probable than otherwise. Harriman with his vast experience of negotiating with the Russians was the best possible American representative. Kennedy, 'with Macmillan's loyal help, arranged to have the American delegation lead for the West in the negotiations' (Sorensen). Lord Hailsham, very much restored to Macmillan's favour and full of brilliant ebullience, was well able to propound the British standpoint. There seems no particular justification for Schlesinger's opinion that he was 'overanxious to reach a treaty at all costs'.

Khrushchev was all smiles with Harriman and Hailsham. It was clear from the beginning that a comprehensive treaty covering tests of *all* kinds was not yet negotiable. The USA/UK limited plan to ban nuclear tests in all environments *except under ground* was the basis for the Western negotiators. Soviet Foreign Minister Gromyko offered a less detailed draft which Harriman felt left too many questions in doubt. With these two drafts on the table the leaders embarked on ten days of intensive discussions.

Macmillan heads his chapter on the Test Ban Treaty 'Breakthrough in Moscow' and takes pardonable pride in the British contribution. From his point of view the difficulties lay on the American side. He mentioned some of them, including the overingenious question of what would happen if governments wished to adhere to the treaty but were not in diplomatic relations with the three original parties.

At the finish the conventional tributes to Harriman and Hailsham were undoubtedly well-earned. For Kennedy and Macmillan it was the high point of their collaboration. Macmillan takes pleasure in recalling that as the climax was reached, 'At last I got a talk with the President on the telephone at 5.30 pm. He told me that he had abandoned the American position and that he had told Harriman not to insist. Indeed, he said that the treaty was just being initialled. He might have told us before and saved us a lot of anxiety!'

And so it all came right in the end. It should be realized that the most awkward questions, those relating to the inspection of *underground* tests, were disposed of by the simple device of leaving these tests out of the agreement. It was, therefore, a case of half a loaf, but it was certainly far better than an absence of bread. Kennedy and Macmillan had now to sell the agreement to their respective countries: for Macmillan this was roses, roses all the way, as far as the conventions of British politics permitted. Kennedy seemed likely to have a hard internal struggle, but threw himself into it, heart and soul. And he carried the day convincingly.

At the beginning of July, that is, before the negotiations started, the President had paid a flying visit to Macmillan at his home in Sussex, in the course of his European tour. 'From the very first moment', he writes, 'when the President's helicopter flew in and landed in the park, until his departure, there was a feeling of excitement combined with gaiety which has left an indelible memory for all concerned and indeed for the whole neighbourhood. I can see him now, stepping out from the machine; this splendid, young, gay figure, followed by his team of devoted adherents.'

At the time when Macmillan fell from power or, more precisely, resigned the premiership on the grounds of ill health, Kennedy wrote to him:

Dear Friend,
> This morning as I signed the instrument of ratification of the Nuclear Test Ban Treaty, I could not but reflect on the extent to which your steadfastness of commitment and determined perseverance made this Treaty possible. . . . History will eventually record your indispensable rôle in bringing about the limitation of nuclear testing. But I cannot let this moment pass without expressing to you my own deep appreciation of your signal contribution to world peace.

John Kennedy's visit to Ireland has a certain quality of timelessness. Chronologically it took place during his European journey in June 1963, after his visit to West Germany and before England and Italy. In the few months that remained to him it had already assumed a large significance. On the plane back to Washington after the assassination, his wife said to Ken O'Donnell and Dave Powers, 'How I envied you being in Ireland with him. He said that it was the most enjoyable experience of his whole life.'

Arthur Schlesinger writes convincingly, 'I imagine that he was never easier, happier, more involved and attached, more completely himself' than in those few days.

When plans were being made for the visit to Europe he told O'Donnell unexpectedly, 'I've decided that I want to go to Ireland.' O'Donnell at once protested. 'Ireland?' he said, 'Mr President, may I say something? There's no reason for you to go to Ireland. It would be a waste of time. It wouldn't do you much good politically. You've got all the Irish votes in this country that you'll ever get. If you go to Ireland, people will say it's just a pleasure trip.' 'That's exactly what I want, a pleasure trip to Ireland,' said the President. In spite of McGeorge Bundy supporting O'Donnell the latter was told to get on with it and make the necessary arrangements.

The reaction of O'Donnell, a real Boston Irishman, king (if anyone was) of the so-called Irish Mafia, will be surprising to most Irishmen in England or Ireland. But the story brings out revealingly the utter absorption of Kennedy's aides in his interests *as they saw them*; some aspects of the real man eluded them. The title of the chapter in which O'Donnell tells most vividly the story of the Irish visit (it also supplies the title of his book) is *Johnny, We Hardly Knew Ye*. The reference is to an Irish ballad which was recalled to the President as he left Shannon Airport. Of all Kennedy's devout disciples O'Donnell and Powers were perhaps the closest to him. But they have the humility to admit the limitations of their knowledge.

Before setting off for Europe the President soaked himself in all things Irish, especially the history of the Kennedys and Fitzgeralds. 'He's getting so Irish', said Dave Powers, 'the next thing we know he'll be speaking with a brogue.' Dave showed him a Kennedy family tree from the Library of Congress which traced his descent from a member of the royal Brian Boru family. He was fascinated by verses describing the plight of the 'Wild Geese', Irish exiles who included his ancestors:

> War battered dogs are we,
> Gnawing a naked bone,
> Fighting in every land and clime,
> For every cause but our own.

The unforgettable atmosphere of the President's visit to Ireland can never be appreciated to the full by anyone not present. For one afternoon I was privileged to share in the emotion, though in this instance the crowd was relatively small, consisting only of President de Valera's invited guests. The overwhelming point is that the fervour was two-way, mutual. In Berlin a million or so beleaguered citizens had hailed their saviour; but there was no suggestion of his being one of their number. He was the one man who could guarantee their physical security. In Dublin Kennedy had nothing to bring the Irish people except himself, and himself as profoundly Irish, in all respects one of them. He felt it; they felt it; they felt that he felt it; he felt . . . the *rapport* was total and beyond comparison or description.

O'Donnell's account begins by referring 'to the happy, carefree crowds along O'Connell Street, Dublin, in stark contrast to the tense anxiety just left behind in Berlin'. The President stayed with the American Ambassador to Ireland, whose house looked out on the matchless Phoenix Park. 'Mat,' he said to the Ambassador next morning, 'this is a much better place than the White House.' He announced that in 1968 he would support the Democratic candidate who would promise to appoint him Ambassador to Ireland.

The first item was a talk with Sean Lemass, the Irish Prime Minister. Then came the flight by helicopter to County Wexford and the real excitement. There was a civic welcoming ceremony at the New Ross Riverside Docks. It was at those docks that the President's great-grandfather had boarded the ship to America. 'When my great-grandfather left here to become a cooper in East Boston,' Kennedy said, 'he carried nothing with him except two things, a strong religious faith and a strong desire for liberty. I am glad to say that all of his great-grandchildren have valued that inheritance.' But as always, and most of all during this Irish visit, he lightened the grave with the gay. He pointed across the river at the Albatross Fertilizer Plant and said, 'If my great-grandfather had not left New Ross, I would be working today over there at the Albatross Company.' Continually during those days the crowd roared their appreciation.

The most sentimental moment was the visit to Mary Kennedy Ryan's cottage at Dunganstown. Mary Ryan and several other third and fourth cousins were there to welcome the President. A bright fire was burning in the fireplace; a platter of cold salmon, a silver pot of tea and a tray of brown bread were laid on the table.

Jack Kennedy was in his element. He lifted his cup of tea and said, 'We want to drink a cup of tea to all the Kennedys who went and those who stayed.' By special request he planted a juniper tree without mishap. O'Donnell and Powers were apprehensive; they remembered all too well the injury to his back the last time he planted a tree, in Ottawa in 1961. But there was no problem this time. As the President was leaving he kissed Mary Ryan warmly on her cheek. His sisters Eunice and Jean, according to O'Donnell, 'stared at him in wide-eyed astonishment'. This sort of public demonstration of affection was not his usual style.

A visit to Cork followed. The Freedom of the City was conferred on the President in front of more than 100,000 people. He knew instinctively the humour appropriate to the occasion. He pointed out Dave Powers who was sitting with seven local first cousins: 'Dave looks more Irish than his cousins,' said the President. A bold sally, but he couldn't go wrong. 'I also', he went on, 'want to introduce Monsignor Michael O'Mahoney, the pastor at the church I go to, who comes from Cork. He is the pastor of a poor, humble flock in Palm Beach, Florida.' The crowd laughed louder and louder.

Back in Dublin he entertained President de Valera and Prime Minister Lemass at the American Embassy. Then came what he afterwards described as the highlight of the tour: he attended a memorial service at Arbour Hill in Dublin for the executed leaders of the 1916 Easter Week Rebellion and watched the drill ceremony performed from Ireland's Military College at Curragh. 'Those cadets', he said afterwards, 'were terrific. I wish we had a film of that drill so that we could do something like it at the Tomb of the Unknown Soldier.' Jackie realized later how much the performance had meant to him. On the way back from Dallas she made arrangements to have the same group of Irish cadets at the President's grave during his burial.

Kennedy's address to the combined Houses of Parliament was the perfect mixture of culture, wit and moving tributes to the courageous history of Ireland and her contributions to the life of America. 'Irish volunteers', he said, 'played so predominant a rôle in the American Army during the War of Independence that Lord Mountjoy commented in the British Parliament, "We have lost America through the Irish".' And much more, equally acceptable. He quoted Benjamin Franklin, Charles Stewart Parnell, Yeats,

Henry Grattan, Bernard Shaw and, not least, James Joyce, who had described the Atlantic as 'a bowl of bitter tears'.

At Dublin Castle he was invested as a Freeman of the City and received honorary degrees from both the National University and Trinity College. As usual he lived up to the solemnity of the occasion without missing the opportunity for arousing hilarity. 'I want to say how pleased I am to have this association with these two great universities,' he said. 'I now feel equally a part of both, and if they ever have a game of Gaelic football or hurling, I shall cheer for Trinity and pray for National.'

President de Valera entertained him at a small dinner party on his last evening. We are told that 'the conversation was sparkling and the laughs plentiful'. Certainly Mr de Valera retained very happy recollections of the President, as I myself can testify. O'Donnell attributes to de Valera this comment on the British: 'Only if you are reasonable will they reason with you, and being reasonable with the British means letting them know that you are willing to throw an occasional bomb into one of their lorries.' O'Donnell was there and I was not, but somehow it does not sound quite like Mr de Valera's language. When Kennedy mentioned that he would be leaving Ireland from Shannon Airport the next day, Mrs de Valera (then in her middle eighties) recited to him an old poem about the Shannon River. He copied the lines on his place card and memorized the words the next morning while he was eating his breakfast.

On the way to Shannon they stopped at Galway where Kennedy addressed a cheering crowd of 80,000, and then at Limerick where these were almost his final words: 'Last night somebody sang a song, the words of which I am sure you know –

Come back to Erin, Mavourneen, Mavourneen,
Come back arue to the land of thy birth;
Come with the shamrock in the springtime, Mavourneen . . .
This is not the land of my birth, but it is the land for which I hold the greatest affection and I will certainly come back in the springtime.'

At Shannon where the aeroplane was waiting, he referred to the poem that Mrs de Valera had given to him. 'Last night', he said, 'I sat next to one of the most extraordinary women, the wife of your President, who knows more about Ireland and Irish history than any of us.' He had told her he was going to Shannon; she had

quoted the beautiful words of a poem and he had written them
down. He went on to recite them:

　'Tis the Shannon's brightly glancing stream,
　Brightly gleaming, silent in the morning beam, oh! the sight
　　entrancing.
　Thus return from travels long, years of exile, years of pain
　To see Old Shannon's face again,
　O'er the waters glancing.

What other political leader who had, incidentally, nothing to gain
from it, would have been capable of either the thought or the deed?

'Well,' he concluded, 'I am going to come back and see "Old
Shannon's face again"; and I am taking, as I go back to America, all
of you with me.' A supremely Irish ending to his Irish adventure.
It was through no fault of his own that he never saw Old Shannon's
face again and did not come back with the shamrock in the
springtime.

In his search for peace John Kennedy was by no means concerned
only with the relationships of the greatest powers. His objective, he
stated, was a stable community of free and independent nations
throughout the world. His policy required those countries blessed
with wealth to help those desperately short of it.

Richard Walton's book *Cold War and Counterrevolution* (New
York, 1972) is described on the cover of the paperback as 'a biting
criticism'. He returns again and again to Kennedy's anti-Com-
munism and what he considers his counter-revolutionary obsession. In my last chapter I come back to Walton and seek to correct
what seems to me a distorted perspective. But even Walton does
not question Kennedy's genuine sympathy for undernourished
and downtrodden peoples. 'Although', says Walton, 'Kennedy's
ventures into the Third World were motivated by his anti-
Communist impulse, as well as by his humanitarian concern, that
concern was real.' He stresses Kennedy's affection for the Africans,
his understanding of the non-aligned point of view, his support for
the United Nations in the Congo, his institution of the United
Nations development decade.

We have been told by more than one writer that Kennedy gave
top priority to America's programme for the new and developing
nations. But in the event he was continually thwarted. Each year
the congressional opposition to foreign aid increased and along

with it the indignation of the President. Not unimportant gains could be pointed to, but each year the gap between the rich and the developing nations increased (to the despair of their citizens and the despair of John Kennedy).

Two specialized efforts were more successful. The Food for Peace programme, initiated during the previous administration, was nearly doubled. And Kennedy promoted entirely on his own initiative one far-reaching scheme of which he had every right to be proud. The Peace Corps, starting with a few hundred and later comprising several thousands of young volunteers, carried American energy and skills to some of the peoples most in need of them. It had an enormous influence and effect upon the youth in America in the sixties. To many of that generation it still epitomizes what they thought about the Kennedy years. To an amazing extent it captured their hearts and enthusiasm. Kennedy had advocated it in his 1960 campaign and he created it in his first hundred days. It was a fine conception enthusiastically given effect to. There was no lack of opposition from liberals who treated it as a gimmick and conservatives who regarded it as a nonsensical dream, and Communists who denounced it as pure espionage. The outcome may be described as limited. But the volunteers who worked as teachers, doctors, nurses, agricultural agents, carpenters and technicians of all kinds served indubitably, to make use of Sorensen's phrase, as most effective ambassadors of idealism.

Sorensen refers to Kennedy 'presiding over a new era in Latin American relations'. No doubt that was his intention and he went some way to achieve it. No continent was more consistently in his mind and eventually no continent appreciated his exertions more warmly. Initially there was a good deal of suspicion in Latin America. They seemed to have heard it all before; the struggle against Castro and more widely against Communism seemed to them less urgent than their own desperate poverty. But later they came to realize that he meant what he said when he called them 'the most critical area in the world'.

We are told by Schlesinger that after the war the United States 'simply forgot Latin America, preoccupied with the recovery of Europe and the war in Korea'. But in the course of his presidential campaign in 1960, Kennedy heralded a new approach altogether. Repeatedly he dwelt on the plight of the Latin-Americans and the need to assist them in their penurious condition. The name 'A

New Alliance for Progress' and the essence of the subsequent programme were published after a speech at Tampa, Florida, though the speech was not actually delivered in full. The title reappeared in the inaugural address, but the official launching came on 13 March 1961. The Ambassadors from the South American states were summoned to the East Room of the White House. Kennedy unveiled for them a far-reaching ten-point programme. 'Our unfulfilled task', he said, 'is to demonstrate ... that man's unsatisfied aspiration for economic progress and social justice can best be achieved by free men working within a framework of democratic institutions. ... Let us once again transform the [Western Hemisphere] into a vast crucible of revolutionary ideas and efforts.'

A year later he proclaimed: 'The Alianza is more than a doctrine of development ... it is the expression of the noblest goals of our society.'

Meanwhile a major conference at Punta del Este in August 1961 had ended on a note of lofty optimism.

The claim that John Kennedy introduced a new emotional relationship with Latin America was justified to the full at the time of his death. He had been received with wild enthusiasm on his visits to that continent. So was Jacqueline – even more so, if possible. She usually accompanied him and spoke to the people in Spanish. When he died the whole continent went into mourning. The genuineness of his concern was indeed manifest. But twelve years later, what did his legacy amount to?

Jerome Levinson and Juan De Onis entitled their thorough-going study of the working of the Alliance *The Alliance That Lost Its Way* (New York, 1970). By the end of the decade it was difficult not to accept their discouraging assessment. 'A decade of the Alliance for Progress', they wrote, 'yielded more shattered hopes than solid accomplishment, more discord than harmony, more disillusionment than satisfaction.' This was how it seemed in Latin America and this was how it came to appear to the United States. 'At the end of the 1960s US policy in Latin America had virtually abandoned the Alliance principle.'

As always it can be claimed that if Kennedy had lived things would have been different and better. Levinson and De Onis, however, detect from the beginning a fundamental flaw in the conception. In their view, the failure of the Alliance resulted in large part from a failure to make the distinction between development objectives and security considerations. If the Alliance were to develop an inspirational driving force, social change had to be a large part of its essence. But how could that be brought about in a climate likely to promote American capital investment and to repress incipient Communism? Walton quotes Ronald Steel's *Pax Americana* (New York, 1970) not unfairly: 'The Alianza was also hobbled by its preoccupation with Communism. When the chips were down, the oligarchies and the generals who backed them up knew that Washington's fear of Communism was even greater than its desire for reform. . . .'

Within the first four years of the Alianza civilian governments were overthrown by the military in seven countries: the Dominican Republic (twice), Guatemala, Ecuador, Bolivia, Argentina, Peru and Brazil. Levinson and De Onis give a credit mark to a new development consciousness in Latin America. But the 'extreme optimism of those who initiated the Alliance, so characteristic of the Kennedy régime, left in its wake a profound disillusionment when the performance lagged so far behind the promises'.

The same criticism has been applied with varying justice elsewhere. South America provides the clearest instance.

12

Justice for blacks – and whites

We left Civil Rights in May 1961 with the relative success of the Freedom Riders. The government took many helpful steps during the following year; a major departure was the resolute support for the Negro James Meredith when he registered at the University of Mississippi and troops were sent to put down riots on the campus. But a tremendous drama had been played out before this result was effected.

By Sunday 30 September the President had issued a proclamation and an executive order preliminary to federalizing the Mississippi National Guard and deploying other troops. He issued a high appeal to the students at the university: 'You have a great tradition to uphold, a tradition of honour and courage.' But the students, whatever their attitudes may have been, were no longer the main element.

'Roughnecks and racialists', in Sorensen's words, 'from all over Mississippi and the South had been coming together, carrying clubs, rocks, pipes, bricks, bottles, bats, fire bombs and guns. As rioting raged through the night a newsman and a townsman were shot dead. Two hundred marshals and guardsmen were injured. Vast damage was done.' The President at last ordered into action the troops standing by. We are told he looked drawn and bleak. Through the long night of waiting and telephoning he cursed himself for not ordering the troops any sooner. Once they arrived they poured in to the tune of some 20,000. The mob was dispersed; the town was quietened. The President had won a victory but did not glory in it. 'I recognize', he said, 'that it has caused a lot of bitterness against me, but I don't really know what other rôle they did expect the President of the United States to play. They expect me to carry out my oath under the Constitution, and that is what we are going to do.'

As we saw earlier the civil rights groups, including the enlightened Negro leaders, withheld much serious criticism of the Kennedy administration during the first two years even though election promises certainly had not been honoured. On this point, Sorensen is more charitable than Schlesinger. 'There was no indifference to campaign pledges', writes Sorensen, 'but success required selectivity. He would take on Civil Rights at the right time, on the right issue.'

Schlesinger uses a rather franker expression. Kennedy had at this point 'a terrible ambivalence' about Civil Rights. He had a wide range of presidential responsibilities and a fight for Civil Rights would alienate southern support he needed for other purposes, including bills of direct benefit to the Negro. . . . What Kennedy said in public was, 'When I feel that there is a necessity for a congressional action, with a chance of getting that congressional action, then I will recommend it to the Congress.' Realistic possibly, but certainly unheroic.

The black population was not going to wait indefinitely. Martin Luther King was still the outstanding leader but more militant forces were straining at the leash. In May 1962 the main organizations had decided to launch a massive campaign against segregation, although action was not to start until 1963. It was to centre on Birmingham, Alabama. At Birmingham King had this to say: 'It is the most segregated city in America. All the evils and injustices the Negro can be subjected to are right there in Birmingham.' In the preceding five years there had been seventeen unsolved bombings of Negro churches and homes. Local racists, as Mrs King recalls, intimidated and even killed Negroes with impunity. In January 1963 Martin Luther King with two colleagues had a conference with President Kennedy and Attorney-General Robert Kennedy to urge the Federal Government to initiate civil rights legislation in that year. The Kennedys were, in Mrs King's words, 'sympathetic as always but they said they had no plans for proposing civil rights legislation in 1963'. The main excuse given apparently was that other legislation would be in peril. King was very disappointed. He felt he had no choice but to go ahead with his plans to force a confrontation in Birmingham so that the Federal Government would have to act. He warned the President accordingly.

Kennedy was not the man to fold his hands and do nothing in the face of impending crisis. On 28 February he presented to Congress a civil rights bill which carried his policy a good way forward, although it was quickly overtaken by events. The message began in his starkest style:

The negro baby born in America today ... has about one-half as much chance of completing high school as a white baby born in the same place on the same day – one-third as much chance of completing college – one-third as much chance of becoming a professional man – twice as much chance of becoming unemployed – about one-seventh as much chance of earning $10,000 per year – a life expectancy which is seven years less – and the prospects of earning only half as much.

But the legislative proposals were limited. They contained piece-meal improvements in voting, legislation for technical assistance to school districts trying to desegregate and an extension of the life of a civil rights commission. The champions of Civil Rights, white and black alike, were disappointed. The agitation continued to gather force.

In April the non-violent resistance campaign led by Martin Luther King got under way in Birmingham, Alabama, in a determined effort to force the desegregation of public facilities. Police Commissioner Eugene Connor responded violently. More than 3,000 blacks were taken to prison while others were assaulted with fire hoses, police dogs, clubs and fists. As more black homes were bombed and burned, more and more pressure was brought upon the White House while the new civil rights bill proceeded through the congressional committees.

'Overnight', say Schwab and Shneidman, 'Kennedy was educated in terms of black affairs.' But this seems less than accurate. Sorensen referring to the historic speech delivered by Kennedy on 11 June 1963 at the American University, says, admittedly, 'at the last minute the President decided that this was the incomparable moment'. But in a larger sense the speech 'drew on at least three years of evolution in his thinking, on at least three months of revolution in the equal rights movement, on at least three weeks of meetings in the White House' (Sorensen). On 4 May the news-papers in the United States and indeed all over the world carried a horrifying photograph of a police dog lunging at a Negro woman. The President received that morning a deputation of 'Americans for Democratic Action'. He said that the picture had made him sick. He regretted that the Birmingham demonstrators had not waited for the new city administration to come into office. Then he added, 'I am not asking for patience. I can well understand why the Negroes of Birmingham are tired of being asked to be patient.'

But sympathetic words of this kind buttered no parsnips. On 18 May he went a little further. At Vanderbilt University in Tennessee, 'No one', he said, 'can gainsay the fact that the deter-mination to secure (their full rights as Americans) is in the highest traditions of American freedom.' What Schlesinger and others have called the 'Negro Revolution' flowed on. The President's remarks seemed to give his sanction to non-violent resistance. In Nashville, Tennessee; in Raleigh and Greensboro, North Carolina; in Cam-bridge, Maryland; Albany, Georgia and Selma, Alabama, Negroes marched, prayed and 'sat-in' for their rights. During the summer 14,000 demonstrators were arrested in the states of the Old Confederacy.

On 9 June 1963 speaking in Honolulu to the United States Conference of Mayors, Kennedy seemed to promise at last more positive action. 'The events in Birmingham', he said, 'have stepped up the tempo of the nationwide drive for full equality. What we can do is seek through legislation and executive action to provide peaceful remedies for the grievances . . . to give all Americans, in short, a fair chance for an equal life.'

The pace quickened and quickened again. On 11 June he again had to federalize a State National Guard, this time in Alabama. The governor, George Wallace, had refused to allow two black students accepted by the state university on to the campus. The troops once again, as in the case of Meredith, protected the students from white mobs and succeeded in securing their entry into the school. It was on this day that the President delivered a speech which ranks, with his speech of the previous day on World Peace, as his noblest utterance. It represented his irrevocable commitment to the pro-position that race has 'no place in American life or law'. One or two sentences at least must be quoted:

It is better to settle these matters in the courts than on the streets, and new laws are needed at every level. But law alone cannot make men see right.

We are confronted primarily with a moral issue. It is as old as the Scriptures and is as clear as the American Constitution. . . .

Now the time has come for this nation to fulfil its promise. . . . We face a moral crisis as a country and as a people. It cannot be met by repressive police action. It cannot be left to increased demonstrations in the streets. It cannot be quieted by token moves or talk. It is a time to act. . . . Those who do nothing are inviting shame as well as violence. Those who act boldly are recognizing right as well as reality.

On 19 June 1963 he sent to Congress the most comprehensive and far-reaching civil rights bill ever brought forth. Now he had fairly and squarely put his hand to the plough. There would be no going back. He spared no effort to acquaint the nation with the deepest issues involved and at the same time sought to achieve his purposes by an unprecedented series of meetings at the White House with selected persons of influence.

The mounting wave, however, of Negro demonstrations presented Kennedy with a testing problem. Mrs King remembers telling her husband, 'People all over the nation have been so aroused by the impact of Birmingham that you should call a massive march on Washington DC to further dramatize the need for legislation to completely integrate the black man into American society.' But Republicans and Southern Democrats warned Kennedy that further pressures would defeat the bill. The Negroes not unnaturally declined to abandon collective protest, their principal weapon. They talked of a 'massive march' on the Senate and House galleries. The President chose a middle course which was at once firm and also understanding. He was careful not to decry the value of peaceful demonstrations, 'but violence', he said, 'is never justified. And while peaceful communication, deliberation and petitions of protest continue, I want to caution against demonstrations which can lead to violence.'

His words bore fruit and still more perhaps his known attitude, as well as the implicit goodwill in his relationships with Negro political leaders. What followed was a triumph for the cause of Civil Rights and all concerned with it.

The sit-in proposed to take place in the legislative galleries was abandoned. Provocative steps were deliberately avoided. The 'day of destiny' 28 August 1963, proved a glorious occasion. The President and the whole viewing world marvelled at the spirit and self-discipline of the largest public demonstration ever held in Washington. Coretta King describes the whole vast green concourse alive with 250,000 people representing all parts of the nation. Almost a fourth of that enormous crowd was white. It was, as she says, a beautiful sight, and nothing arose to mar it.

The high point of the day was naturally the address by Martin Luther King, made forever memorable by his use and reiteration of the phrase 'I have a dream. . . .'

I have a dream that one day this nation will rise up, live out the true meaning of its creed. . . . We hold these truths to be self-evident that all men are created equal. I have a dream that one day on the red hills of Georgia the sons of former slaves and the sons of former slave-owners will be able to sit down together at the table of brotherhood. I have a dream that one day the State of Mississippi, a state sweltering with the heat of oppression, will be transformed into an oasis of freedom and justice. I have a dream that my four little children one day will live in a nation where they will not be judged by the colour of their skin, but by the content of their character.

Later in the day when President Kennedy received Martin Luther King and other leaders, he found instinctively the perfect greeting: 'I have a dream.' But by this time none of them were inclined to discount it as clever politics or brilliant courtesy. They were aware that, as Sorensen puts it exactly, 'his dream was theirs'.

The march on Washington, though perfect in ideal and execution, worked in Schlesinger's phrase, 'no miracles on the bill'. Some members of Congress thought it went too far and others not far enough. The President never relaxed his pressure. The Judiciary Committee of the House of Representatives approved the bill on 29 October and reported it to the House on 20 November. Two days later President Kennedy set out for Dallas. A bill very similar to the one for which President Kennedy and his brother Robert had worked so intensely was passed in the following year.

Martin Luther King spoke of 'Kennedy's ability to respond to creative pressure', Kennedy frankly acknowledged that he was responding to mass demands and did so because he thought it was right to do so. 'This is the secret of the deep affection he evoked. He was responsive, sensitive, humble before the people and bold on their behalf.' There are in theory higher forms of statesmanship than that to which tribute is paid here. But Martin Luther King does not seem to think so.

In so far as the American people voted for a single idea when they elected President Kennedy, they voted for Activism. Professor James L. Sundquist sums this up well in his comprehensive study *Politics and Policy: Eisenhower, Kennedy and Johnson Years* (1969). 'It was the activist approach to public problems – open-minded, innovative, willing to employ the powers of government that characterized the Democratic program developed in the 1950s and both the attitude and the substance of the Kennedy campaign.' It was the mandate for such an approach that Kennedy was accorded.

Sundquist places Kennedy's social programme under six main headings: the unemployed, the poor, education, Civil Rights, health care for the old and a better outdoor environment. More than two years after President Kennedy was elected James McGregor Burns could write with general acceptance, 'We are mired in governmental deadlock as Congress blocks or kills not only most of Mr Kennedy's bold proposals of 1960, but many planks of the Republican platform as well.' Yet two years later the Speaker of the House of Representatives John McCormack could say of the 89th Congress elected at the end of 1964 that it was 'the Congress of fulfilment'. It is the Congress of 1964 and 1965 (that is during the first two years of the Johnson Presidency) which expressed the national purpose in bold and concrete terms – to outlaw racial discrimination in many of its forms, to improve educational opportunity at every level, to eradicate poverty, to assure health care for old people, to create jobs for the unemployed, to cleanse the rivers and the air and protect and beautify man's outdoor environment.

A cataclysmic change had occurred and it is not easy to draw the right conclusion, for two accidents of history had intervened. First in importance the assassination and secondly an election that was at once a presidential and a Democratic landslide. But the assassination itself involved two obvious consequences: the enormous sympathy which President Johnson inherited and the fact that he was a totally different man – more successful, it must be acknowledged, than his predecessor in dealing with Congress.

A few words must be said about the main headings listed by Sundquist. On fiscal policy and the attack on unemployment

President Kennedy had foreshadowed an approach of expansion and boldness. Soon after he was elected he took a number of particular steps referred to earlier to improve employment and went some way to develop industrial planning. But for a long time he followed a cautious line. He went out of his way to re-affirm at the bottom of an acknowledged recession the basic Eisenhower fiscal doctrine of the balanced budget. Some explanation seems necessary and there is no need to seek it in any failure of Kennedy's economic understanding though, as mentioned earlier, he was something of a novice when elected President.

His main reason seems to have been a desire to convince the nation that the Democratic Party, so often accused of reckless spending, was indeed fiscally responsible. It seems also that he regarded his call for national sacrifice as inconsistent with a policy of handouts. Whatever the explanation the up-to-date Keynesian economists in the administration did not take their defeat lying down. Beaten at first, in Sundquist's words, they were wholly successful two years later.

Kennedy began to reveal his conversion to 'the New Economics' of tax reduction and if necessary deficit spending in June 1962. He spelt out these ideas more fully at the Economic Club of New York on 14 December in that year. In October 1963 his tax reduction bill was carried through the House of Representatives by 271 votes to 155. It passed through the Senate in January 1964. A year later the business world paid its homage. 'It isn't often', said *Business Week* magazine, 'that the United States can look back on a major change in government policy and find absolutely no grounds for criticism.' Kennedy was the Moses who looked into the promised land into which Joshua led the people. And so it was with Civil Rights. The far-reaching measure initiated by Kennedy passed into law in July 1964 under Lyndon Johnson. Schwab and Shneidman insist that 'it is not certain that Kennedy would have found the same success. The new southern President with many southern friends in Congress used the after-effect of the assassination to force passage of the bill'.

It was Johnson who told the Congress in 1965 that, 'a prime national goal must be an environment that is pleasing to the senses and healthy to live in'. One cannot deny him the main credit there. But in regard to the attack on poverty the responsibility can be shared more equally. 'This administration today, here and now,' said Johnson in his first State of the Union message, 'declares unconditional war on poverty in America.' On the face of it, therefore, we must allow Johnson all or most of the glory.

There seems no doubt however that if he had lived Kennedy would have tried to strike the same note. Sorensen tells us that Kennedy started working on a comprehensive, co-ordinated attack on poverty more than a month before he went to Dallas. On 19 November, three days before he died, he gave a flat 'yes' to the question of whether anti-poverty measures would be in the 1964 legislative programme and asked to see the measures themselves in a couple of weeks. Regarding education and medical care for the old one cannot give the same confident answer. The plan for federal aid to education initially presented in 1961 was never passed. The fear of a growing federal government and the issue of the inclusion of aid to church schools raised too many complications and suspicions. The whole programme got voted down. Congress also refused his proposals for 'Medicare' for the aged. Here again the southerners and Republicans resented the growth of federal power, and they had plenty of allies in denouncing the scheme as too costly and smacking of socialism.

The education story deserves some treatment on its own. Kennedy had made a strong point of education during the election in the television debates and denounced Nixon and the Republicans for killing the Democrats' bill which would have raised teachers' salaries. Moreover he devoted a whole speech to education. He boldly promised that 'in 1961 a Democratic Congress under the leadership of a Democratic President will enact a bill to raise teachers' salaries. . . .' as well as 'an adequate bill for school construction'. Nothing of the kind occurred; Kennedy was defeated by the religious issue, the question of government help to church schools which in the United States, unlike Britain, had not hitherto been accorded. It was held to be opposed to the fundamental American notion of the separation of Church and State as embodied in the US Constitution.

Kennedy's personal views on what, if any, help should be given to Catholic education are not very clear; but as the first Catholic President he was worse placed to help his Church than would have been a Protestant. In Sundquist's vivid phrase, 'he was locked in, as were the non-Catholic hierarchy also locked in, as were the non-Catholic organizations'. Throughout the three years of the

Kennedy administration a major educational reform never had a chance.

And yet a way round was in fact discovered within two years of Johnson's coming to power. The new President's War on Poverty provided the context. Why not, it was argued, help children in need instead of arguing about schools of one kind or another? On this basis a solution, at least of a provisional kind, was reached. The special purpose was declared to be the education of poor children, but in practice virtually all of the nation's school districts would benefit. The official Catholic spokesman gave it qualified approval: 'the cause of children in need will benefit'. So did the other religious bodies. Johnson was able to say with some justification that in one year Congress did more for the cause of education in America than all the previous 176 regular sessions of Congress put together.

But it was indeed ironical that one palpable result of electing a Catholic President was to retard the advancement of Catholic schools.

Johnson carried far-reaching measures in education and Medicare as in other areas. Everything became easier after the Democratic triumph in the elections of 1964. But Sundquist considers that the legislative achievements in 1964, that is before the elections, were still more remarkable. No one, as he points out, can determine how much of the result was attributable to the wave of emotion that followed the assassination, and how much to the skill, energy and resourcefulness of President Johnson himself. Yet after his very detailed investigation, his verdict must be recorded: the considerable progress of the Kennedy programme prior to November suggests that most of what happened would have happened, more slowly perhaps, but ultimately, if Kennedy had lived.

This conclusion depends on the opinion that Kennedy's spirit of activism could not be expected to succeed at the first assault but created an atmosphere that would prevail in the end. As so often with the unfinished life of President Kennedy there is room for plenty of speculation. But here it is in danger of not being fair to President Johnson. If Kennedy had lived, he would still have been the first Catholic President; thus would he not still have laboured under a special handicap in regard to Catholic schools?

13

Who will rid me? -
plots against foreign leaders

The issue of Kennedy's alleged connection with the assassination of certain foreign leaders cannot be passed over in silence. In November 1975 appeared a Senate document entitled 'Alleged Assassination Plots involving Foreign Leaders'. It was also styled 'An Interim Report of the Select Committee to Study Governmental Operations with respect to Intelligence Activities'. It takes its place amid the flood of revelations and allegations about the Central Intelligence Agency which are now pouring out almost daily. This book is a biography of Kennedy, not a history of the CIA; but a few facts about the organization must be provided briefly.

The CIA was set up in the time of President Truman under the National Security Act of 1947 (later amended and amplified). Its original purpose was to co-ordinate the 'Intelligence-collection programmes' of the various governmental departments and agencies. Even the most savage critics of the CIA have not objected to an attempt of this kind to improve the supply of vital information; but as soon as an intelligence agency becomes an operational weapon, as the CIA rapidly did, a passionate argument breaks out at once ethical and strategic. What *covert operations* are to be regarded as legitimate and what illegitimate? Should indeed these covert operations (apart from the collection of information) be allowed at all? If allowed, how can they be made answerable to Congress? Victor Marchetti and John D. Marks in their arresting book *The CIA and the Cult of Intelligence* (1974) are not the most objective of witnesses. But to say the least they raise many questions which demand an answer, though not necessarily from me. The issue at hand, as they say, is a simple one of purpose. Should the CIA function in the way it was originally intended to – as a co-ordinating agency responsible for gathering, evaluating and preparing foreign intelligence of use to governmental policy-makers? or should it be permitted to function as it has done over the years, 'as an operational arm, a secret instrument of the Presidency and a handful of powerful men, wholly independent of public accountability, whose chief purpose is interference in the domestic affairs of other nations (and perhaps our own) by means of penetration agents, propaganda, covert paramilitary interventions, and an array of other dirty tricks?'

The Senate Select Committee stress the distinction between the general purposes and performance of the CIA on the one hand and certain abuses which crept in on the other. They defend the first on reasonable lines and roundly condemn the second.

Even Marchetti and Marks concede that what they consider the evil methods employed by the CIA have been practised just as ruthlessly by the Russians. The Senate Committee point out calmly enough that concern over the expansion of an aggressive Communist monolith led the United States to fight two major wars in Asia. In addition it was considered necessary to wage a relentless Cold War against Communist expansion wherever it appeared in the 'back alleys of the world'. This called for a full range of covert activities in response to the operations of Communist clandestine services.

They go on to say that they believe it still to be in the national interest of the United States to help nations achieve self-determination and resist Communist domination. However they insist that 'this interest cannot justify resorting to the kind of abuses covered in this report'. Their special concern was with assassination. The Committee indicate their firm resolution that steps must be taken to prevent those abuses from happening again.

Kennedy's responsibility for the performance of the CIA during his Presidency must be assessed with caution. It had been operating for over twelve years before he became President. It is still with us thirteen years after his death. He presided over it for less than three years out of its twenty-nine. After the Bay of Pigs fiasco he moved quickly to tighten White House control of the Agency. He vowed, so it is said, to 'splinter the CIA in a thousand pieces and scatter it to the winds'. But he seems to have been infuriated by its *inefficiency* rather than by its ethical standards.

On the face of things he shook it up drastically. He soon purged three of the Agency's top officials; in particular in the autumn of 1961 he replaced Allen Dulles with John McCone, a defence contractor who had formerly headed the Atomic Energy Commission. On his instructions General Maxwell Taylor, special military adviser to the President and soon to be Chairman of the Joint Chiefs of Staff, undertook a thorough study of United States intelligence. Robert Kennedy was a member of his small committee.

It seems difficult, however, to resist the conclusion of Marchetti and Marks that after the initial public outcry any steps taken by President Kennedy had little effect. 'The CIA went back to operating essentially in the same way it had for the previous decade with at least a tacit acceptance of the American public.' It was not till the total failure of the war in Vietnam and the scandal of Watergate that the whole issue of the CIA was dragged into glaring publicity. Kennedy probably exerted a closer supervision over the CIA than any previous President, but this is a claim which his admirers may be diffident about pressing in the light of abuses, including the attempts at assassination which have since been uncovered. When all is said the thing did not start with him.

The Senate Committee investigated alleged United States involvement in assassination plots in five foreign countries. They set it out in this way:

Country	Individual involved
Cuba	Fidel Castro
Congo (Zaire)	Patrice Lumumba
Dominican Republic	Rafael Trujillo
Chile	General Rene Schneider
South Vietnam	Ngo Dinh Diem

In a biography of President Kennedy we are only concerned directly with three of these, the target figures being Castro, Trujillo and Diem (also his brother-in-law). Of the three killings relevant to our purpose that of Diem is on a different footing from the other two. There is no reason to doubt the sincerity of Kennedy's grief when the news reached him that Diem and his brother-in-law had been murdered.

The Senate Report describes the assassinations of these two

leaders as a spontaneous act which occurred during the coup and was carried out without United States involvement or support. The President had come to regard Diem and his brother-in-law as considerable nuisances, but not as enemies. It may fairly be held that the President and still more his officials had lent encouragement to the coup; but the murders had not been foreseen. They do not throw light, therefore, on the American attitude to assassination.

This leaves us with Trujillo and Castro where Americans were certainly involved, though, in the latter case, most unsuccessfully. Trujillo was shot by Dominican dissidents on 31 May 1961. For over a year the United States government had been supporting these dissidents. Some American officials knew that the dissidents intended to kill Trujillo. Three pistols and three carbines were furnished though it is not certain 'whether the weapons were knowingly supplied for use in the assassination'. The day before the assassination a cable, personally authorized by President Kennedy, was sent to the United States Consul-General in the Dominican Republic stating that the United States government as a matter of general policy could not condone political assassination. At the same time they indicated that the United States continued to support the dissidents and stood ready to recognize them if they were successful in their endeavour to overthrow Trujillo.

On a charitable view this last-minute cable exonerates the President from a share of the moral responsibility for the assassination. Less charitably considered it more or less does the opposite. What is more significant (a point stressed by the Committee) is that no one apparently took any steps following Trujillo's assassination to reprimand or censure any of the American officials involved either on the scene or in Washington, or to otherwise make known any objections or displeasure about the degree of United States involvement in the events which had transpired. The staff of the CIA had some excuse for drawing the conclusion that assassination was not rejected on the highest levels.

It was Castro, however, who received the maximum of crude attention. We have found, say the Committee, evidence of at least eight plots involving the CIA to assassinate Fidel Castro. Although some of the assassination plots did not advance beyond the stage of planning and preparation, one plot involving the use of underworld figures reportedly twice progressed to the point of sending poison pills to Cuba and dispatching teams to commit the deed. Another plot involved furnishing weapons and other assassination devices to a Cuban dissident. Suggested assassination devices included poison pens, deadly bacterial powders and other still more weird gimmicks.

I am not, I repeat, writing the history of the CIA but rather investigating John Kennedy's responsibility. The Committee begin by pointing out: 'Whether or not the Presidents (Eisenhower, Kennedy, Johnson) knew of or authorized the plots, as chief executive officer of the United States, each must bear the ultimate responsibility for the activities of his subordinates.' But after what appears to be a very thorough investigation they tread warily in their conclusion. 'In view of the strained chain of assumptions and the contrary testimony of all the presidential advisers, the men closest to both Eisenhower and Kennedy, the Committee makes no finding implicating Presidents who are not able to speak for themselves.'

The report continues: 'Helms and McCone testified that the Presidents under which they served never asked them to consider assassinations.' That covers Eisenhower, Kennedy and Johnson, but in the case of the last-named the exoneration was more positive.

A dispassionate student of the report is entitled to go a little further. We are told that CIA officials in the targetted assassination attempts testified that they had believed that their activities had been fully authorized.

The Committee conclude that those officials were remiss in not seeking express authorization for their activities but that their superiors were also at fault for giving vague instructions and for not explicitly ruling out assassination. This last point is crucial in the present writer's view. 'No written order', we are told, 'prohibiting assassination was issued until 1972.' That order was not issued by the government but was an internal CIA directive. One is forced to conclude that the question of whether assassination was or was not permissible was deliberately left to the CIA themselves to decide.

The Committee took evidence from all living high officials in the Kennedy administration who dealt with Cuban affairs. No doubt with absolute sincerity they not only denied any personal knowledge of assassination plans but did not believe that 'President Kennedy's character or style of operating would be consistent with approving assassination'. Some who rise from a study of the report would wonder whether a similar overall denial could be extended to Robert Kennedy. Even in regard to the President himself the picture, as the Committee says, is not a clear one. They find that 'the system of executive command and control was so ambiguous that it is difficult to be certain at what levels assassination activity was known and authorized'.

There was in operation a curious system of 'plausible denial'. This was originally intended to implement covert action in a manner calculated to conceal American involvement if the actions were exposed. It led to the use of circumlocution and euphemism in speaking with Presidents and other senior officials. Words like 'assassinate', 'murder' and 'kill' were avoided if possible. The Committee is very severe on these practices.

Presidents Eisenhower and Kennedy are not then explicitly blamed. On the evidence, however, one feels that those in the CIA and elsewhere who concluded that assassination was a method of performing their duty and would, if successful, be welcomed on the highest levels, had no little excuse. Many of the plans that were discussed and 'often approved contemplated violent action against Cuba'. The Bay of Pigs invasion had the approval of two Presidents. Thereafter Attorney-General Kennedy insisted that 'a solution to the Cuban problem carried top priority. No time, money, effort or manpower to be spared'. Subsequently Operation Mongoose involved propaganda and sabotage operations which were aimed at spurring a revolt of the Cuban people against Castro. Mongoose ran from November 1961 until 1962 when it was superseded by more elaborate arrangements. It would not be particularly easy for CIA agents to distinguish between those violent actions involving death and destruction which were in order and those which were forbidden. The Kennedy brothers obviously exerted strong pressure on the CIA. Helms, DDP in the CIA, recalled that during the Mongoose period it was made abundantly clear to everybody involved in the operation that the desire was 'to get rid of the Castro régime and to get rid of Castro'. The point was that no limitations were put on this injunction.

This dialogue followed during the Committee investigations:

Senator Mathias: Let me draw an example from history. When Thomas Becket was proving to be an annoyance, as Castro, the King said 'Who will rid

	me of this man?' He didn't say to somebody, go out and murder him. He said 'Who will rid me of this man?' and let it go at that.
Mr Helms:	That is a warming reference to the problem.
Senator Mathias:	You feel that spans the generations and the centuries?
Mr Helms:	I think it does, Sir.

Later Mr Helms added, 'I think that any of us would have found it very difficult to discuss assassinations with the President of the US. I just think we all had the feeling that we had to keep those things out of the Oval office.' (That is the office of the President.)

There is no reason to suppose that President Kennedy consciously authorized assassination at any time, although many rumours to that effect have been circulated. But how much he, and still more his brother, knew of what was going on must forever remain mysterious. As far as we can tell he never clarified in his own mind the ambiguity of his moral position. It is extremely unlikely that the President would have desired an assassination in the later stages at the same time as he authorized talks to explore the possibility of improved relations with Castro.

Since the appearance of the Senate Committee Report much interest has been concentrated on someone who figures in the report simply as 'a friend of the President' but who has since been revealed, and has indeed revealed herself, as a lady who had what she called 'a close friendship' with the President. She acknowledges without apparent shame that she also had close friendships with two leading members of the Mafia, who were being employed at that time by the CIA to assassinate Castro. There is at the time of writing no evidence that the President knew of this association of hers. For the purposes therefore of the Senate Committee his friendship with this lady can still be treated as irrelevant.

14
Vietnam: the Achilles heel

'The evidence is inconclusive', says Henry Brandon in his *Anatomy of Error* (Boston, 1969), 'whether, despite his seemingly deepening commitment, Kennedy would have tried to extricate himself from the war in Vietnam.' In the closing months of his life he and his brother were beginning to question the fundamental assumptions of United States involvement. 'Nevertheless,' says Brandon, 'those who worked for him differ sharply on whether he would have followed more or less the same policy that President Johnson pursued in Vietnam.' The question will never be settled. Those who take the view that Kennedy would have extricated the United States long before he found himself in Johnson's extreme dilemma, base their opinion on their character assessment of the two men.

Brandon writes for example: 'One reason why I think he would not have followed as stubbornly and steadfastly the same course as Johnson is that he was a more temperate, more pragmatic man, neither as dogged and unyielding as Johnson, nor as prestige conscious.' He concludes that Kennedy would have been more impatient with the political instability of the Saigon régime. 'As they would have proved manifestly incapable of helping themselves, Kennedy would have found in this a sufficient excuse for disengagement.' On the other side of the argument is the undeniable fact that the advisers so carefully chosen by Kennedy continued to advise Johnson. It is plausible to suppose that they would have led Kennedy into the same tragic position that they led Johnson.

'Kennedy', says Brandon, 'assumed the war was going well in

1961 and 1962. But by the autumn of 1963 he seemed sick of it and frequently asked how to be rid of the commitment.' On one point Brandon seems quite clear enough. 'Kennedy knew he could not get out of Vietnam before the elections in November 1964 without inviting his own political eclipse.' If this is right there would have been another year of commitment in Vietnam. In that time there would have been inevitably a significant and perhaps a fatal escalation.

Brandon tells us that early in 1964 a complete reassessment of America's commitment in Vietnam would have been possible. Instead the war that summer moved into a new phase and the commitment deepened. It was not until July 1965 that in his opinion the most crucial period of the war occurred. There was therefore time, but only just time, for Kennedy to have effected the extrication before too late. All this remains speculation, however intriguing.

Those who wish to disparage the Kennedy achievement naturally concentrate on the sequel in Vietnam and put the main blame for it on Kennedy. Some of these critics are manifestly unfair, but Schlesinger, most sophisticated of hero-worshippers, on this one topic makes little attempt to defend the record. He appears to have completed his mighty volume *A Thousand Days* by February 1965. There is no hint in his 1965 book, or in that of Sorensen of similar date, of the moral and material disasters to follow. Yet Schlesinger in that same book refers to Kennedy's depression about Vietnam in autumn 1963. 'No doubt', he said, 'the President realized that Vietnam was his *great failure* [my italics] in foreign policy and that he had never really given it his full attention.' In a later essay on Kennedy in *History Makers* (London, 1973) Schlesinger admits in effect that Kennedy's attitude on Vietnam remained ambiguous to the end.

On the one hand he said as late as July 1963, 'for us to withdraw would mean a collapse, not only of South Vietnam, but of South-east Asia'. On the other hand Kennedy was never happy about the commitment of American troops to the Asian mainland. His plan for the phased withdrawal of American forces by the end of 1965 was still national policy four months after his death. Schlesinger agrees with Brandon that Kennedy, once the United States was committed in Southeast Asia, would have gone a long way to prevent South Vietnam falling into the hands of the Communists, but 'how far he would have gone to prevent this outcome, no one can know'. Once again we are left to speculate as we wish.

David Halberstam offers a prolonged and scathing indictment of the whole American performance in Vietnam. In his book *The Best and the Brightest* (1973) he lays considerable blame on Kennedy for creating the atmosphere of commitment in which the unfortunate Johnson would have to operate. 'By the end he [Kennedy] had grave doubts', says Halberstam, 'whether we should be there at all', but he had never shown those doubts in public. He had expressed doubts about the Diem régime but not about the commitment generally. His very eloquence in this field had had damaging consequences. His speeches and pronouncements had raised the importance of Vietnam in American minds. His commitment had, by the publicity he gave it, become that much more vital. Halberstam accuses him, with some show of justice, not only of markedly increasing the American involvement but working to conceal the truth about Vietnam from the public. He had left a brilliant, activist 'Can-Do Kennedy Team' without Kennedy to restrain them. His record, according to Halberstam, was largely 'one of timidity'. In other words he handed on a dreadful legacy to Johnson, who was soon to make his way into the mire deeper and deeper.

To understand these judgments, the record must be recited briefly. The simplest fact is that there were 17,000 American troops in Vietnam at the end of 1963 compared with 2,000 at the end of 1960. Under Johnson the commitment rose to over 500,000. Seventy-three Americans were killed during the three years of the Kennedy period. In the end 210,000 Americans were killed or died of wounds. But behind those simple statistics, which sound quite all right from Kennedy's standpoint, lies a wretched story of misunderstanding and frustration.

Roger Hilsman was Director of the Bureau of Intelligence and Research in the State Department under Kennedy and later his Assistant Secretary of State for Far Eastern Affairs. His memorable if hardly dispassionate book *To Move a Nation* was published in 1968. He finishes it with this poignant tribute to his beloved master whose death led to his speedy resignation from the Foreign Service: 'John F. Kennedy was a leader. And he was a hero as well.' We are not likely to be unfair to Kennedy if we follow the general thread of Hilsman's narrative.

We might, it is true, be somewhat less than fair to McNamara, Rusk and some others. But if we are to give Kennedy full credit, as we do elsewhere for successes in the economic field where his personal interest was small, we must debit him likewise for the alleged inadequacies of McNamara and Rusk. After all he had selected them without ever having met them before, and he supported them without wavering till the day he was murdered.

Hilsman tries to argue that Kennedy had the right ideas about Vietnam. He mentions Senator Fulbright as suggesting that President Eisenhower's original commitment to South Vietnam was a mistake and that so was President Kennedy's renewal of that commitment in 1961. But Hilsman does not share Fulbright's view by any means. Once it is accepted that the commitment was to be continued, he claims that Kennedy's mind worked on the right lines. 'If', says Hilsman, 'Vietnam does represent a failure in the Kennedy administration', and he is loath to admit it, 'it was a failure in implementation.'

With hindsight I cannot accept that as a sufficient comment. De Gaulle was no less anti-Communist than Kennedy, and in Paris in May 1961 he gave Kennedy a dire warning as a result of French experience: 'You want to rekindle a war that we ended. I predict to you that you will, step by step, be sucked into a bottomless military and political quagmire despite the losses and expenditures that you may squander.' Khrushchev gave similar advice in Vienna immediately afterwards, from whatever suspect motives.

But Kennedy and his advisers equated the defence of South Vietnam, under the Diem dynasty installed by the Americans, with resistance to the onward march of Communism and with the discharge of an ineluctable responsibility for world peace.

The truth is that American intervention in Vietnam was doomed, whoever was President. But in 1961 this was recognized by few Americans in high places. Kennedy was wrong from the start, but wrong in excellent company.

When Kennedy turned his attention to Vietnam in the spring of 1961, matters were approaching a crisis. A set of recommendations prepared during the previous administration to increase American support in Vietnam, military and economic, was confirmed in April. In May the President sent Vice-President Johnson on a tour of the Far East to reassure the Allies in Asia. Johnson felt it necessary to hail President Diem publicly as the Sir Winston Churchill of Southeast Asia. He recommended a major effort to help South Vietnam and the other countries of Southeast Asia to defend themselves, but at the same time urged social and economic reform. The situation, however, grew worse rather than better. In October, Kennedy sent out General Maxwell Taylor, accompanied by Walt Rostow, McGeorge Bundy's deputy on the White House staff, and various advisers. Hilsman and others have stressed the failure of Dean Rusk to make sure that the State Department was adequately represented. From now on the influence of the military in Vietnam was supreme. For this, as for many other errors of omission or commission, the ultimate responsibility must fall on the President.

If the President took definite action at this time it was of a negative character. The Taylor Report envisaged, among other steps, the introduction into Vietnam of over 10,000 regular American ground troops and accepted the possibility that as many as six full divisions might eventually be required. The President, while approving the increase of military and economic aid and the pressure for social reforms, did not approve the commitment of American ground troops. But he did not meet the proposal with a direct 'No'. He merely let the decision slide. At the same time he ordered the preparatory steps for introducing troops if they should come to be needed.

The search went on for a strategic concept. Hilsman's war-time experience of guerrilla operations led to the President's calling on him for suggestions. Hilsman was convinced that large scale conventional military operations were not effective against guerrillas and the way to fight the guerrilla was to adopt the tactics of the guerrilla. At all times the support of the local population had to be secured. Some such doctrine was adopted in theory but in practice the military in Vietnam, and indeed the top brass at home, never gave effect to it wholeheartedly.

As 1962 wore on, David Halberstam and other leading journalists on the spot insisted that the war could never be won with President Diem and his brother-in-law Nhu in charge, and that the position was steadily deteriorating. Yet official optimism was maintained by the authorities in Vietnam. Hilsman cannot be held blameless for his own appreciations during this period. After a further visit to Vietnam at the request of the President at the beginning of 1963 he reported to the President, 'Our overall judgment in sum is that we are probably winning, but certainly more slowly than we had hoped.' In March he found himself at a conference in Honolulu where General Harkins, American Military Chief from Saigon, 'thought he could say that by Christmas it would be all over'. Secretary of Defence McNamara was elated and reminded Hilsman that it was only a year and a half 'since it had all looked so black'.

The summer brought traumatic and unexpected happenings. On 8 May Buddhist priests and their followers paraded in protest at government orders which forbade them to fly the British flag or to use the local radio station to broadcast a statement. Amidst a certain amount of confusion the armoured vehicles of the government opened fire, killing nine people and crushing some of the bodies under their wheels. From May to August the repression mounted and so did the protests. On 5 August came the second Buddhist suicide by burning. On 21 August Vietnamese military units attacked major pagodas in a number of cities. Religious statues and holy relics were desecrated. Many of the monks were wounded and some of them thought to be killed. In Washington a public statement from the American government denounced the assault on the pagodas as a direct violation by the Vietnamese government of assurances that it was pursuing a policy of reconciliation with the Buddhists. The statement marked a clear severance of relations between the United States and the Diem régime but in itself it solved no problems.

There began what Hilsman has called 'the agonies of decision'. But 'agonies of indecision' would be a better description. Kennedy's advisers could not make up their minds what on earth to do. Nor could he. The end came in a fashion that shocked even the American leaders who had been anxious to see the end of the Diem régime and whose point of view was not unknown to the South Vietnamese generals. A military coup chased Diem and Nhu from power, a full scale attack being launched on the palace. The fleeing leaders were trapped in a small Catholic church, taken to headquarters in an armoured personnel carrier and shot and killed on the journey.

There is no excusing, though it is not difficult to explain, the paralysis of American policy during the months of September and October 1963. Its origins went further back. The dilemma for the

Americans was how to pressurize Diem and Nhu into a reform programme without damaging the war effort. Hardly two American
politicians, soldiers or officials could agree on how this should be
done and no way of doing it was discovered.

Once again a fact-finding mission had been adopted as a substitute for immediate action when General Krulak and Joseph
Mendenhall of the State Department returned from Vietnam. They
had disagreed so totally as to how things were going that President
Kennedy could only look quizzically from one to the other. 'You
did visit the same country, didn't you?' McNamara had conducted
yet one more whirlwind tour of Vietnam. At last he began to doubt
some of his own statistics. But the report that he submitted,
written by himself and General Taylor, maintained even at this
hour that the shooting war was making great and continuing progress. They gave it as their considered judgment that the major
part of the United States military task could be completed by the
end of 1965. An agreed statement was issued by the government. It
accepted the military assessment. In return the military accepted
the need for intensive pressures on Diem and his brother-in-law to
bring about the essential changes.

But it was all too late if it was ever a viable policy. As we have
seen the South Vietnamese generals took the law into their own
hands. Diem and Nhu were murdered; so three weeks later was
President Kennedy. With the disappearance of Diem and Nhu the
real facts about the military situation began to emerge. They confirmed the worst fears of the American pessimists.

One can feel strong sympathy for a President misled as consistently as was Kennedy by his advisers, or most of them, at home and
in Vietnam. It remains unclear as to whether he ever had a policy
for Vietnam of his own. If so he was never at much pains to impose
it. The final verdict must be that right up to the end he underestimated the significance of the problem and never brought to
bear on it his marvellous energy or fine intelligence.

15

Struck down at noon-day

The assassination

John Kennedy's assassination was an immense tragedy for himself, for his family, for the multitudes of those who loved him and, on the assessment of him given here, for humanity at large. But for many, perhaps for most people, the terrible incident will always contain a large element of mystery.

In 1967, Pierre Salinger, devoted Press Attaché to the President, wrote an Introduction to *The Truth about the Assassination*, by Charles Roberts, a White House Correspondent who rode in the President's motorcade that day in Dallas. Salinger's introduction to a book which broadly endorses the conclusions of the official inquiry contains this passage: 'Neither this book, nor any book like it, will ever still the doubts about the assassination of John F. Kennedy.' The fact asserted seems incontestable. Even more so than in the case of Lincoln, though even there suspicions have not yet disappeared. There is never likely to be general agreement that the full truth has emerged about Dallas.

The official inquiry was carried out under Chief Justice Warren. Mr Gerald – now President – Ford was among its distinguished members. It heard 552 witnesses and received more than 3,000 reports from Law Enforcement Agencies which had conducted 26,000 interviews. The evidence filled twenty-six volumes.

The Commission concluded that the assassination was the unaided work of a single gunman, Lee Oswald, himself murdered two days later when in police custody by a Dallas night club owner, Jack Ruby. It was concluded further that Ruby was himself, like

Oswald, acting entirely on his own. In this they are supported by the author of the most comprehensive work on the subject, William Manchester; and by much well-informed opinion. Salinger, writing in 1967, asserts that 'the damage that has been caused and the hatred that has been spawned by the muckrakers of the Kennedy assassination deserves some careful answer'. Up till then he acknowledged 'they have pretty much had the field to themselves'. Since then the argument has continued and shows no sign of abating.

The critics of the Warren Commission have given us their own versions in about two dozen books on the estimate of Louis Heren, a dispassionate and well-informed commentator. Novels, feature films and countless television programmes have followed. A biography of President Kennedy should be a picture and assessment of his personality and performance. It should not stand or fall by its assassination theory. Whatever the identity and motivation of the assassin, it does not affect our view of the President. Yet the author should at least indicate his present suppositions as to what actually happened and what lay behind.

To me it still seems quite likely that the President was shot at and killed by only one man, Lee Oswald. Whether the latter fired two or three shots does not seem important. All attempts to overturn this part of the official findings have run into trouble. For example what was said to be the figure of a rifleman on a grassy knoll in front of the President's car was demonstrated to be the shadow of a tree. A film seemed to suggest that Kennedy was shot at least once from the front. Some experts are now satisfied that a head wound of this kind would almost instantly move the head back in the direction from which the bullet came, in other words to the rear. Mr Harold Weisberg continues to reject what may now be called the orthodox account of the actual happenings. Having written nine books on this one subject he is entitled to respect, but in his last book *Post Mortem* he indicates that his main interest is 'the story of how the crime was left unsolved by those whose responsibility it was to develop all the relevant facts and reach conclusions'. He himself, he admitted, 'makes no pretence of attempting to solve the crime' so he does not help us as much as one could wish. On the other hand a still more recent book, *November 22* by Michael Eddowes, based on eleven years of research, is emphatically orthodox about the actual shooting (in a moment we shall come to his wider theory). 'The President was mortally wounded by two bullets fired from behind. Three single bullets had been fired in about seven seconds by a young man' passing under the name of Lee Harvey Oswald. Up to this point the Warren Commission has not been disposed of. But there is no certainty yet.

Still less must one put out of one's head any so-called conspiracy theory, or accept the unqualified verdict that Oswald, and later Ruby, were assassins acting entirely on their own.

Roberts quotes a member of the Secret Service as saying: 'If this is a conspiracy, it's really a big one. It's got to include those doctors at Parkland, all those doctors at Bethesda, the entire Warren Commission, the Warren Commission staff, the Justice Department and finally the Attorney-General (Robert F. Kennedy), or it just won't work.' But that is trying to prove too much. One could imagine much less extravagant types of instigation of, or assistance to, the assassin.

At various times the real culprits, the men behind the assassination, have been allegedly discovered in all sorts of directions. The ultimate blame has been fastened on Americans supposedly hostile to Kennedy including the authorities in Dallas and the CIA; on South Vietnamese leaders in revenge for the murder of Diem and his brother-in-law; on Soviet Communists in pursuit of world power; on Castro as a counter-blow to the supposed attempts of the Kennedy brothers to liquidate him. This last hypothesis seems later to have been held by President Johnson. Indeed he said this very thing to a friend of mine. Against this there are some grounds for thinking that if Kennedy had lived he and Castro might have begun to move towards an understanding. If this is so the anti-Castro Cubans would be the more likely assassins. (For the conclusions of Mr Dawney see Acknowledgements.)

Nothing that could be called serious evidence has been produced to substantiate any of these hypothesis. But it is at least possible that one of them in fact might contain the truth without hard evidence emerging. Those who continue to cling to a conspiracy theory of some kind can fairly point out that, as soon as the assassination occurred, those closest to Kennedy and Johnson, and for that matter Johnson himself, assumed that a concerted plan lay behind the shooting. Whether its authors were Communists or right wing men of Dallas was an open question. The need to get out of Dallas without a moment's delay lest worse befall was recognised as imperative.

If the lone gunman verdict is the final truth, it was the unexpected truth and, of course, it has also turned out to be the convenient truth. Any uncovering of guilty participation, either by a foreign power or by American elements, might well have led to an uncontrollable reaction in American public opinion. Nevertheless, the fact must be repeated – no coercive evidence has come to light up to the present which would support a conspiracy theory.

If the assassination of the President was the more horrifying of two murders (supposing that one murder can be more horrifying than another), that of Oswald performed in full view of television and in front of seventy policemen will always seem the more astounding. Physically there was nothing incomprehensible about the picking off of the President from a slow moving car by a trained marksman about ninety yards away. But how on earth a well-known, if far from reputable, citizen like Ruby could walk into a police basement and shoot a prisoner in front of all those policemen – if one did not know that this happened, one would not believe it possible. Except on one assumption. It could of course be that the Dallas police welcomed and connived at the extraordinary incursion. The official line was not to blame the Dallas police force for more than negligence. One must retain one's own suspicion of darker motivations.

But here the psychological hypotheses become confused and hard to follow out consistently. Dallas, or the majority of its citizens, hated Kennedy in spite of the warm demonstration by the minority in his favour. Dallas had a grim record of murderous conduct. Ninety-eight murders had already been committed there that year. It is reasonable to surmise that Kennedy would not have been murdered in any other American city at that time; though Robert Kennedy and Martin Luther King were to be murdered elsewhere. One can reasonably think of Oswald responding to the hate spirit of Dallas, even though he was so much an outsider in that city.

Once we conclude that Ruby obtained special facilities for his murder of Oswald, it is natural to believe that important elements in Dallas were happy to see Oswald disappear. But if they hated Kennedy so much, why were they so reluctant to protect his assassin?

An answer could lie, I suppose, in their conviction that he had brought disgrace on the town, even though their hostility to the President had been and remained so formidable. Alternatively and more obviously, those behind Ruby may have had some special reason for wanting Oswald out of the way before he began 'spilling the beans' about their own involvement. But again it may all have been emotional and unpremeditated.

Mr Michael Eddowes, as the most up-to-date investigator at the time of writing and certainly a very ingenious one, deserves a few words on his own. He concludes that the assassin was a Russian agent masquerading as Lee Oswald, that Ruby was privy to the plot and that Ruby liquidated Oswald to prevent the truth emerging at the trial of the latter. Louis Heren reviewing this book in *The Times* points out a glaring fault. Eddowes would have us believe that the Chinese were joined to the Russians in a plan to assassinate Kennedy en route to the conquest of the world. But by 1963 the idea of Sino-Russian collaboration of this kind was quite inconceivable.

I myself feel, however, that Mr Eddowes' argument does not depend on the myth of Chinese participation. One must read his book to form a fair opinion. Personally, I cannot swallow the hypothesis of a pseudo-Lee Oswald deceiving his family for a year and a half after returning to America. In the narrative that follows I shall assume therefore that we are dealing with the real Lee Oswald and not an imposter. This is not to deny that Eddowes makes many telling points against the Warren Commission. Even Louis Heren who does not like this book, or another recent one, *They Killed the President* by Robert Sam Anson, considers that the time has come when another full scale inquiry should be held. Otherwise the suspicions and ever more far-fetched explanations will rumble on for ever.

But suppose at the end of a further inquiry new and unpleasant truths emerged and the finger of accusation was left pointing at Russia or Cuba or others nearer home? Would not the price paid for 'arriving at the truth' be too high? On balance I cannot think so.

Let us turn to a narrative of the public facts about which there is relatively little argument. Even a critic like David Halberstam concedes, and he makes few concessions, that 'the months of September and October were very good ones for John Kennedy, rich in themselves, full of promise for the future. Above all the beginning, perhaps just the beginning of an end to a particularly rigid era of the Cold War'. Halberstam's primary concern, of course, is with Vietnam and he is soon qualifying the tribute just paid with a grim reminder about the situation in Southeast Asia. 'Vietnam,' he says, 'which he (Kennedy) had conceived of as part of the price of making American power and determination credible to the Communists, was coming apart even as the US–Soviet balance seemed to be stabilizing.' That is as maybe. It was not in many people's minds.

On 13 November Kennedy had summoned a conference of his chief strategic advisers to discuss the coming campaign for the Presidency. They agreed that prospects for a landslide victory against Goldwater were encouraging. The economy was flourishing, its rate of growth was higher than that of either Russia or Europe, the new Saturn rocket to be launched in the following month would at last put the United States ahead of the Soviet Union in the manned spacecraft race. The world looked very good to John Kennedy and to the ever larger numbers who shared his ideals. And so on 21 November he set off for Dallas.

'Most Americans', we are told by Manchester in *The Glory and the Dream*, 'didn't even know that the President was in Texas. His visit was only of local interest there; he had come down to make peace between two feuding delegates, Senator Ralph Yarborough, the liberal, and Governor John B. Connally, Jr, the deviate.' O'Donnell rejects this reason for his visit. 'He was thinking', he says, 'of a bigger thing – his own votes.' Texas and Florida were the two States where President Kennedy was planning to make his strongest effort in the 1964 campaign and, according to O'Donnell, he was in high spirits. 'I feel great,' he said, 'my back feels better than it's felt in years.' A new treatment of calisthenics had strengthened his back muscles and he was able to play golf again for the first time since he had crippled himself planting a ceremonial tree at Ottawa in the spring of 1961. Along with his good health, 'Dave and I', writes O'Donnell, 'never saw him in a happier mood'.

Salinger's report, based on an interview the day before the President set off, is different. 'The President,' he writes, 'looking tired, was sitting behind his desk signing letters, his glasses perched precariously on his nose. He wore these glasses in the privacy of his office but carefully tucked them into his pocket when appearing in public.' (A pardonable foible perhaps in the case of such a young-looking President.) 'I wish I weren't going to Texas', he said. Salinger insists that Kennedy did not say this with any sense of uneasiness about the trip or fear for his life. 'He said it with an air of fatigue.' It is possible that the President was readier to confess to human frailty in front of the plump, easy-going Salinger than of the super-fit O'Donnell, the old Harvard football captain. Or it may be that fatigue vanished once the action had started. In the case of anyone less intrepid than Kennedy one could understand a certain shrinking.

Dallas was a city of hatred and violence and most reactionary. It was only four weeks since Adlai Stevenson had gone to Dallas for a meeting on United Nations Day. The day that Stevenson spoke, handbills with photographs of the President of the United States were scattered round Dallas with the message: 'Wanted for treason. This man is wanted for treasonous activities against the United States.' Stevenson was booed and heckled and as he left the meeting jostled and spat on. A woman crashed a sign down on his head. Stevenson, wiping his face with his handkerchief, said coldly, 'Are these human beings or are these animals?' Stevenson himself and those who knew Dallas well were anxious to persuade Kennedy not to go, though Schlesinger seems to have held up Stevenson's warning and Stevenson later withdrew it. But as Kenneth O'Donnell said later, 'The President could not possibly go to Texas and avoid Dallas.' Kennedy would be the last of all Presidents to avoid Dallas after the roughing up of Stevenson.

He had, however, one consolation which he had not expected: his wife had decided to come with him. In the summer of that year they had suffered the appalling loss of an infant son, Patrick Bouvier Kennedy, forty hours after birth. Both father and mother were utterly stricken; she had wanted to stay with him and the children. Curiously, as it may now seem, he had persuaded her to try to forget her wretchedness in a cruise in a Greek millionaire's yacht. Curious idea or not, it worked splendidly. She returned in the middle of October in far better spirits than she or anyone had expected. She said to her husband, 'I'll campaign with you anywhere you want'. And when he asked her whether that included 'the expedition with Lyndon' she opened her engagement book and wrote 'Texas' against 21, 22 and 23 November. It was the first time she had campaigned with him since he became President. He was visibly excited, anxious lest she might not enjoy it and determined that she should look her best.

Dallas was not his first port of call in Texas. In San Antonio he was greeted with high enthusiasm. In Houston the crowds were still larger and more enthusiastic, though the breach between Governor Connally and Senator Yarborough showed no signs of being healed. On to Fort Worth for a dinner and the night. Before retiring to bed Jacqueline Kennedy joined her husband. 'You were great today', he said, as indeed she had been. And so had he, but by this time that was expected.

Next Morning the *Dallas Morning News* made unpleasant reading. It ran a full page advertisement headed 'WELCOME MR [*sic*] KENNEDY TO DALLAS'. It posed a whole series of questions designed to suggest that the President was systematically pro-Communist, if not a traitor. Kennedy pushed the paper aside with disgust. He asked, 'How can people write such things?' with unusual bitterness. He spoke in friendly fashion to a crowd in front of the Texas Hotel, then he chatted with Jacqueline and Kenneth O'Donnell about the limited power of the Secret Service to protect a President. If somebody really wanted to kill the President perched on a high building with a telescopic rifle there was nothing anybody could do to defend a President's life. O'Donnell said afterwards that Kennedy regarded assassination as an occupational risk of his job, 'It didn't disturb him at all'. On the short trip to Dallas the President discussed fanatical hatreds in a spirit of detachment. He detested fanaticism but he laid the chief blame on those who stirred it up rather than its rank and file exponents.

Now before he begins his final drive through Dallas, we must turn to the humble fanatic, if he was that, or at least the practitioner of hatred who was to end the President's life in the immediate future, Lee Oswald. Whether he acted alone or in concert with, or under the influence of others, the main facts of Lee Oswald's life are fairly well known after microscopic inquiry. His mother, Margaret Oswald, had had three husbands. One had died, two had left her, in the last case after she had physically assaulted him. Her younger son Lee was of more than average ability, with an IQ of 118; but he has been described under such labels as tense, withdrawn, maladjusted. A school psychiatrist concluded that his withdrawal was a form of protest against neglect by his mother.

Entering the Marines he qualified as a sharp shooter with the M1 rifle. This was and remained his only skill and a disastrous one it was to prove. In 1959 he had appeared in Moscow and applied to renounce his American citizenship. But by 1962 he informed the American Consulate that he had seen the light; he returned to Texas with a 'lynx-eyed' Russian wife, Marina, and a small girl. He was accustomed to describe himself as a Marxist though his knowledge of Marx has been questioned. It was not this factor, but a general inadequacy, which seemed to prevent him getting or keeping jobs. He tried to migrate to Cuba but was refused a visa.

Manchester describes him with some plausibility as the most rejected man of his time. If so we can regard him as the total antithesis to John Kennedy, the most accepted. Oswald's rejection extended to his home. After a good many comings and goings his wife had gone to live with a dominant Quaker woman called Ruth Paine. Oswald only paid visits on sufferance. His wife Marina concealed astonishingly from Ruth Paine that a brown-green blanket roll in the Paine garage contained Lee Oswald's rifle. *A fortiori* she concealed the fact that earlier in the year Oswald had tried to assassinate General Walker, the reactionary Dallas leader. In other words he had what can only be called 'assassination leanings'.

It is asserted with some show of proof that Oswald had suffered from a mental illness of paranoia, or in the colloquial phrase, persecution mania, since childhood. There seems no doubt that when he visited his wife in Ruth Paine's house on the evening of 21 November, he encountered what seemed a final rejection. On the same day he appears to have learnt that the President would be passing under his windows the next morning.

The above gives the psychological explanation of Oswald's motives. Those who prefer an ideological interpretation will be interested in a quotation from a memorandum to the Warren Commission sent in April 1964 by Edgar Hoover, Head of the FBI. Regarding Oswald he wrote that after he had returned to America

he had subscribed to 'The Worker', had distributed pamphlets for the Fair Play for Cuba Committee and had admitted publicly that he was a Marxist. He had been in contact with the Soviet Embassy in Washington, DC; and it was reported, but not confirmed, that he had been in contact with the Soviet Embassy in Mexico. The reason indicated for his contacts with the Soviet Embassies was to obtain visas to re-enter the Soviet Union.

Hoover concluded that there was no reason at this point to regard him as a 'threat to the personal safety of the President'. That was how it seemed to the head of the FBI at the time. Whatever the strange events that were occurring in Oswald's mind there was no doubt about the steps which he took in the external world. He collected his rifle from its place of hiding and when he set off in the morning for Dallas his purpose must have been formed.

The flight from Fort Worth to the Dallas airport was only about thirteen minutes in the air, but the President made good progress with one of his purposes; within a few minutes Governor Connally was agreeing to invite Senator Yarborough to the reception and to put him at the head table at the dinner. 'How could anybody say No! to that man?', said Connally.

'So we landed in Dallas', says O'Donnell, 'with everybody on the 'plane in love with each other and the sun shining brightly.' The President peered out of the window at the gathering excited crowd and remarked to O'Donnell, 'this trip is turning out to be terrific. Here we are in Dallas, and it looks like everything in Texas is going to be fine for us'. They reached the airfield shortly after half past eleven, Dallas time. Certainly the liberal minority in Dallas, if that is what they were, made a brave showing.

The President and Mrs Kennedy walked about fifty yards smiling and touching fingers. 'How do you like campaigning?', Chuck Roberts of *Newsweek* asked her. 'It's wonderful', she replied. To more experienced eyes the city remained on edge. Gonzales, a local representative, commented, 'I sure wish somebody had invented a spit-proof mask . . . and I forgot my bullet-proof vest'. The President lingered for another five minutes. Ronnie Dugger, Editor of the *Texas Observer*, wrote in his notebook: 'Kennedy is showing he is not afraid.' At 11.55 am the cavalcade moved off, the Presidential car following the lead car and three motor cycles. The six passengers were in their usual places. Agent Kellerman beside Greer the driver, Governor Connally and Mrs Connally in the 'jump' seats, the Governor on the right, the Kennedys in the rear. The next car was full of agents; the Vice-President, Lyndon Johnson, was sitting in the left rear of the fourth car.

The reception was generally reassuring. The people on the outskirts, Kenneth O'Donnell said later, were not unfriendly nor terribly enthusiastic. 'They waved but were reserved, I thought.'

As they drove on, the roar of goodwill swelled, rising and

rising. Mrs Kennedy heard the President saying 'Thank you! Thank you! Thank you!' They couldn't hear him. Why did he bother?

But he had been brought up to be gracious.

As they moved out of Main Street, Mrs Connally turned round delightedly to Kennedy. 'You can't say Dallas doesn't love you, Mr President.' Or on one account, 'You can't say that the people of Dallas haven't given you a nice welcome'.

Kennedy smiled and answered 'No you can't'. Now they were passing into Elm Street where the crowds had thinned out. Nellie Connally pointed to the underpass ahead and said to Jackie, 'It's just beyond that.' Jackie thought how pleasant the cool tunnel would be. They drew near the Texas School Book Repository.

About a quarter of an hour earlier (on Manchester's account rejected by others), a young man named Arnold Rowland had seen a figure, in fact Lee Oswald, silhouetted in a window of that building holding what appeared to be a high-powered rifle across his body at port arms, like a Marine on a rifle range. He assumed that the figure must be protecting the President and said to his wife, 'Do you want to see a Secret Service Agent?' 'Where?', she asked. 'In that building there', he said, pointing. Shortly afterwards Robert Edwards and Ronald Fischer of the County Auditor's Office also noticed Oswald but his weapon was below their line of sight. They were struck by something peculiar in his stance and expression. He never moved, he didn't even blink his eyes. He was just gazing like a statue. Finally, Howard Brennan was seated on a three and a half foot high white cement wall forty yards beneath Oswald. He looked upwards and saw the pinched face of Lee Oswald. He also wondered why the young man was standing stock still.

There was what Manchester has called 'a sudden, sharp, shattering sound', whether produced by one shot or two is still disputed. Not all who heard it recognized it as gunfire.

It is just conceivable that if evasive action had been immediately taken a further shot could have been avoided. But for five seconds Kellerman, the agent, and Greer, the driver, were motionless. The President was wounded but not fatally. A bullet had entered the back of his neck, bruised his right lung, ripped his windpipe and exited at his throat; continuing its flight it seriously wounded Governor Connally. Roy Kellerman thought that he heard the

President call out 'My God, I'm hit'. Now it was too late for evasive action to save the day.

Howard Brennan, already mentioned, saw Oswald take deliberate aim for his final shot. His target was eighty-eight yards away which for an expert marksman was all too easy. He squeezed the trigger. Jacqueline Kennedy leant towards the President; his face, we are told was quizzical. In a gesture of infinite grace he raised his right hand as though to brush back his chestnut hair. But in Manchester's words, 'the motion faltered, the hand fell back limply. He had been reaching for the top of his head, but it wasn't there any more'.

Jacqueline Kennedy saw a piece of his skull detach itself. In a moment there was nothing but blood spattering her and everyone. Jackie embraced her stricken husband, cried out towards the sidewalk. 'My God, what are they doing? My God, they've killed Jack. They've killed my husband! Jack! Jack!'

The President's car was driven at reckless speed to the Parkland Memorial Hospital, the drive taking perhaps four minutes. By the time they arrived it was clear that the President was dead.

Manchester devotes more than two-thirds of his massive work on the assassination to the period following the murder. In a life story of the President there is no need to follow that pattern. The events which followed immediately, though they give rise to no little controversy, are more a matter for the biographer of Johnson than of Kennedy. The sublime refusal of Jackie Kennedy to leave her husband's body made an ineradicable impression. Otherwise it is inevitably on Johnson, the new President, that the spotlight falls.

Manchester can reasonably be criticized for being less than fair to Lyndon Johnson in connection with these terrible hours. Johnson was in a position of exceptional difficulty. On the one hand it was his imperative duty to reassure America and the world at large that there was no break in continuity and that a strong man had taken charge. On the other hand, to those who had loved Kennedy, it seemed almost sacrilegious that a successor should step too promptly into his shoes. In my view the balance actually struck by President Johnson could not have been improved upon.

Johnson and his aides were desperately anxious to escape without a moment's delay from the hate city of Dallas. Who knew where the next blow would fall? The idea of a lone gangster had occurred at that point to no one. It might be a Communist or a right wing conspiracy. In either case, they must get away as soon as possible.

In this matter there was no difference between them and those closest to the dead President, Kenneth O'Donnell and Larry O'Brien. There was an extraordinary scene at the hospital when the coroner, Dr Rose, attempted to prevent the body being removed until an autopsy had been performed. O'Donnell and O'Brien heard a Justice of the Peace say, 'It's just another homicide case as far as I am concerned'. The effect on O'Donnell was instantaneous. Thrusting his head forward until their noses grazed, he said: 'We're leaving.' A policeman tried to interfere. Jerking his head, O'Donnell rasped out, 'Get the hell over. We're getting out of here. We don't give a damn what these lawyers say.' Agent Kellerman snapped, 'Wheel it out.' It became 'us against them' and 'we' (that is the Kennedy men) prevailed.

But that was not the end of conflicts and misunderstanding. Johnson became convinced, not unreasonably it would now seem, that he should take the Presidential oath *before* the aircraft left for Washington. He honestly believed after a telephone conversation with Robert Kennedy, the Attorney-General, that the latter held the same opinion. He quoted him to that effect in arguing against O'Donnell, who chafed at the delay while a Judge was being brought to the aeroplane. That and other misunderstandings loomed large at the time.

Johnson and his wife showed tender sympathy towards Jackie Kennedy in the unbelievable situation. Through no fault of hers or theirs, and for reasons easily understood, the relations between the Johnson men and the Kennedy men on the flight back were distressing. 'The impression', says O'Donnell, 'that there was a wall of coldness between us and Johnson on the plane rose simply from the fact that we remained during the flight with Jackie, beside the casket.'

Johnson came back once to talk to them and said that he wanted O'Donnell and O'Brien to stay with him at the White House. 'I need you now,' he said, 'more than President Kennedy needed you.' Later one of his advisers asked them to join the President for a talk about arranging a Congressional leadership meeting. O'Donnell explained that they did not want to leave Jackie. The adviser, Bill Moyers, said agreeably, 'We understand perfectly'. But the seeds of subsequent resentment were being sown.

The talk with Jackie was full of warmly sentimental reminiscences. Jackie remembered how much Jack had loved the singing of Luigi Vena, a tenor from Boston at their wedding in Newport, and she decided then and there that Vena would sing Schubert's *Ave Maria* and Bizet's *Agnus Dei* at the President's funeral Mass, as he did. Of course, she added, their good friend Cardinal Cushing, who married them, would say the low requiem Mass, 'which Jack liked better than the solemn high ritual'.

The flight took less than two and a half hours. The Kennedy party followed the coffin to Bethesda; the autopsy continued through most of the night. It was 4.34 am when the casket, now covered by an American flag, was carried into the White House and placed upon the catafalque in the East Room. Mrs Kennedy knelt beside it and buried her face in the flag's field of stars.

On Monday, 25 November, the coffin was taken to St Matthew's Cathedral for a funeral Mass and thence to Arlington, the National Cemetery. Delegations from ninety-two nations had come to participate in the funeral. Afterwards they attended two receptions, one at the State Department and another, much smaller, at the White House where Mrs Kennedy received them.

Throughout these days she was love and courage incarnate. Never had the death of a national leader evoked quite such worldwide lamentation. The manner of his death and his youthfulness no doubt contributed. When he died Roosevelt was half as old again and in failing health. Churchill was twice his age when he died and long retired. Whatever special factors may have been at work the sense of loss in Kennedy's case was profound and universal. In Ireland it was said, 'Ah! they cried the rain down that night'. David Bruce, wisest and most experienced of diplomats, reported from London: 'Great Britain has never before mourned a foreigner as it has President Kennedy.' In West Berlin people lighted candles in darkened windows. In Poland and Yugoslavia the grief was just as intense. In Moscow Khrushchev was the first to sign the book and Soviet Television relayed the funeral including the service in the church. Latin America, in Schlesinger's phrase, 'was devastated'. Streets, schools, housing projects were named after him, shrines were set up in his memory. Castro was not undignified. 'This', he said, 'is bad news.' In a few moments he stood up and said: 'Everything is changed. I'll tell you one thing. At least Kennedy was an enemy to whom we had become accustomed.'

It is impossible to summarize the endless expressions of heartfelt distress and admiration in the United States. One must at least mention that Cape Canaveral was rechristened Cape Kennedy. Idlewild International Airport was renamed. The Treasury began minting fifty million Kennedy half dollars, which were soon being hoarded as souvenirs. In every part of the country committees and councils were altering local maps to pay honour to his name. The United Kingdom set aside three acres of the meadow at Runnymede where Magna Carta was signed as a Kennedy shrine. In May 1965, Queen Elizabeth presided at the ceremony dedicating the tract to the President 'whom in death my people still mourn and whom in life they loved'.

I myself attended the ceremony as Leader of the House of Lords. Everyone present seemed to be united by their personal grief and their own private imaginings.

16
Fulfilment and promise

John Kennedy possessed a phenomenal power of appealing to his fellow humans. That, at least, should be plain from the foregoing. His charm – his charisma – call it what you will, operated naturally on old and young, on black and white, on Americans and foreigners. We have come across it first in his mother's recollections of his early years. We find it in his otherwise unsatisfactory school days; in his gay life in London, and at Harvard, though there he was a relatively unobtrusive figure. It was the same in the Navy; in his endless contacts, individual and collective, on his way to the Presidential summit. In the early days there were many references to his shyness, but that disappeared with the ever-increasing acclaim.

When he emerged in the full light of the international stage he had admittedly large advantages to help him carry his immense responsibilities. He was the leader of the most powerful country in the world. His youth, his huge success, his lovely wife, by that time conferred on him a special glamour. But long before that the magical quality had been steadily emerging.

The walls of Jericho did not fall down in front of him. In the Presidential election he scraped in by a minimal margin. There came a moment when the world held its breath while he and Khrushchev stood 'eyeball to eyeball'. But any dispassionate consideration of Kennedy must begin with his amazing power of arousing devotion and (frequently though not invariably) of reducing antagonism. Benjamin Bradlee, who knew one side of him at least so intimately, described him as 'graceful, gay, funny, witty, teasing and teasable, forgiving, hungry, incapable of being corny, restless, interesting, interested, exuberant, blunt, profane, and loving . . . all of those and more'. Many others have said the same or the equivalent.

Bradlee could not bear Nixon. No one did more than Bradlee, by now Editor of the *Washington Post*, to destroy him through the Watergate exposure. He harped on Nixon's alleged lack of style compared with Kennedy and Kennedy himself referred to Nixon's 'want of class'. But Theodore White insists convincingly that Nixon actually *liked* Kennedy. There is no reason to doubt the sincerity of what he wrote to Jacqueline after the assassination:

Dear Jackie,
    In this tragic hour Pat and I want you to know that our thoughts and prayers are with you.
While the hand of fate made Jack and me political opponents I always cherished the fact that we were personal friends from the time we came to the Congress together in 1947. That friendship evidenced itself in many ways including the invitation we received to attend your wedding.
   . . .
If in the days ahead we could be helpful in any way we shall be honored to be at your command.

Sincerely,
Dick Nixon

John Kennedy was adored by many men and not a few women. His relations with the latter were always the subject of strong rumours and have lately been dragged into full daylight. I am bound to record my opinion that here was a serious defect in his character. One is aware that Mr Gladstone said that he had known eleven British Prime Ministers of whom seven had committed adultery. One does not admire them for that, but does not dismiss on that account alone their claims to greatness.

None of these relationships went deep. His marriage underwent many strains and became at one moment precarious, but not for this reason. Bradlee tells a significant story:

'You haven't got it Benjy', said Kennedy to him on one occasion. 'You're all looking to tag me with some girl, and none of you can do it, because it just isn't there.' 'Jackie', goes on Bradlee, 'just listened with a smile on her face. And that is the closest I ever came to hearing him discuss his reputation as what my father used to call "a fearful girler".'

It seems certain that Jack and Jacqueline came closer and closer together at the White House and at the time of his death were more in love than ever previously. He was an utterly devoted father to his daughter Caroline and his son John. Like Jackie he was heartbroken at the death of his infant son Patrick.

It is not easy but we must do our best to distinguish the personal magic of Jack Kennedy from the collective mystique of the family. Even without the supreme career of the President, even if he had died at sea or retired early from politics on health grounds, Joe Kennedy, Rose Kennedy and the children would have left a memorable imprint. The hypothesis becomes unreal; we cannot be sure how far Bobby and Teddy would have gone without their brother to pave the way for them. But Joe Kennedy senior made many enemies, as indeed did Bobby. The legend that Joe, the eldest brother, was in some all round sense superior to Jack is hard to believe. Teddy has not yet approached the President's standard. The women, including the marvellous mother, do not enter the comparison. One seeks to isolate a factor in Jack that was not simply a family characteristic, though he indubitably shared with them a number of important qualities, including good looks, dynamic energy and the will to win.

He shared also, of course, their Irish origins. We have quoted earlier from a poem written by Jackie soon after their marriage, which contained the line:

> He would call New England his place and his creed
> But part he was of an alien breed
> Of a breed that had laughed on Irish hills
> And heard the voices in Irish rills.

Ten years later the Irish strain figured even more potently. Ben Bradlee gives us a poignant picture of Jackie after the assassination. 'She entered the hospital suite on the arms of the Irish Mafia in the form of Larry O'Brien and Kenny O'Donnell, men she had never really understood or appreciated, but to whom she turned and clung now, strong men from the Irish political side of the dichotomous Kennedy whom Jackie had never met on equal terms but who now seemed to comfort her more than any of the rest of us.'

Certainly when I met Kennedy for the first and only time at

President de Valera's reception a few months before he died, I felt with absolute assurance that he had indeed come home. The fact of his Irishness loomed larger and larger and would have loomed larger still.

The English influences on him and his pro-British sentiment are harder to delineate. If his father had never been Ambassador in London, he would not have developed his English friendships. But in fact those English friendships while not numerous were enduring. When he left Ireland in June 1963 he was at heart more Irish than ever. I saw as much with my own eyes. But his next appointment was a visit to his sister's grave at Chatsworth; after that he stayed with Harold Macmillan at his country house in Sussex. The change from County Wexford was about as complete as could be.

Macmillan, with expert sagacity, had established for himself the status of a highly entertaining uncle, with additional merit as a better ally than any other available. David Ormsby Gore, now Lord Harlech, whose mother's sister was Macmillan's sister-in-law, was one of the President's oldest and remained one of his closest friends. The President played no small part in his appointment to Washington in succession to an outstanding professional in Harold Caccia. Ormsby Gore enjoyed an intimacy with Jack Kennedy never approached by an Ambassador in Anglo-American history on either side of the Atlantic.

No one can say what all this amounted to in terms of American policy. Kennedy obviously felt that Macmillan and *a fortiori* Harlech were capable of looking at his problems from his own point of view as well as theirs. On that account he valued their advice all the more highly. We can be sure that British interests and British ideas would receive a high priority. Much that passed between Kennedy and Harlech will not be known, at any rate until Lord Harlech writes his memoirs.

We can reasonably conclude with Louis Heren, for example, that Kennedy's special relationship with British leaders prolonged for another two or three years the special relationship between the United States and the United Kingdom. The latter relationship did not long survive his death.

Jack, we are told, was the only member of the family who was fond of reading. The reference is no doubt to the reading of books. All who make any headway in public life are compelled to read newspapers and documents continuously. Jack, it seems, was the only one who had literary tastes. It is hard to be sure how far this went with him. When he was 'a rather sickly boy' (his mother's phrase) he read many romantic stories. Later we hear of a few of his favourite books: Churchill's *Marlborough* among them. Above all David Cecil's *Melbourne* and John Buchan's autobiography (Ian Fleming in lighter moments).

Schlesinger and Sorensen, the former a first-class historian, the latter well-informed and studious, seem to strain the evidence to maximize the width and depth of his culture. It is true that literary and historical allusions are worked into some of his speeches, no doubt with the help of Sorensen and other assistants. But in the records of his conversation there is hardly an indication of anything he is reading at the time. In so far as he did read at all widely it was in biography and political history which are, after all, a small part of a civilized education. David Harlech mentions, however, that he never lost his interest in poetry; he became well-versed in political oratory, Edmund Burke being a particular favourite.

We are told that we must admire his wit and humour. His humour yes. But about his wit one is more doubtful. Humour depends on a God-given attitude, a special angle of comprehension; wit on verbal felicity. Though a man's wit can often be judged by the wit he appreciates in others. Bradlee and his wife went to supper with the Kennedys within a few hours of his being elected President. Bradlee's wife and Jackie Kennedy were both *enceinte*. We have recorded earlier Kennedy's greeting: 'Okay girls, you can take out the pillows now. We won.' The wit involved was not very distinguished, but the humorous approach to life comes through, and that indeed was an enviable asset. His awareness of the contrasts between his own aspirations and achievements, the contrasts also between his standpoint and that of the 'other fellow' kept his humour constant and genuine. All who knew him well agree that he was extremely amusing, and unselfishly so.

His wit was no doubt better than the wit of nine politicians out of ten, but when one reads through the anthology called *The Wit of President Kennedy* one cannot regard its compilation as a service to his memory.

He would never have wished to compete with Mark Twain or Oscar Wilde; he did not possess the image-making power of Churchill or the gnomic intuitions of Lincoln. Whenever he had any kind of contact with Harold Macmillan, the British Prime Minister, a real wit in his day, he came away with an anecdote which pleased him enormously.

On one occasion they had been discussing Laos and their yacht pulled alongside a small flotilla of acorn shells from a local high school. 'Ah, what have we here?' Kennedy quoted Macmillan as saying, 'Looks like the Laotian navy.' Adequate for the purpose of the moment. We must assume that the more subtle pleasantries were not recorded.

One accepts absolutely his mother's conviction that he remained throughout a practising Catholic who continued up to and during his Presidency to say his prayers. Paul Fay gives a vivid picture of Kennedy's religious observances, including regular attendance at Confession. 'In general,' says Fay, 'Jack felt about his religion as many Catholics his age feel. Life was full and demanding and the need for religion generally seemed remote. But the basic faith acquired as a child in a Catholic family instilled in him a total allegiance to his faith that only real faith brings.'

What is striking and rather dismaying for Christian admirers is his apparent lack of interest in Catholic thinking and religious thinking in general. Fay assures us that Kennedy's faith did not keep him from questioning his Church on positions that seemed in conflict with the needs of society.

But there he seems to be claiming more than the facts justify. Bradlee recalls a conversation when everyone was against capital punishment except the President. 'I asked him about the Catholic precept against taking a life, including abortions, and he said that he saw no conflict. He said he was all for people solving their problems by abortions and he didn't seem to equate execution with the taking of life in the doctrinal sense.' Very likely he would not have maintained these positions if he had given the matter serious thought.

Apart from a 'mother's knee' Catholicism, his education had been secular. He found it all the easier to reassure an American public, still fearful of electing a Catholic President, just because his ideas were so uninfluenced by Catholic social ideology.

It was said of de Valera by his former chaplain, that he would have made an excellent Protestant. This of a man who was a daily communicant. Kennedy was no daily communicant or anything like it. He was, as mentioned above, a practising Catholic. But apart from his loyalty to the Catholic Church as an institution, it might be said that he was indistinguishable from a public-spirited Protestant. It was surely no coincidence that the first Catholic President of the United States was so well equipped by nature and nurture to share the attitude to religion of the average American.

One quality at least can be eulogized without a quibble. The sheer quickness and sensitivity, the sureness of touch with which he responded to and thereby influenced large crowds, small groups and individuals. The Woman's Editor of the *Irish Press* told me that when she visited Washington in 1963 she attended one of President Kennedy's press conferences but she was quite unable to 'get in' her question. She came away feeling very much ignored. When Kennedy held a press conference in Dublin she was on her own ground and she knew how to assert herself. 'President Kennedy', she began, 'when I was in Washington you wouldn't even *see me*.' 'Ah', he flashed back quicker than light, 'but I felt your presence.' Most politicians imagine that they can give answers of that kind at will. I have never met one who could.

Let me spell out the point. It was not just the speed and the verbal neatness but the immediate personal response to a total stranger that made sure she would never forget the encounter. And no doubt she was one of thousands. When we talk of his immediate response we are referring to a quality even more moral than mental, to an instinctive sympathy with all he met which was felt and returned and felt and returned again.

An old friend of his described him to me as a loner, but another old friend, David Harlech, who saw still more of him in his last years, does not care for that word. You could say of him as of any man of real distinction that he possessed an aura of reserve, an inner sanctuary which no one could penetrate, but he was immensely and joyously gregarious. He had only to enter a room to make everyone present feel happier and more alive, and himself to draw fresh life from the company.

It is one thing to charm, another to inspire. In Britain Anthony Eden did the first, Sir Winston Churchill (once the war came) did the second. Jack Kennedy did both. He was an immensely popular man who could not only please but move his audiences, large or little. He himself was no doubt fully aware of his rare attractiveness, as any sane man must have been. But what really concerned him, what indeed he craved for, was achievement. It was as a man who had achieved things that he longed to go down in history.

Some part of his secret must always elude us but at least we can credit him with a kind of vision, an ideal of something much greater than himself or any other individual, which stirred the modern world as it has not been stirred in peacetime.

But what was that vision? And how far did his deeds live up to it? Here again we are halted. Sorensen, in his arresting book *The Kennedy Legacy*, tries to give meaning to the concept named in the title. But even with the introduction of Bobby to supplement Jack, the legacy evaporates into the broadest generalities, which hardly any politician of any persuasion could fail to subscribe to. Certainly in England they would be equally agreeable to the Conservative, Liberal and Labour parties. It is a fact that the leaders of all those parties have admired Kennedy equally.

When all is said the word 'pragmatic' emerges as the residual label which could mean much or nothing. Yet in his lifetime Jack Kennedy showed an instinctive understanding of the world's problems, such evident concern for its peoples, that the peoples in question were for the most part enchanted to follow him in the search for solutions.

Take then the pragmatic creed, the test of verification by performance, a test which he accepted readily. How will he emerge in the long perspective of history? The achievement which cannot be denied him is that he was the first Catholic to become President of the United States and the youngest President. He was, beyond all argument, 'the hell of a candidate'. His performance as President was cut so tragically short that no amount of further research or subsequent happenings will ever produce an agreed assessment. He himself, says Salinger, was not at all satisfied with the record of his administration. He regarded the Nuclear Test Ban Treaty as his most important achievement and Vietnam as the most frustrating of his foreign policy endeavours. He was disappointed that he had not been able to push either Medicare or a comprehensive civil rights' bill through Congress.

Words like 'hope' and 'promise' are freely employed to enhance his glory. We are told that they have not been approached since his death. But there are many ambiguities here and hostile critics are quick to turn the phrases round and accuse him of arousing expectations which could never, in fact, have been fulfilled. 'Hope', however, remains in theology one of the supernatural virtues. We are better with it than without it. If Kennedy stirred far-reaching hopes in America and the rest of the world (and there is no doubt that he did so) that must surely be counted for righteousness, unless the hopes themselves can be dismissed as dangerous illusions. And here the argument will continue raging.

Even a dedicated admirer like Schlesinger admits today the dangers inherent in some of the language of the Inaugural. He refers to a counter-insurgency mystique which nourished the belief in the American capacity and right to intervene in foreign lands, and brought out the worst in the over-confident activism of the New Frontier. He calls our attention to the development of an Imperial concept of the Presidency. In that connection I would suggest that he is too kind to Kennedy.

I have devoted a chapter to Kennedy and Vietnam. I have concluded that he underestimated the significance of the problem, and never gave it a proper share of his attention. The critics, however, will not be content with the acknowledgment of administrative defect. They will insist that the philosophy of the Inaugural prepared the way for the ultimate tragedy and the horrifying legacy bequeathed to Johnson. The latter would find himself advised for the most part by the nominees of Kennedy. The inflexible believers in Kennedy will acknowledge relative failure in this area, but will insist that Kennedy, if he had lived, would have found a way out of the dilemma which defeated his successor. No dogmatism is possible here but it seems to me that on the whole the critics have the best of the argument.

As regards Soviet Communism his policy cannot be disposed of on its own away from East/West history. No serious student of Kennedy can fail to study the mighty tomes of Schlesinger and Sorensen. But having done so he must cast his eyes on the so-called 'biting assessment' of Richard Walton. Walton concludes *inter alia* that the Berlin crisis was fabricated in Washington. He totally rejects the thesis that the Cuban missile crisis was the occasion of Kennedy's greatest triumph. 'I believe', he writes, 'that Kennedy's decision to go to the brink of nuclear war was irresponsible and reckless to a supreme degree.'

His conclusions, or should we call them assumptions, are in glaring contrast to those which have governed the policies of the United States and Great Britain since the end of the war. It has been assumed in America and Britain, not to mention other

Western countries, that the West has been threatened throughout this period by Soviet Russia and for that reason it has been necessary for vast armaments to be maintained. Certainly they have not been maintained for any other reason. Personally, I accept this assumption, which is not to underwrite in all respects the policies followed. But Walton evidently regards the whole assumption as pure fantasy. 'A respectable argument can be made', he writes, 'that Russia never intended a military adventure into Western Europe, that there was simply no need for NATO, and that its existence did more to increase tension than to preserve the peace.' It is not only my conviction but that of those I have looked up to most in Britain and America since the war that this is pure delusion.

I myself was Minister for Germany from 1947 to 1948. I sat beside Ernest Bevin at the Council of Foreign Ministers in December 1947. The other leaders were General Marshall, Monsieur Bideault, and Mr Molotov. Monsieur Bideault never knew from day to day whether France would collapse under Communist pressures internal and external. Mr Molotov, on instructions from home, but it seemed to suit his personality well enough, made all agreement impossible. Not long afterwards Soviet Russia tried to starve West Berlin into submission. She was thwarted, though only just, by the Allied air-lift. Ernest Bevin once said of Stalin in my hearing 'he's just a working chap like you and me.' But that was his humour. He really looked on him as a deadly and all too powerful opponent. No Western democrat at that time could question the physical menace of Communism. NATO was produced as a desperate defence measure at the eleventh hour.

If we are to be told that Russia turned over a new leaf with the departure of Stalin there is overwhelming evidence to the contrary in Hungary, Poland and most noticeably in recent times, Czechoslovakia. Indeed as long as she holds down Eastern Germany one cannot take seriously her pretensions to respect the freedom of other nations, whose freedom she respects as little as that of her own citizens. Her bitter dispute with China has admittedly opened up possibilities of at least friendly co-existence with the West. But the need for the continuance of NATO has been equally great at the time that it was founded, during the Kennedy years and in 1976. No one can force Mr Walton to accept this way of looking at things, but if one cannot even treat it as a tenable hypothesis it is impossible to understand Kennedy or assess him fairly.

This is not to say that every move made by Kennedy in his dealings with Khrushchev was ethically inspired and every move by Khrushchev devilish. It is frequently argued today that the vast expansion of American armaments under Kennedy produced their inevitable reaction on the Soviet side and were of no ultimate benefit to anyone. Without going to that length one can agree that Kennedy would seem to have over-reacted in his rearmament, once he knew – as he did on becoming President – the extent of the American nuclear superiority. But having said that I cannot fail to hold Khrushchev solely responsible for the Berlin crisis of 1961/2. He was quite shamelessly trying to drive the Western Allies out of Berlin. Again I hold the unshakeable conviction that it was Khrushchev, not Kennedy, who was responsible for the missiles crisis (autumn 1963). Kennedy handled it (assisted it may be by wise British counsel) in so statesmanlike a fashion that peace between the great powers became and remained more assured than at any time since the war. With a magnanimity very much in character, Kennedy exploited this triumph to build a new understanding with Khrushchev and to pave the way to a Test Ban Treaty the following year.

Even Walton ceases 'to bite' when he deals with Kennedy's great speech of 10 June 1963 at the American University. He calls it 'magnificent', as it was, though Walton continues to think of Kennedy as a Jekyll and Hyde statesman, Jekyll being the reconciler and Hyde the cold warrior. He questions whether Hyde was really dead. It is true that not every speech delivered by Kennedy between 10 June and the assassination was pitched in the same key but even when he seemed to be departing from the peace message, as in one of his Berlin speeches, his general trend was unmistakable. He had always believed in the double line, 'the arrows and the olives'. But he had learned much since the far-off days of the Inauguration; by firmness and restraint he had reached a point where he could give effect to his peaceful vision of friendly relations with Russia.

One cannot be equally flattering about his attitude to China or his comprehension of developments in that country. His intimates have insisted that if he had lived and been re-elected he would have set himself to bring about a rapprochement between China and the

United States. It may be so. But there is nothing in the record to suggest it. Schlesinger tells us that the problem of China by 1963 was 'increasingly in the President's mind' but this meant, it seems, that 'Kennedy and Macmillan were reaching the conclusion that China presented a long term danger to the peace.' One day when they were discussing the problem of a new Commander for NATO Macmillan said whimsically, 'I suppose it should be a Russian'. Officials present had some difficulty in realizing that this was a joke. A new American approach to China could not, or at any rate did not, take place until the Sino-Soviet split had gone much further. In that instance at least we must not detract from the credit due to President Nixon.

On the domestic side his economic policy was immensely successful in attacking recession and inflation alike. But as regards the quality of life and social justice he realized before the end that he had hardly begun his task. On the racial question it is easy once again to argue for and against him. Martin Luther King's widow has been quoted in the text as an authoritative witness in his favour. But his postponement of Civil Rights legislation until forced to act seems, looking back, to have provided an atmosphere of frustration and unrest, of which the militant black leaders were not slow to take advantage. Overall the domestic record compares unimpressively with the achievements of 1964 and 1965 under Johnson. It can be argued that the composition of Congress made bolder steps impossible till after the elections of 1964, and that the legislation carried out in 1964 before those elections were the fruit of Kennedy's initiatives. The defence is not very convincing.

There emerges at the finish an extraordinary human being whose sympathies continually widened and who simultaneously became ever more effective in expressing them in political action. One apparent contradiction in his nature confronts us: he was strangely fascinated by men like Melbourne as described by David Cecil, and Raymond Asquith in John Buchan's autobiography – brilliant, sophisticated, sceptical, unsure of their object in life. Kennedy's record in the time available to him was that of a supreme activist, metaphorically ready to set out at every moment to climb Mount Everest.

The psychologists will tell us, indeed they have told us, that the explanation is simple: Jack Kennedy was deeply distrustful of his capacity to live up to the heroic feats expected of him: action was the only opium that could lull his sense of insecurity and potential failure. I cannot see him that way. He was endowed it would seem from the beginning with whatever natural qualities prepare the way for the highest courage. The ill health of his boyhood gave him time to read and think and strengthen his determination to excel. His self-questioning mind helped him in a literary sense to identify with certain famous figures of history, some men of action, some the reverse. But it never weakened his purpose. It added, indeed, a dimension of human understanding, an ability to enter into the minds and to allow for the weaknesses of other men. When his supreme moment arrived he came forth equipped alike with the softer and the tougher virtues.

No one of his time was more obviously cut out for leadership. 'There,' wrote an Irish Nationalist who would have appealed to Kennedy, 'There go the young, the gallant, the gifted, the daring. And there too go the wise.' Not even his harshest critics would deny the first four epithets to John Kennedy. Wisdom is not the first quality one associates with him but he was rapidly acquiring it on his lonely eminence under the impact of harsh reality. Farsightedness about the future of the human race might well have come later to someone with such exceptional insight into human beings as people. His attachment to the works of John Buchan encourages me to finish by drawing on the end of the latter's book *The Half Hearted*. The tribal chief on a lonely hill in Afghanistan, beside the dead body of the fallen hero, pronounces his epitaph:

'This', he said, 'was a man.' And then more explicitly, 'This man was of the race of kings.'

Bibliography

Agee, Philip, *Inside the Company: C.I.A. Diary*, Penguin Books Ltd, London, 1975

Alsop, Susan Mary, *To Marietta from Paris, 1945-60*, Doubleday, New York, 1975

Anson, Robert S., *They've killed the President*, Bantam, New York, 1975

Blair, Joan and Clay, Jr, *The Search for J.F.K.*, Berkeley/Putnam's, New York, 1976

Bradlee, Benjamin C., *Conversations with Kennedy*, W. W. Norton, New York, 1975

Brandon, Henry, *Anatomy of Error: The Inside Story of the Asian War on the Potomac, 1954-1969*, Gambit, Boston, 1969

Clinch, Nancy G., *The Kennedy Neurosis*, Grosset & Dunlap, New York, 1973

Eddowes, Michael, *November 22: How they killed Kennedy*, Neville Spearman, Jersey, 1976

Edmonds, Robin, *Soviet Foreign Policy 1962-1973: The Paradox of Super Power*, Oxford University Press, London, 1975

Fairlie, Henry, *The Kennedy Promise*, Doubleday, New York, 1973

Fay, Paul B., Jr, *The Pleasure of His Company*, Popular Library, New York, 1973

George, Alexander L. & Richard Smoke, *Deterrence in American Foreign Policy: Theory and Practice*, Columbia University Press, New York and London, 1974

Halberstam, David, *The Best and the Brightest: Kennedy-Johnson Administrations*, Barrie & Jenkins, London, 1973

Harrington, Michael, *The Other America: Poverty in the United States*, Rev. ed., Macmillan, New York, 1970

Heren, Louis, *No Hail, No Farewell: The Johnson Years*, Weidenfeld & Nicolson, London, 1970

Hilsman, Roger, *To Move a Nation*, Dell, New York, 1968

Kennedy, John Fitzgerald, *Profiles in Courage*, Taurus Press of
Willow Dene, Bushey Heath, Herts, 1972

Kennedy, John Fitzgerald, *Why England Slept*, Sidgwick &
Jackson, London, 1962

Kennedy, Robert F., *Thirteen Days: A Memoir of the Cuban
Missile Crisis*, W. W. Norton, New York, 1969

Kennedy, Rose, *Times to Remember*, Collins, London, 1974

Khrushchev, Nikita, trans. S. Talbot, *Khrushchev Remembers: The
Last Testament*, André Deutsch, London, 1974

King, Coretta Scott, *My Life with Martin Luther King*, Hodder &
Stoughton, London, 1970

Laing, Margaret, *Robert F. Kennedy*, Macdonald, London, 1968

Lasky, Victor, *J.F.K.: The Man and the Myth*, Arlington House,
New Rochelle, New York, 1966

Levinson, Jerome, and Juan De Onis, *The Alliance That Lost Its
Way: A Critical Report on the Alliance for Progress*, Quadrangle,
New York, 1970

Lincoln, Evelyn, *My Twelve Years with John F. Kennedy*, David
McKay, New York, 1965

Macmillan, Harold, *Pointing the Way, 1959-61*, Macmillan,
London, 1972

Macmillan, Harold, *At the End of the Day, 1961-63*, Macmillan,
London, 1973

Manchester, William, *Death of a President*, Harper & Row,
London, 1967

Manchester, William, *The Glory and the Dream*, Michael Joseph,
London, 1975

Marchetti, Victor, L., and John D. Marks, *The C.I.A. and the
Cult of Intelligence*, Jonathan Cape, London, 1974

Nunnerley, David, *President Kennedy and Britain*, Bodley Head,
London, 1972

O'Donnell, Kenneth P., and David Powers, *Johnny, We Hardly
Knew Ye: Memories of John Fitzgerald Kennedy*, Little, Brown,
Boston, 1972

Paper, Lewis J., *The Promise and the Performance*, Crown
Publishers Inc., New York, 1975

Salinger, Pierre, *With Kennedy*, Doubleday, New York, 1966

Schlesinger, Arthur M., Jr, and Sir John Wheeler-Bennett,
'Kennedy' in *The History Makers*, ed. Lord Longford, Sidgwick
& Jackson, London, 1973

Schlesinger, Arthur M., Jr, *The Imperial Presidency*, André Deutsch, London, 1974

Schlesinger, Arthur M., Jr, *A Thousand Days: John F. Kennedy in the White House*, André Deutsch, London, 1965

Schwab, Peter and J. Lee Shneidman, *John F. Kennedy*, Twayne, Boston, 1974

Sidey, Hugh and Fred Ward, *Portrait of a President*, Harper & Row, New York, 1975

Sorensen, Theodore C., *Kennedy*, Hodder, London, 1965

Sorensen, Theodore C., *The Kennedy Legacy*, Macmillan, New York, 1969

Steel, Ronald, *Pax Americana*, Rev. ed., Viking Press, New York, 1970

Sundquist, James L., *Politics and Policy: Eisenhower, Kennedy and Johnson Years*, Brookings Institution, London, 1969

Tanzer, Lester, *The Kennedy Circle*, Robert B. Luce, Washington, 1961

Walton, Richard J., *Cold War and Counterrevolution: The Foreign Policy of John F. Kennedy*, Viking Press, New York, 1972

Whalen, Richard, *The Founding Father: The Story of Joseph P. Kennedy*, New American Library, New York, 1964

White, Theodore H., *Breach of Faith: The Fall of Richard Nixon*, Atheneum, New York, 1975

White, Theodore H., *The Making of the President 1960*, Jonathan Cape, London, 1962

Index

Wyndham Books are obtainable from many booksellers and newsagents. If you have any difficulty please send purchase price plus postage on the scale below to:

Wyndham Cash Sales,
P.O. Box 11,
Falmouth,
Cornwall

OR

Star Book Service,
G.P.O. Box 29,
Douglas,
Isle of Man,
British Isles

While every effort is made to keep prices low, it is sometimes necessary to increase prices at short notice. Wyndham Books reserve the right to show new retail prices on covers which may differ from those advertised in the text or elsewhere.

Postage and Packing Rate
U.K.
One book 22p plus 10p per copy for each additional book ordered to a maximum charge of 82p.

B.F.P.O. and Eire
One book 22p plus 10p per copy for the next 6 books and thereafter 4p per book. Overseas 30p for the first book and 10p per copy for each additional book.